I08126 79

IMAGES
of America

DINGMANS FERRY

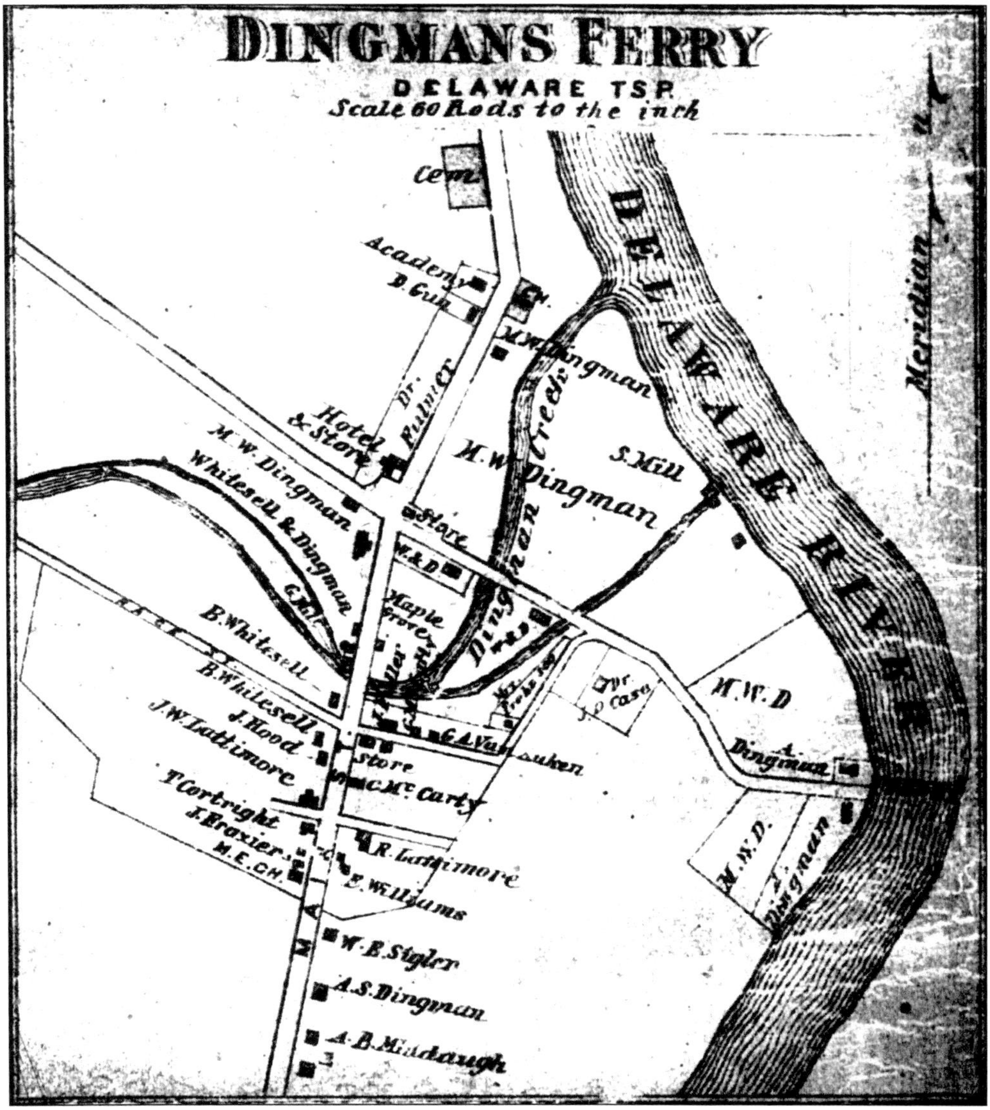

This is an 1870 Beers map of Dingmans Ferry. (Courtesy DF/DTHS.)

IMAGES
of America

DINGMANS FERRY

Matthew M. Osterberg

ARCADIA
PUBLISHING

ISBN 978-0-7385-3873-0

Published by Arcadia Publishing
Charleston, South Carolina

Printed in the United States of America

Library of Congress Catalog Card Number: 2005926946

For all general information contact Arcadia Publishing at:
Telephone 843-853-2070
Fax 843-853-0044
E-mail sales@arcadiapublishing.com
For customer service and orders:
Toll-Free 1-888-313-2665

Visit us on the Internet at www.arcadiapublishing.com

This book is dedicated to Frederick W. White III, who loved his family, Dingmans Ferry, and Pike County. His memories, stories, and passion for local history and family genealogy live on in all who had the honor of knowing him, especially his three sons: Fred IV, Michael, and Joseph.

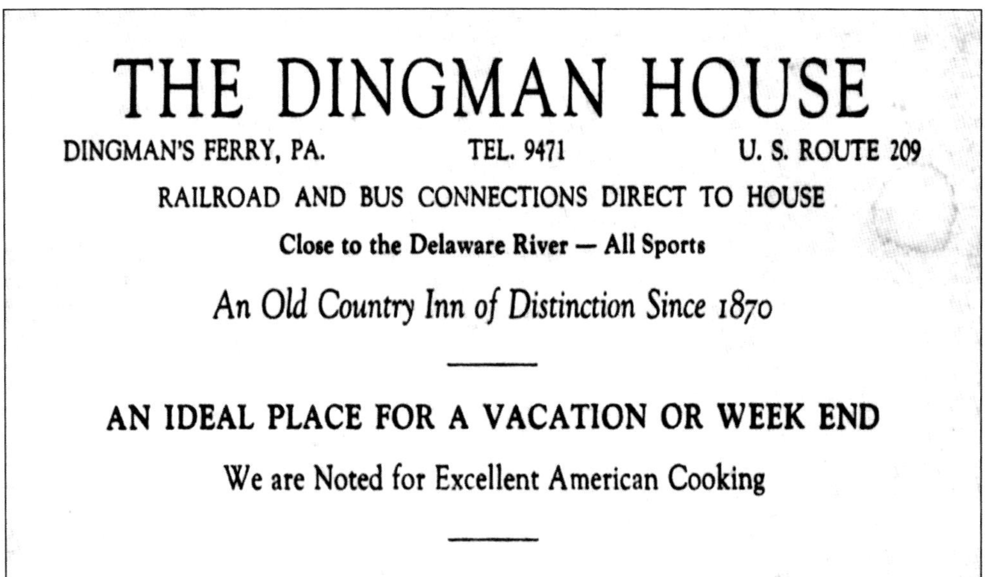

This early-20th-century advertisement card promotes the Dingman House. Its claims still hold true in the 21st century. (Courtesy DF/DTHS.)

Contents

ACKNOWLEDGMENTS

There are many people and organizations to thank for their help in comprising this book. First and foremost is my wife, Carol, who spent countless hours editing and typing captions, and also my children, Stephanie and Michael, who put up with my clutter of papers and total control of the family computer. Their encouragement is what kept me going when sitting up at 2 a.m. writing.

The others to thank are numerous, and if I forget anyone please accept my apology. I am grateful to the many groups and individuals who were generous in sharing their photographs, memories, time, and expertise to help create this book. A very special thank-you goes to the Dingmans Ferry/Delaware Township Historical Society (DF/DTHS), particularly Jo Ann Parsell, Roberta and Leroy Cron, and Mim Carpenter. These four individuals gathered enough photographs and information to publish a thorough book. Their dedication to the history of Dingmans Ferry is incredible and invaluable, and the citizens of Delaware Township should be proud of people like them, who are strongly committed to preserving the stories and communicating the history of Dingmans Ferry. The Pike County Historical Society, especially director Lori Strilecki, provided expertise and allowed the use of the *Column*'s vast photograph collection. For its continued support, I thank the Minisink Valley Historical Society, particularly executive director Peter Osborne. I am also grateful to the following, Mary and James Albright Sr., Carl and Sue Arnold, Harry Arnold, Elsie Bensley, Edwin Brodhead, Kathleen and Stephen Bumball, Viola Kern Canouse, Barbara Bensley Cole, Linda Davis, the Delaware Water Gap National Recreation Area, Laura and Jan de Graaf, Inez Dickison, Jacqueline Dougherty, Barbara Snyder Herman, Marie Hoffman, George and Carolyn Hotalen, Mildred Jagger, the Jagger family, Bill and Patsy Kiger, John Kurz, Joyce Reser Lewis, James Leiser and the Pike County Mapping Office, Sandy Leiser, Helen Malmquist, Audrey Mervine, Sonda and Lee Miller, Sylvia Miller, the Flora Myers family, Marilyn Nestor, Virginia Oliver, Ted Parsell, the Raitt family, the Dorothy Schouppe family, Sean Strub, the Gen Stripple family, Dorthann and Joe White, and Eugene Whitesell.

I acknowledge the individuals who wrote so extensively on Dingmans Ferry and Delaware Township. Their resources, listed as follows, were invaluable in writing the captions for these photographs: Patricia Herbertz's *History of Delaware Township*, William Henn's *River Road*, Matthews's *History of Pike and Wayne Counties*, and Norman Lehde's *History of Pike County*.

Lastly, I give thanks to my dear friend Lizanne Samuelson, who worked so diligently in editing all the captions and the introduction. I am indebted to her, not just for this book but for the last three that I have created; she has always been there to guide and support me.

INTRODUCTION

Traveling along Route 209, south of Milford, is like taking a drive through a country wilderness. It is, in fact, the Delaware Water Gap Recreation Area. But few visitors today realize that just 30 years ago, this route was the main street for the bustling community of Dingmans Ferry, a town of many businesses and beautiful homes. It was a place where families prayed together on Sundays, dogs barked, children played, mothers hung out laundry, and fathers worked. It was a place where neighbors met at local restaurants, tourists bought souvenirs, and children attended school.

In 1976, Dingmans Ferry residents held a community fair to celebrate the country's 200th birthday. It was a bittersweet party, though, for many knew this was their final celebration; after 230 years, the small river village of Dingmans Ferry would soon become history.

Since the 1960s, the United States Army Corp of Engineers had been acquiring property—the family homes, businesses, and farms that comprised Dingmans Ferry—to make way for the proposed Tocks Island Dam Project. The dam was to provide hydroelectric power for the growing New York and Philadelphia metropolitan areas, as well as help protect the valley from flooding and create a recreational area for fishing and boating.

But there was a high price to be paid, as the soul and fabric of this once picturesque village was to be destroyed. All of its beautiful buildings would be lost. Places where families laughed and cried for over 200 years would exist only in cherished memories and old photographs.

When traveling this route today, it is a good idea to pause and reflect. Take a moment to visualize and understand that what remains is the tranquil natural beauty, not unlike that which drew the first European settlers to the area they named Dingmans Choice, later re-christened Dingmans Ferry.

Settled in 1732 by Andrew Dingman, this fertile valley was originally the home of the Leni-Lenape Indians, a peaceful tribe who worshiped and respected the land as sacred. The results of the infamous Walking Purchase treaty shocked and betrayed the Leni-Lenape, as most of Pike County was taken from them. They lost the home sites where they had lived and the land they had tilled for centuries. The tribe revered the fertile and ancient Minisink Valley for its hunting and fishing and its spiritual link to their ancestors who lived and died there. Archaeologists have discovered numerous artifacts of great significance, some now protected in New York City museums. This fraudulent treaty was an important factor in turning the natives against the white settlers, who had driven them from their sacred lands and burial grounds.

Andrew Dingman saw in this area what the Lenape had known and protected for generations: more than just beautiful scenery, but an abundance of natural wealth, including the fertile lands which had already been farmed for centuries and the many streams that eventually powered the many mills that would be built in the area over time.

Dingman and his family created a village that connected the east to the west, for in the 1700s, the mountain range of Pennsylvania beginning just west of the Delaware was the American frontier. Dingman and other early settlers grasped the pragmatic importance of linking this fertile valley to the markets in New York and other cities on the eastern seaboard. The Dingman family facilitated commerce by establishing the first ferry across this part of the Delaware and building a dependable road from Bethany to Dingmans. The trading with New York and New Jersey increased rapidly over time, and eventually, the first of several bridges was built to span the river. The bridge still in use at Dingmans Ferry, owned by the Dingmans Choice Company, was built in 1900 and is the last privately owned span on the Delaware River, now serving commuters more often then the transport of commercial goods.

As the town and the region developed, the Dingman family was involved in practically all matters, which impacted Dingmans Ferry's government, schools, and businesses. Hotels were constructed, and soon visitors from far-off places found this tranquil spot in the foothills of the Pennsylvania Mountains to be a great vacation getaway from city life. Some loved it so much that they moved here permanently to raise their families.

Even to this day, as Pike County grows at a rapid rate, new visitors are discovering what Andrew Dingman saw more than 270 years ago. Today, the area retains much of its original natural environment, as well as a rich cultural history, with families who have been here for nearly 10 generations, as well as the vibrancy brought by newcomers.

This book is a photographic essay that attempts to give the reader a sense of life in Dingmans Ferry. In it, you'll find photographs of the churches where children were baptized and sweethearts were married, and hotels where local residents worked and visitors enjoyed the natural beauty during the summers.

The first five chapters include images demonstrating how a small American village grew. The story tells how the hotel business grew and prospered, when New Yorkers and Philadelphians flocked here for a respite from the hectic bustle of city life; how a wonderful main street, the economic center of a quaint town comprised of mills, blacksmith shops, and later gas stations and stores, served the neighborhood and region; and how the lovely churches and splendid schools drew together this proud and close community. In the final chapter are glimpses into the families who called Dingmans Ferry home, including the Dingmans, Jaggers, Judds, Crons, Whittakers, Bensleys, and Brodheads. We see families at carnivals and parades, children riding bicycles, men enjoying a drink at a local bar, in this look at ordinary life in a treasured, but now lost, small Pennsylvania river village. Dingmans Ferry was the kind of place where when the fire whistle rang, everyone in town had true concern, wondering which of their neighbors was in trouble and how they could help. It is family and neighbors, through fortune and hardship, who bond and sustain a small town. Dingmans Ferry was this type of town. Even now, when asked, people speak about it with a reverent tone. They know what many of us do not: that one time not so long ago, a small town existed along the beautiful banks of the Delaware River, loved and known as Dingmans Ferry.

The next time you drive down Route 209, slow down, imagine what life was like there, and what a great sacrifice these families made. This was their home and they miss it dearly.

One

Boardinghouses and Tourism

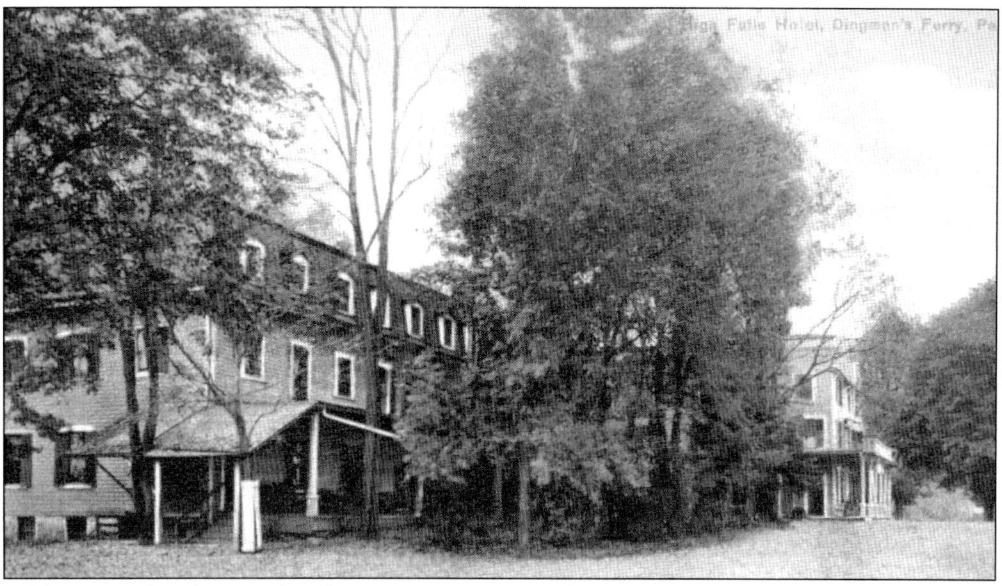

Of the many fine, historic hotels in Dingmans Ferry, the High Falls is considered the oldest. In 1866, Dr. Phillip Fulmer purchased it in its 55th year, when known as the Wayside Inn Dingmans Choice Hotel. Fulmer renovated and expanded the building to accommodate 200 guests and landscaped the hotel's magnificent grounds, while renaming it the High Falls Hotel. For the next 80 years, guests traveled from as far away as New York City and Philadelphia for the elegant rooms and excellent service awaiting them at the splendid High Falls Hotel. (Courtesy Dorothy Schouppe Collection.)

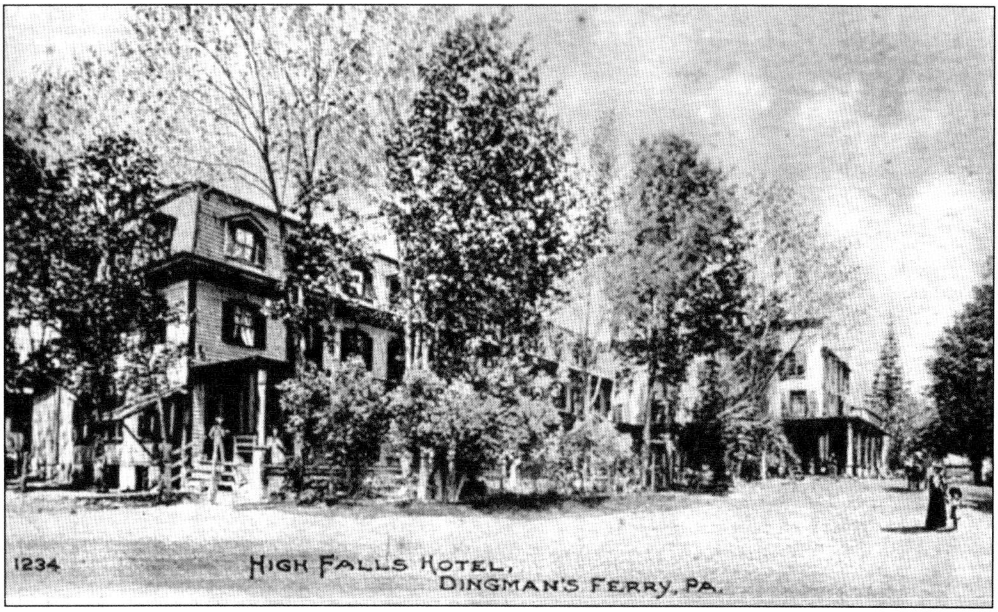

The High Falls Hotel, originally built with just 14 bedrooms, grew rapidly in popularity and by 1870, held 200 guests. Advertised as a place for "lavish parties and vacations," this was the place to stay when visiting Dingmans Ferry. (Courtesy Dorothy Schouppe Collection.)

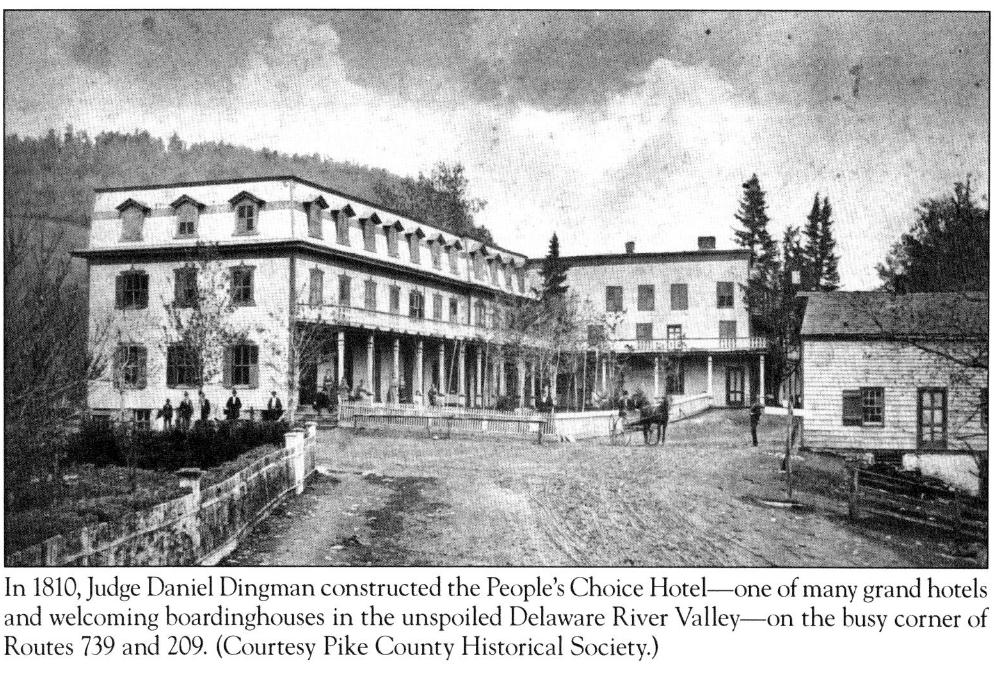

In 1810, Judge Daniel Dingman constructed the People's Choice Hotel—one of many grand hotels and welcoming boardinghouses in the unspoiled Delaware River Valley—on the busy corner of Routes 739 and 209. (Courtesy Pike County Historical Society.)

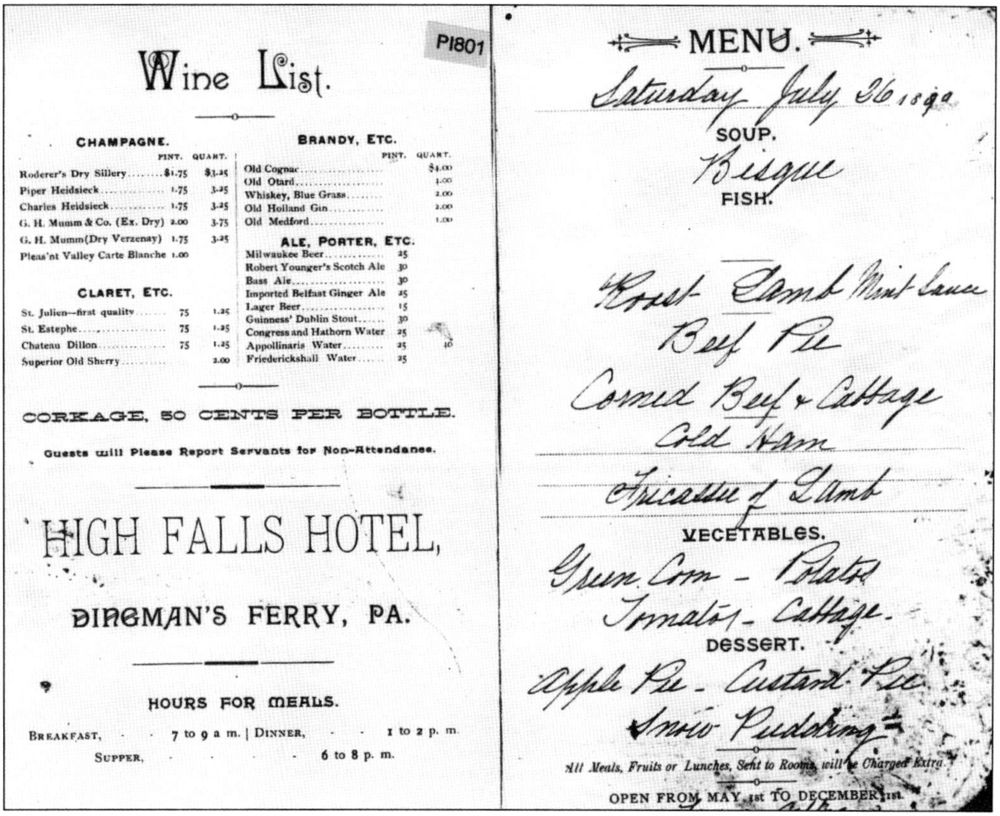

Wine List.

P1801

CHAMPAGNE.	PINT.	QUART.
Roderer's Dry Sillery	$1.75	$3.25
Piper Heidsieck	1.75	3.25
Charles Heidsieck	1.75	3.25
G. H. Mumm & Co. (Ex. Dry)	2.00	3.75
G. H. Mumm (Dry Verzenay)	1.75	3.25
Pleas'nt Valley Carte Blanche	1.00	

CLARET, ETC.		
St. Julien—first quality	75	1.25
St. Estephe	75	1.25
Chateau Dillon	75	1.25
Superior Old Sherry		2.00

BRANDY, ETC.	PINT.	QUART.
Old Cognac		$4.00
Old Otard		4.00
Whiskey, Blue Grass		2.00
Old Holland Gin		2.00
Old Medford		1.00

ALE, PORTER, ETC.	
Milwaukee Beer	25
Robert Younger's Scotch Ale	30
Bass Ale	30
Imported Belfast Ginger Ale	25
Lager Beer	15
Guinness' Dublin Stout	30
Congress and Hathorn Water	25
Appollinaris Water	25
Friederickshall Water	25

CORKAGE, 50 CENTS PER BOTTLE.

Guests will Please Report Servants for Non-Attendance.

HIGH FALLS HOTEL,

DINGMAN'S FERRY, PA.

HOURS FOR MEALS.

BREAKFAST, 7 to 9 a. m. | DINNER, 1 to 2 p. m.

SUPPER, 6 to 8 p. m.

MENU.

Saturday July 26 1890

SOUP.

Bisque

FISH.

Roast Lamb Mint Sauce

Beef Pie

Corned Beef & Cabbage

Cold Ham

Fricassee of Lamb

VEGETABLES.

Green Corn - Potatoes

Tomatoes - Cabbage.

DESSERT.

Apple Pie - Custard Pie

Snow Pudding

All Meals, Fruits or Lunches, Sent to Rooms, will be Charged Extra.

OPEN FROM MAY 1st TO DECEMBER 1st.

The High Falls Hotel menu appealed to elite customers. The hotel served its guests fresh food from its five-acre garden and dairy, attached to the house. Many people of stature, including the president of Princeton University and tennis great Bill Tilden, chose High Falls as their favorite getaway. (Courtesy DF/DTHS.)

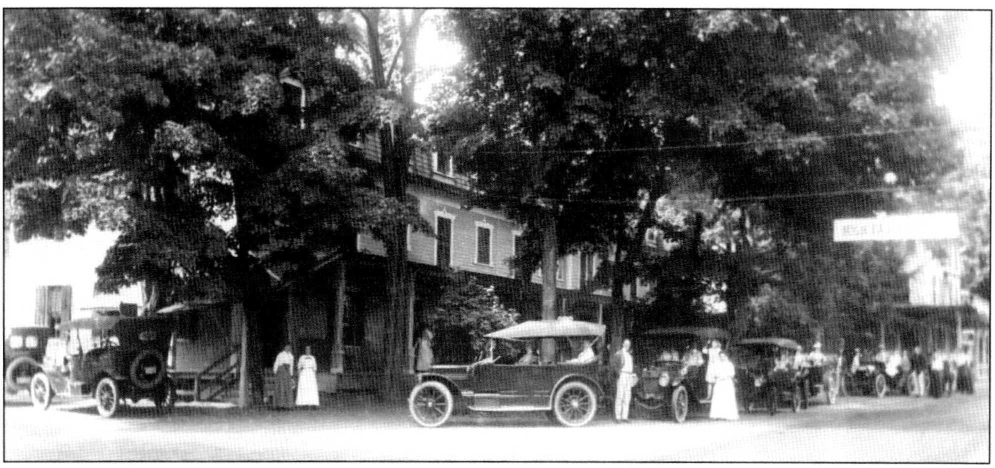

This c. 1915 photograph illustrates the popularity of this grand hotel, which the press nicknamed "the Pearl of Sylvan Retreats." It boasted "clear spring water, bathing houses and boating on the Delaware." It appealed to its upper-class clientele from May 1 to December 1. Like many of the area's spacious hotels, the High Falls's popularity waned in the 1930s, and in 1946, fire consumed it. (Courtesy Pike County Historical Society.)

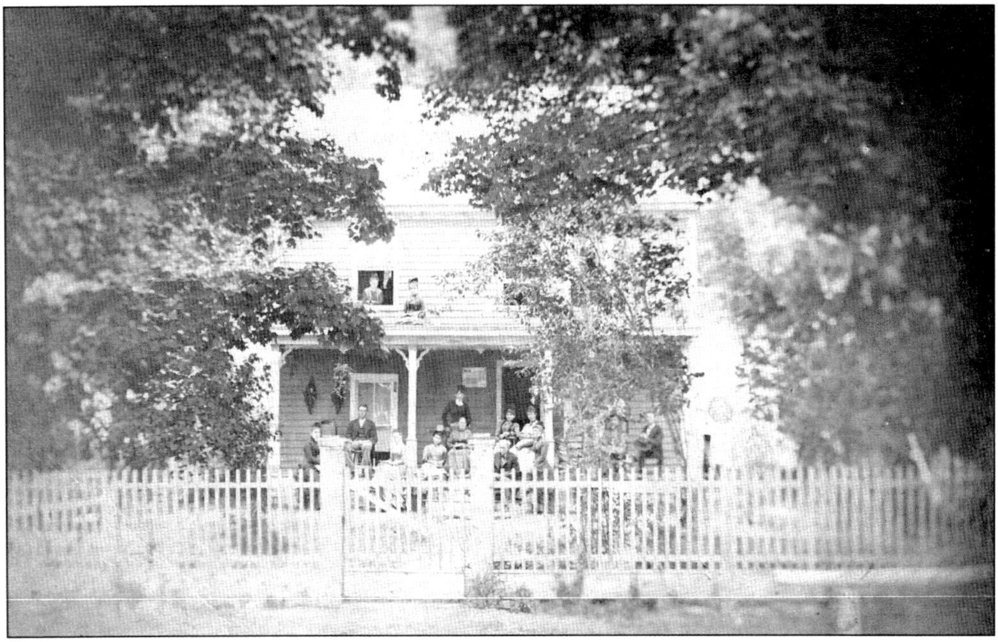

The Conashaugh Spring House was first established by the Van Etten family. Located on Conashaugh Road, the resort grew from a small seven-room house to a grand hotel accommodating 175 guests. The Van Etten family was one of the earliest settlers of Dingmans Ferry when they took ownership of this property in 1745. (Courtesy DF/DTHS.)

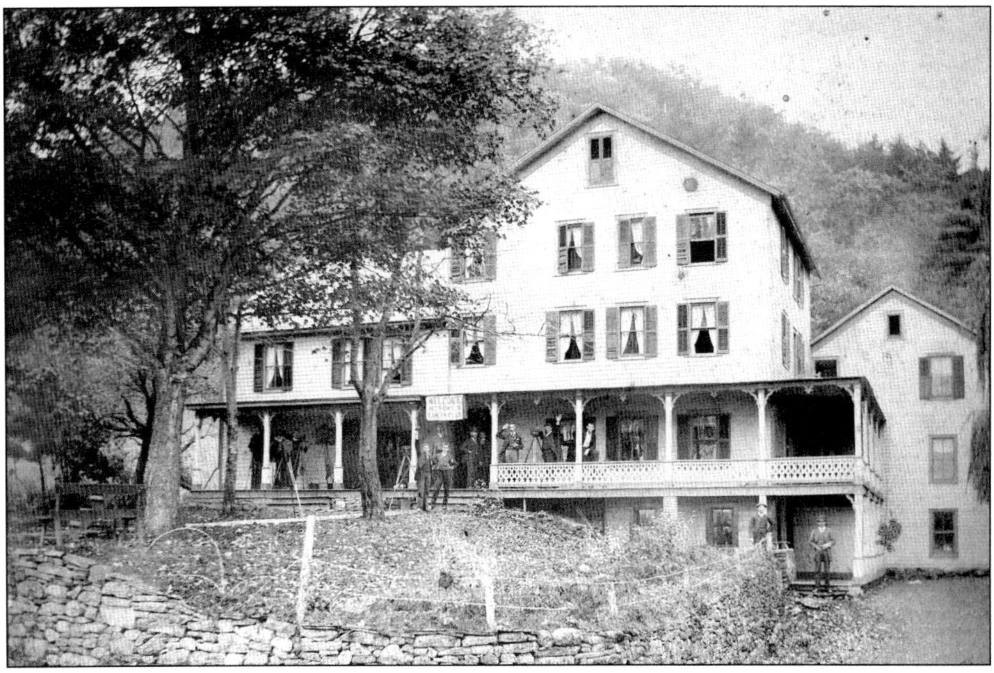

Built in 1837, the Conashaugh Spring House served as a respite for rafters and other travelers. In 1883 and 1884, it was enlarged to 100 rooms, catering to summer guests along the Delaware River north of Dingmans Ferry on Main Street (Route 209). Considered an elite resort, it was known for its famous Conashaugh Spring water. (Courtesy Pike County Historical Society.)

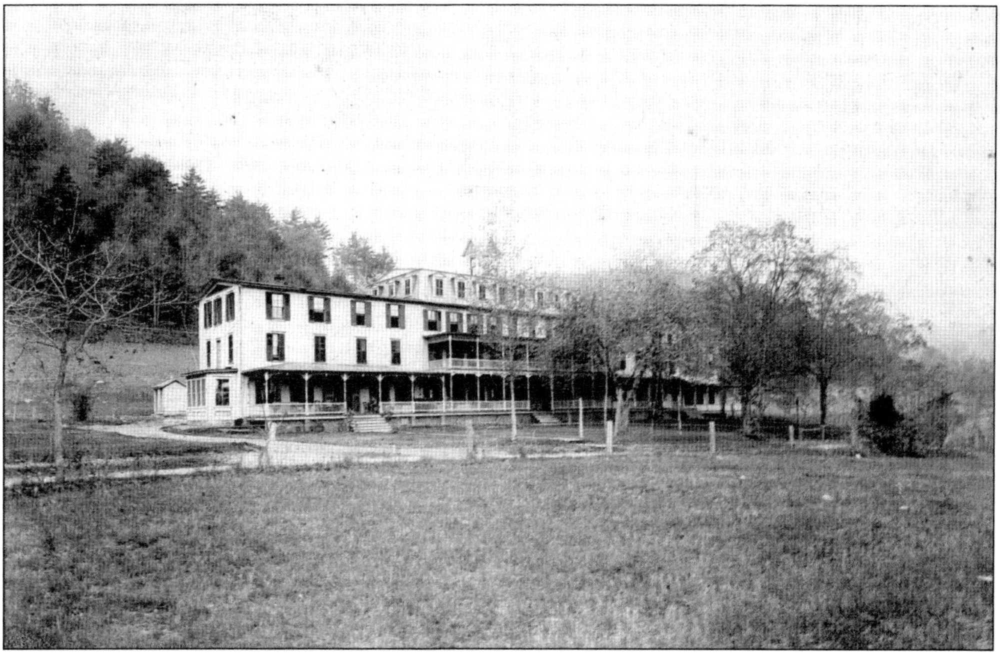

The Conashaugh Spring House, recognized as one of the elite resorts in the region, provided its guests with all of the modern conveniences of the day, including running clear spring water on every floor. In 1915, fire destroyed this grand hotel. (Courtesy DF/DTHS.)

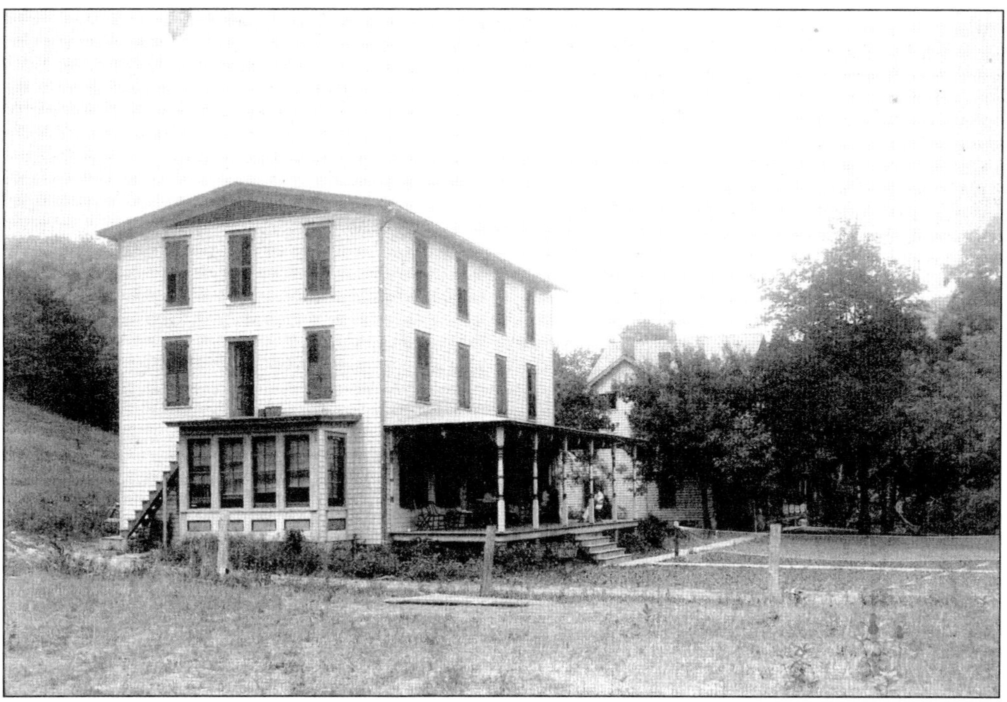

This is an early photograph of the Conashaugh House before the additions of the 1880s. In the distance is the original Van Etten home. (Courtesy DF/DTHS.)

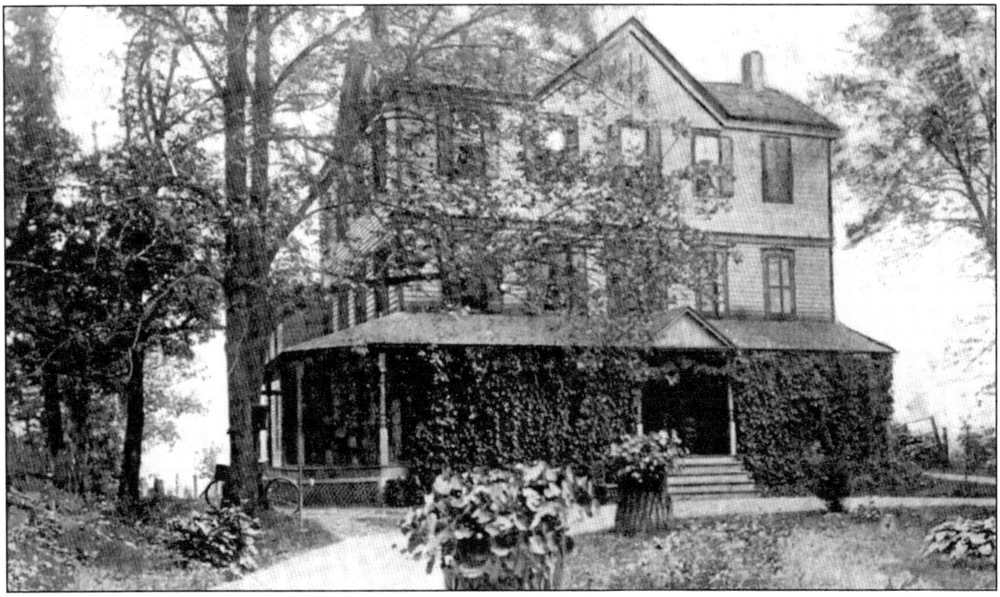

The Adams Brook Inn, built in the 1890s with a grand view of Adams Creek and the Delaware River, served as a boardinghouse for many years. When the original owner, Lafayette Quick, inherited the land from his father, Peter, he constructed this resort on 200 tranquil acres of natural beauty. (Courtesy DF/DTHS.)

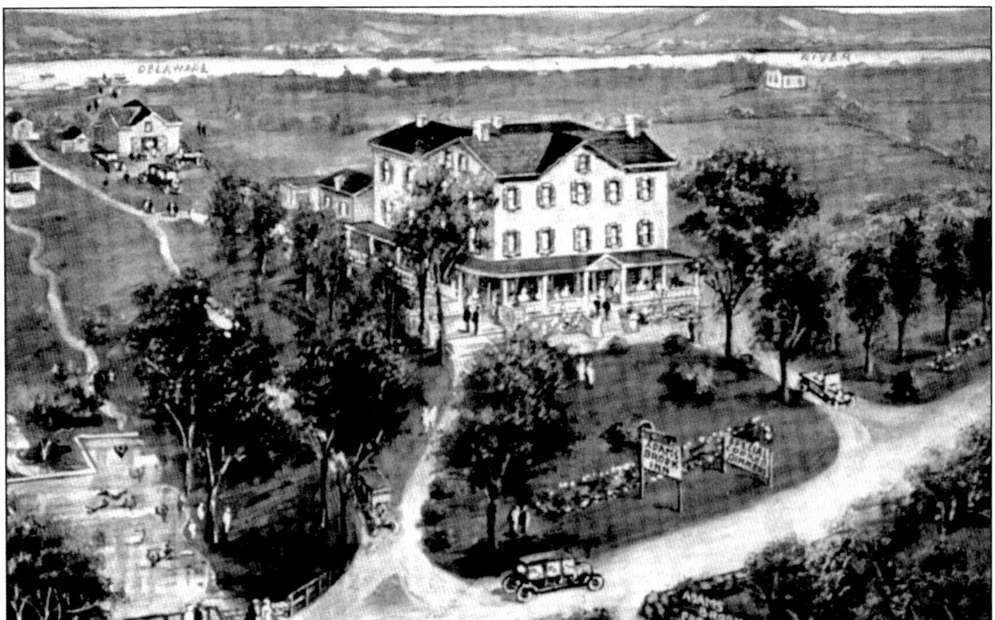

H. R. Ryder owned the Adams Brook Inn when this postcard was published in the early 1900s. At the time, the hotel boasted a garage and electric lights with rooms renting for $25 per week. (Courtesy Kathleen and Stephen Bumball.)

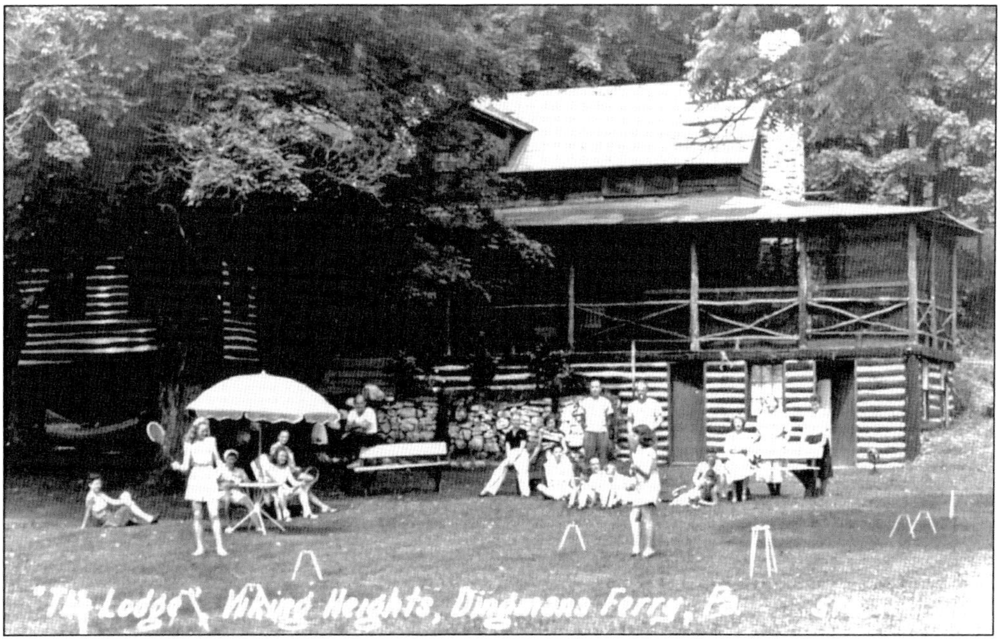

In 1936, the Hedemark family purchased a farm on Briscoe Mountain Road and opened a summer resort there called Viking Heights. They built many cabins to rent to hunters and their families. (Courtesy Kathleen and Stephen Bumball.)

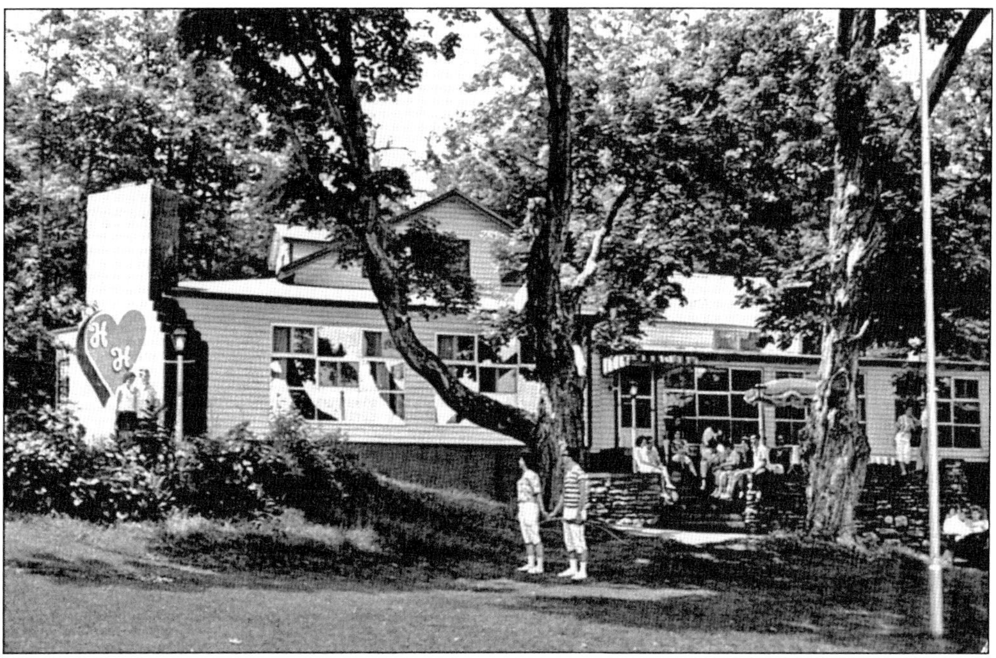

Viking Heights was purchased and transformed into Honeymoon Haven in 1960. This mountaintop resort catered to honeymooners until 1972, when it was purchased by the federal government. Today, this area is the home of the Pennsylvania Environmental Education Center. (Courtesy Kathleen and Stephen Bumball.)

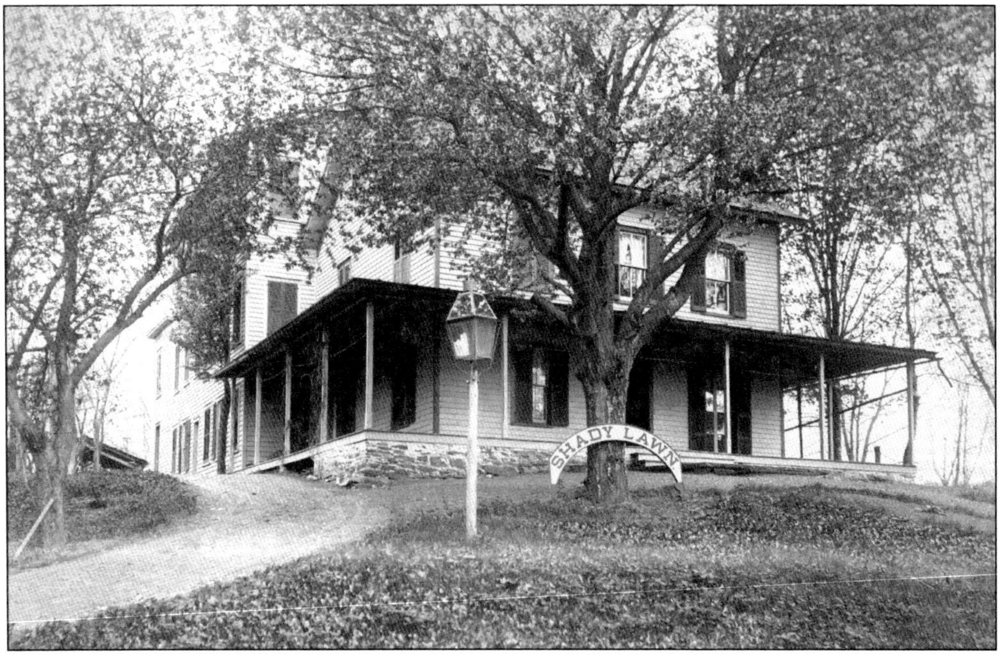

The Shady Lawn's grand porches were a haven for guests. Located next to the Episcopal church on Route 739, this hospitable inn was run by Trudy and Joe DeAngelo for many years. (Courtesy DF/DTHS.)

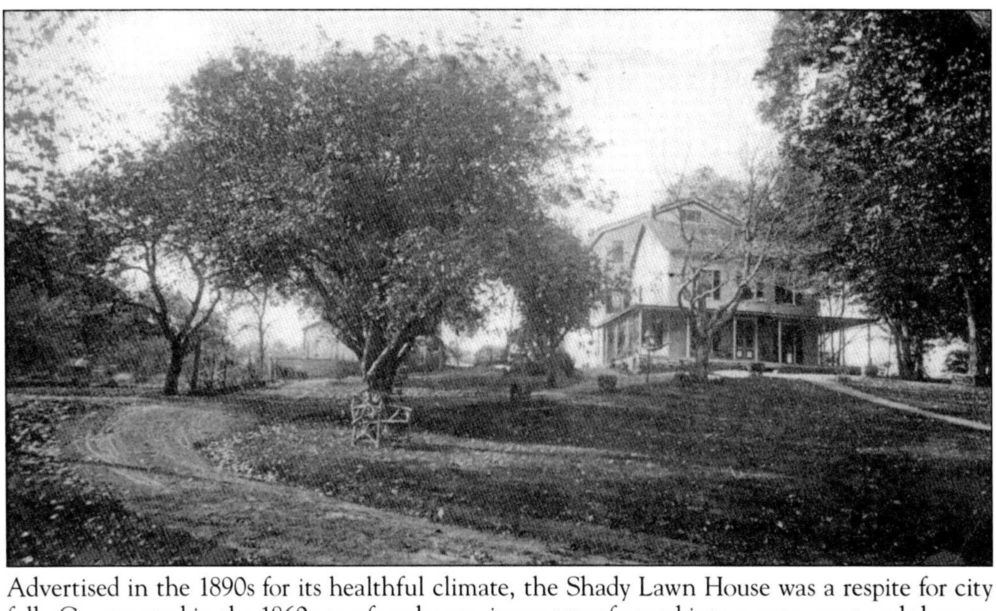

Advertised in the 1890s for its healthful climate, the Shady Lawn House was a respite for city folk. Constructed in the 1860s as a farmhouse, it was transformed into a restaurant and then an inn. By the 1900s, its rooms accommodated 40 guests. (Courtesy DF/DTHS.)

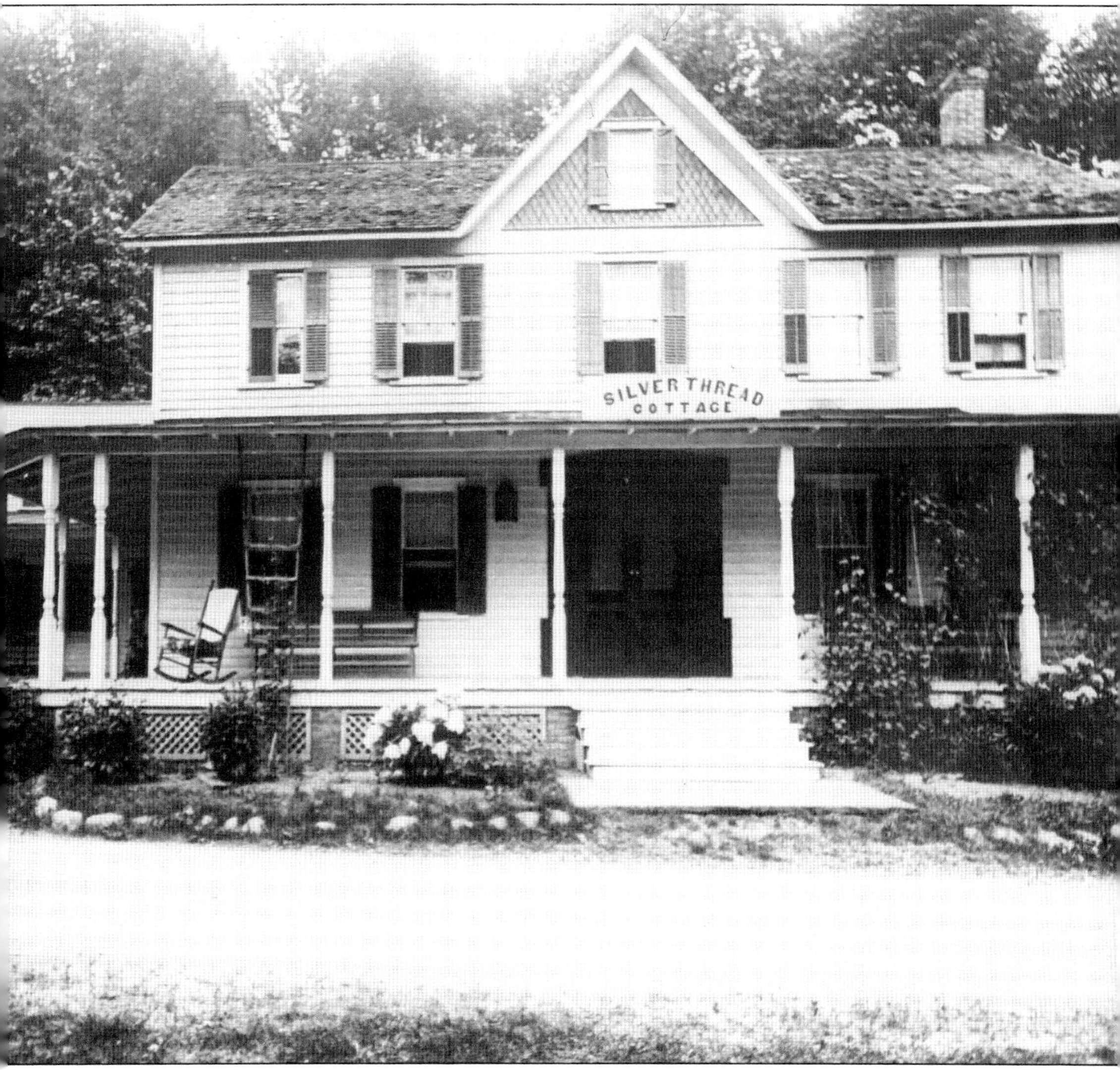

The Silver Thread Cottage, built in the early 20th century on the foundation of the old Mollineaux Mill House on the road leading to Dingmans Falls, was originally named the Laurel Grove Cottage. This tourist destination had rooms for 20 guests and was a favorite due to its proximity to the majestic falls. Like many of the grand resorts in old Dingmans, it was lost to fire in 1950. (Courtesy Pike County Historical Society.)

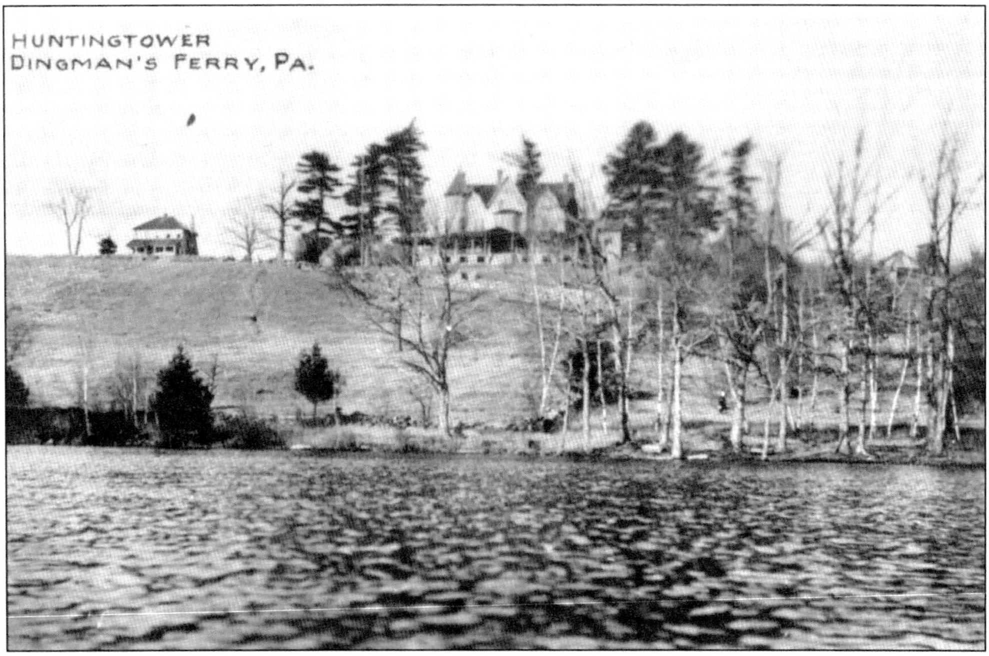

The Hunting Tower, a grand inn on Silver Lake Road across from Camp Massad, was built as a private home overlooking Beaver Dam, later known as Adams Dam. Fire consumed this magnificent building in the 1930s. (Courtesy Dorothy Schouppe Collection.)

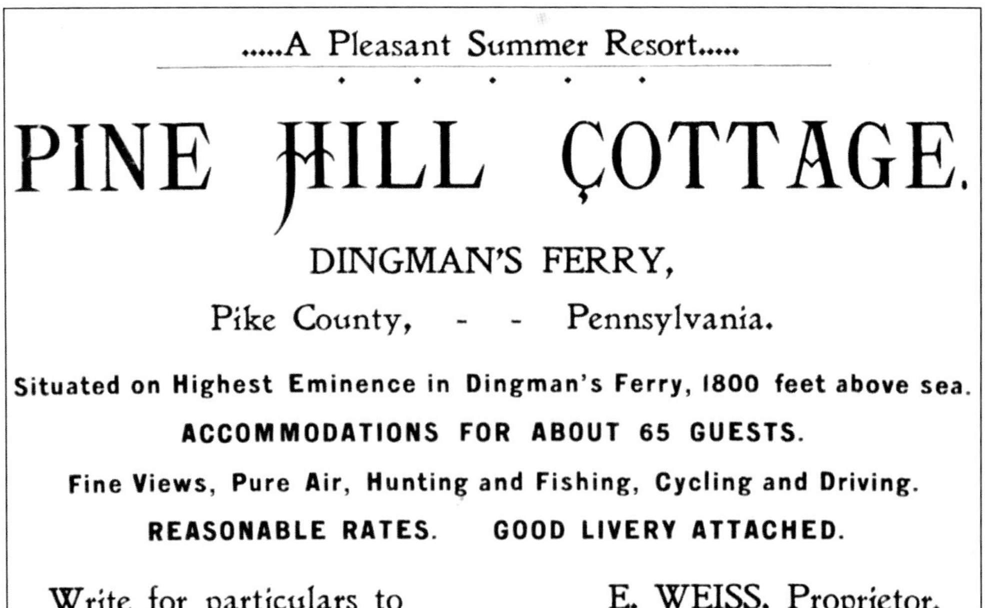

As in most of Pike County, tourism contributed substantially to the Dingmans Ferry economy. The main tourist attraction of "fine views and pure air" still lures visitors to this picturesque and intriguing northeast corner of Pennsylvania. (Courtesy Roberta and Leroy Cron.)

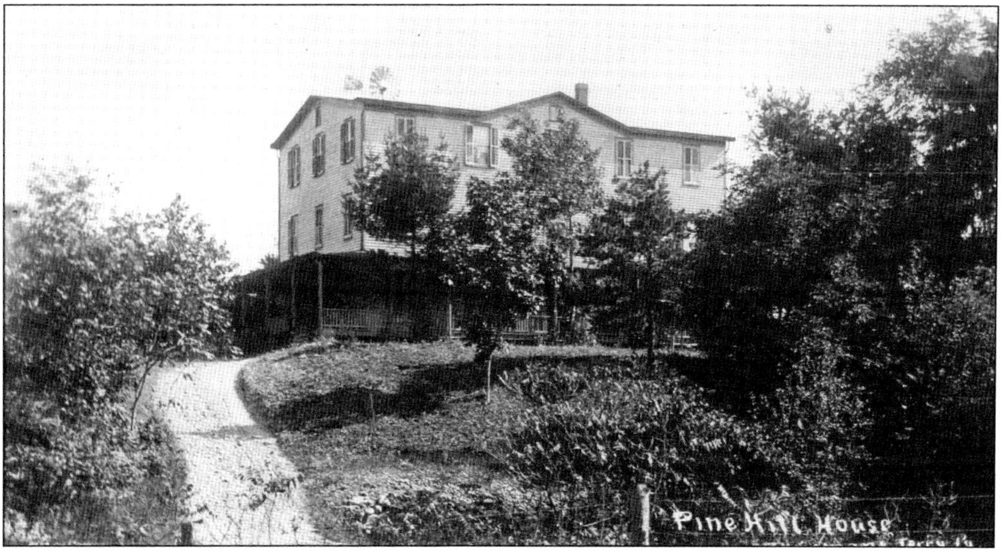

The Pine Hill House was located off of Tie Alley behind the Episcopal church. Built at the dawn of the 20th century, this hotel used a well pumped by a windmill, visible in the rear of the building. (Courtesy Pike County Historical Society.)

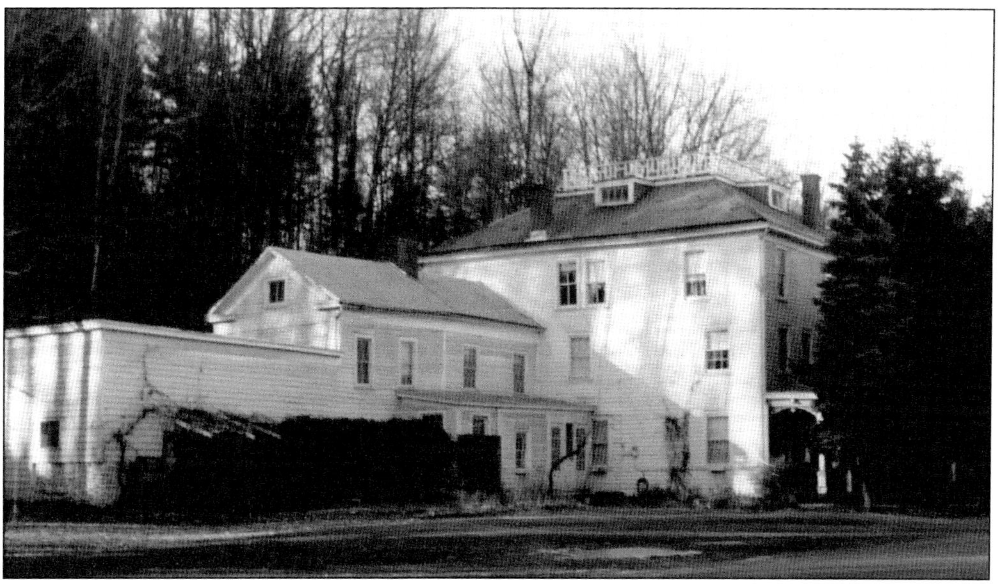

This 1973 photograph shows the Dingman House in its final years. It was only a matter of time before the grand hotel vanished into memory. It is an understated loss, as part of this exceptional structure was in fact one of the first homes built in the village. Opinions differ as to who constructed this beautiful clapboard house—Judge Dingman or William Brodhead, his son-in-law. The later addition to the simple family home transformed it into a splendid inn offering guests hospitality, recreation, rest, and the river valley's natural wonders. (Courtesy George and Carolyn Hotalen.)

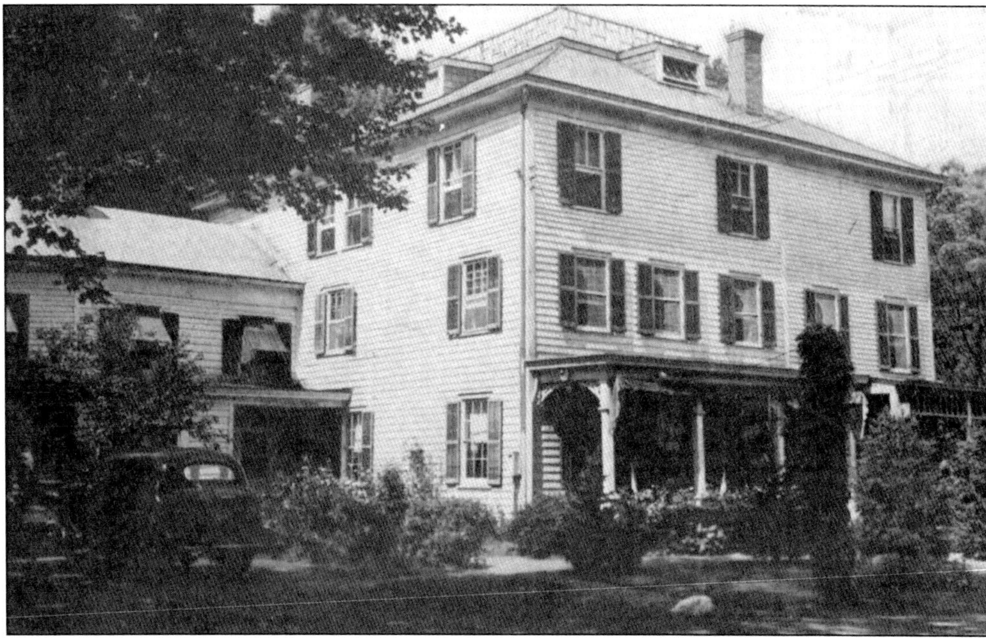

The Dingman House stood across Route 739 from the High Falls Hotel, on the corner of present-day Route 209. A magnificent building constructed in the early 1800s, it was renovated and enlarged from a three-room structure to a hotel serving 35 guests. (Courtesy DF/DTHS.)

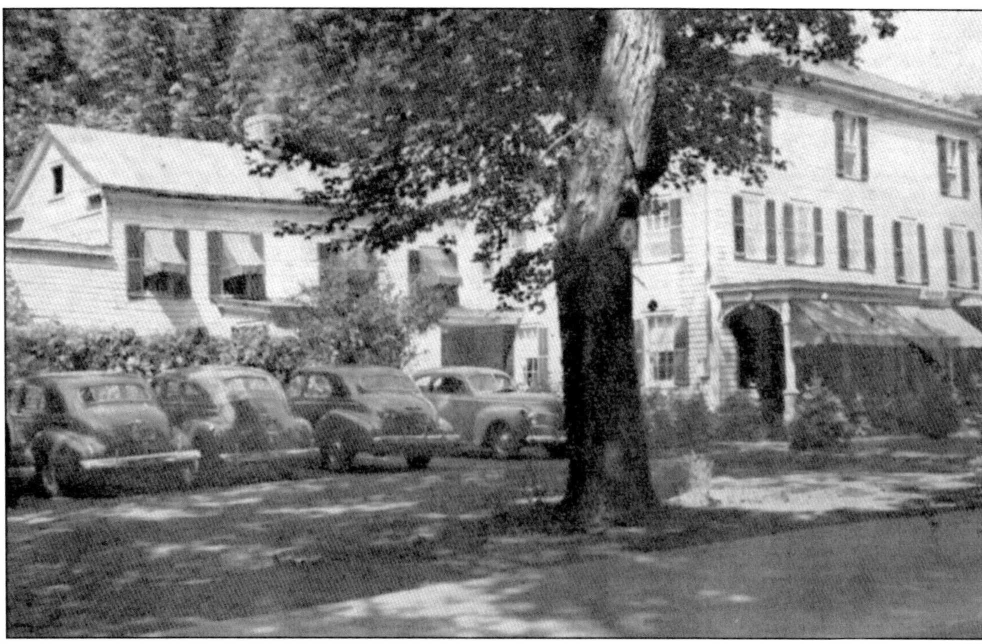

One of many popular local resorts, the Dingman House offered a relaxation for New York and Philadelphia visitors. When a house of temperance in the early 1900s, Sundays were so respected that the horses were not even moved. Its demolition in the 1970s, making way for the Delaware Water Gap National Recreation Area, made the Dingman House one of the last resorts in Dingmans Ferry.

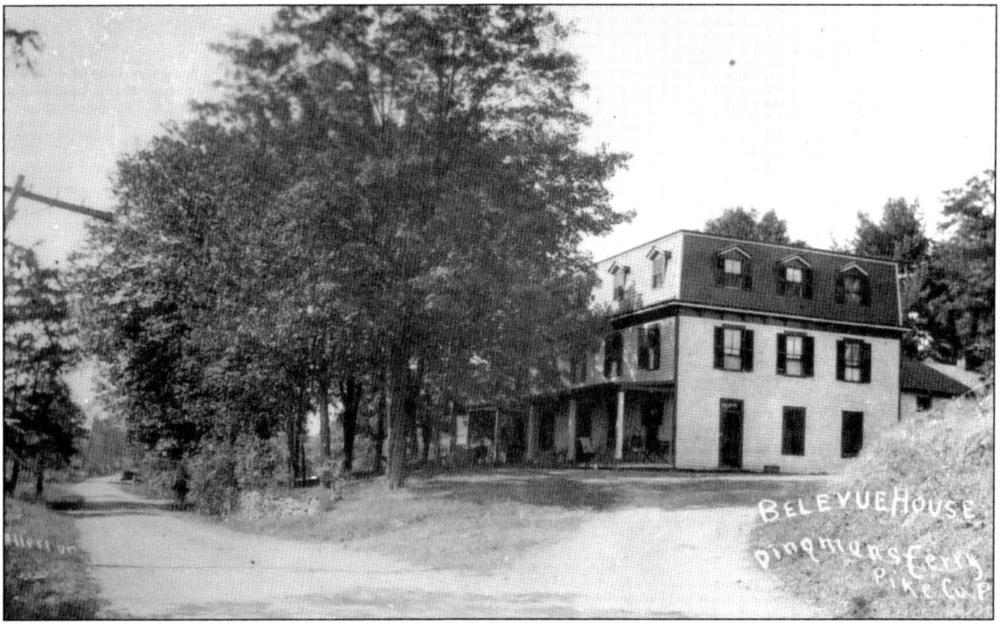

In the early 20th century, W. E. Kern owned the Bellevue. He was the nephew of the nationally recognized artists Richard H., Edward M., and Benjamin Kern. These gentlemen were part of many early western expeditions. During these western tours of the 1850s, most notably the Fremont Expedition, they sketched the terrain of the Rocky Mountains in Colorado. Kern County and Kern River in California are named in their honor. (Courtesy DF/DTHS.)

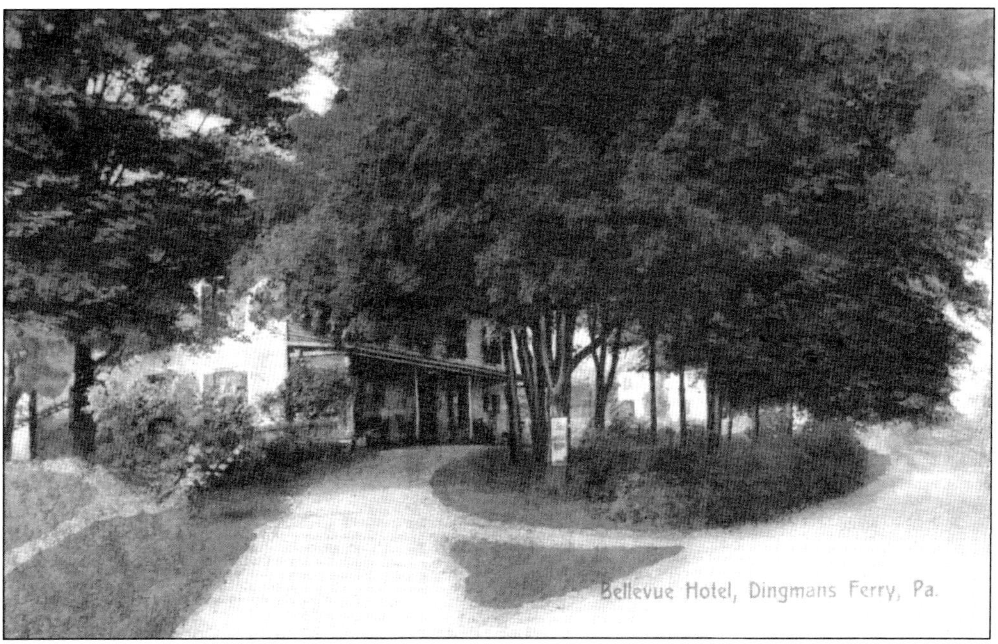

The Bellevue Hotel stood gracefully on Main Street, north of Wilson Hill Road. This hotel accommodated 25 guests and provided its visitors with fresh vegetables from the garden. A stay in 1902 cost $8 to $10 a week. The last owners of this hotel were Fred and Ann Cron. (Courtesy DF/DTHS.)

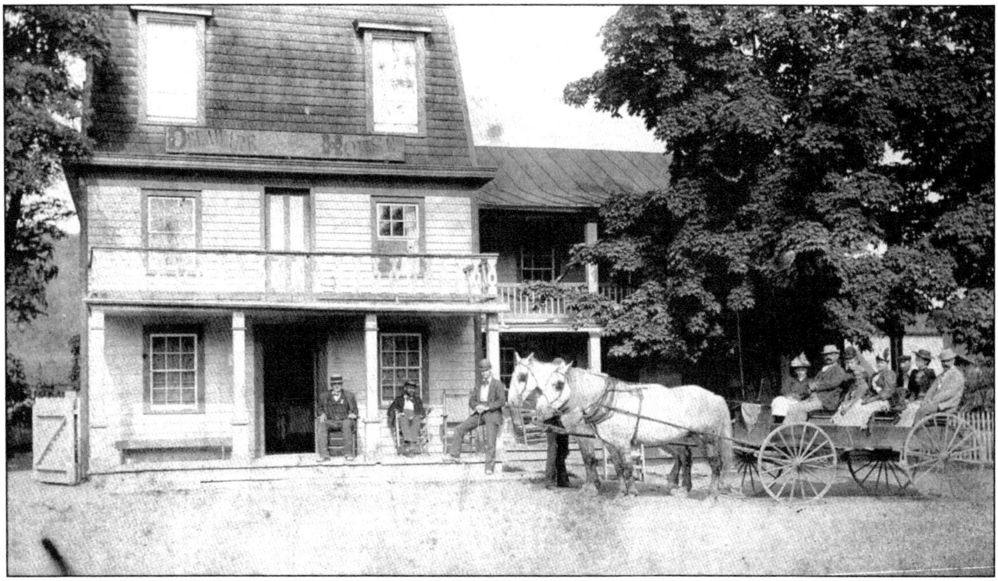

This is an incredible early view of the popular Delaware House, built just south of Johnny B. Road on the right side of Route 209. A celebration ball requiring "proper attire" followed the November 21, 1866, grand opening. Van Gordon, known for his "down to earth hospitality" operated this successful inn from 1870 until 1937. In 1970, it became one of the last grand and historic hotels to close in the once thriving village of Dingmans Ferry. (Courtesy Roberta and Leroy Cron.)

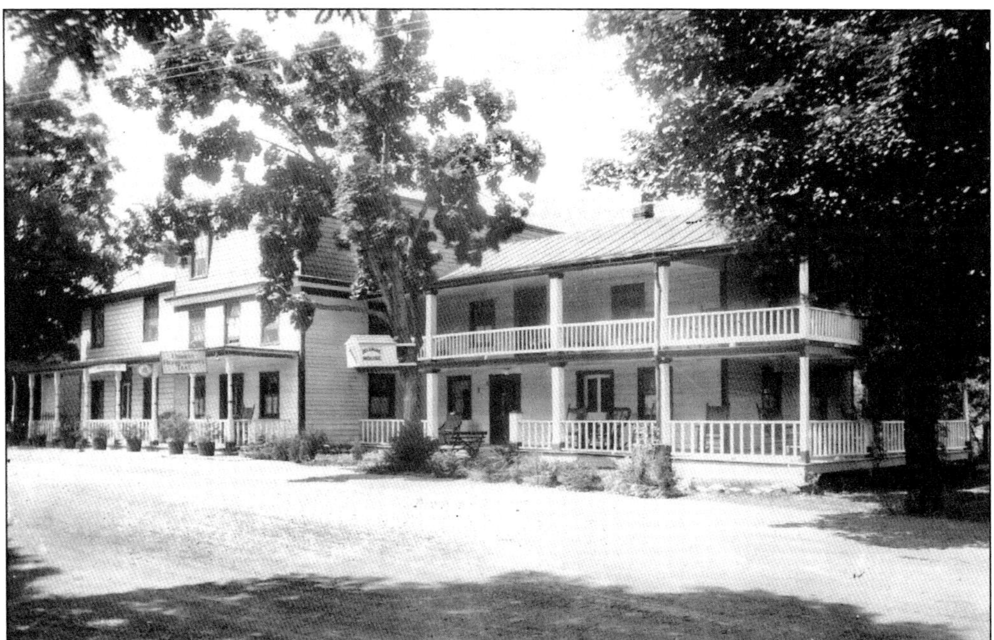

The Delaware House, like many hotels of its day, had spacious, comfortable porches where visitors could rock the day away. This hotel served 20 guests at $7 a week, as advertised in 1907. (Courtesy DF/DTHS.)

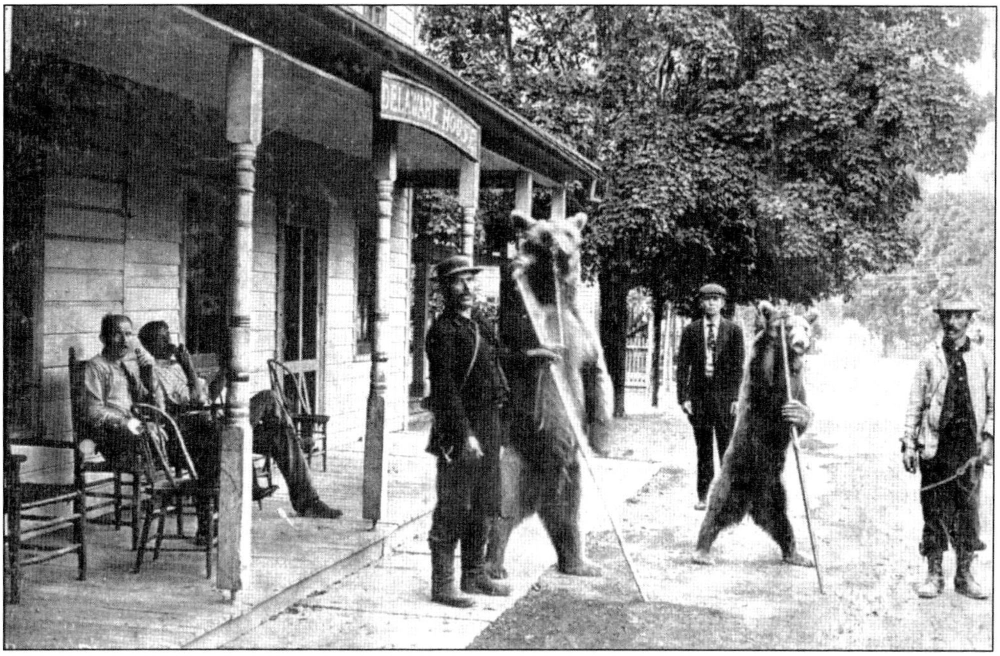

In the 1890s, a traveling show came to Dingmans Ferry, entertaining the locals with trained dancing bears at the Delaware House. (Courtesy DF/DTHS.)

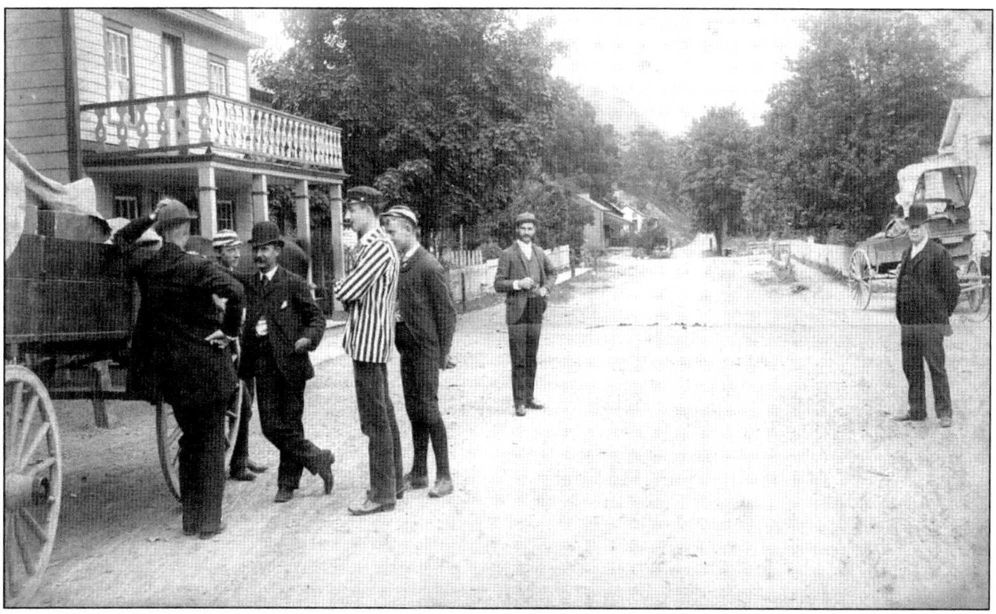

The Delaware House was a hot spot for activity in Dingmans Ferry and Delaware Township from the beginning of its existence. If bicyclists were not visiting, bears dancing, or a baseball game occurring, there was always time for political discussion and local gossip, as shown here about 1890. (Courtesy Roberta and Leroy Cron.)

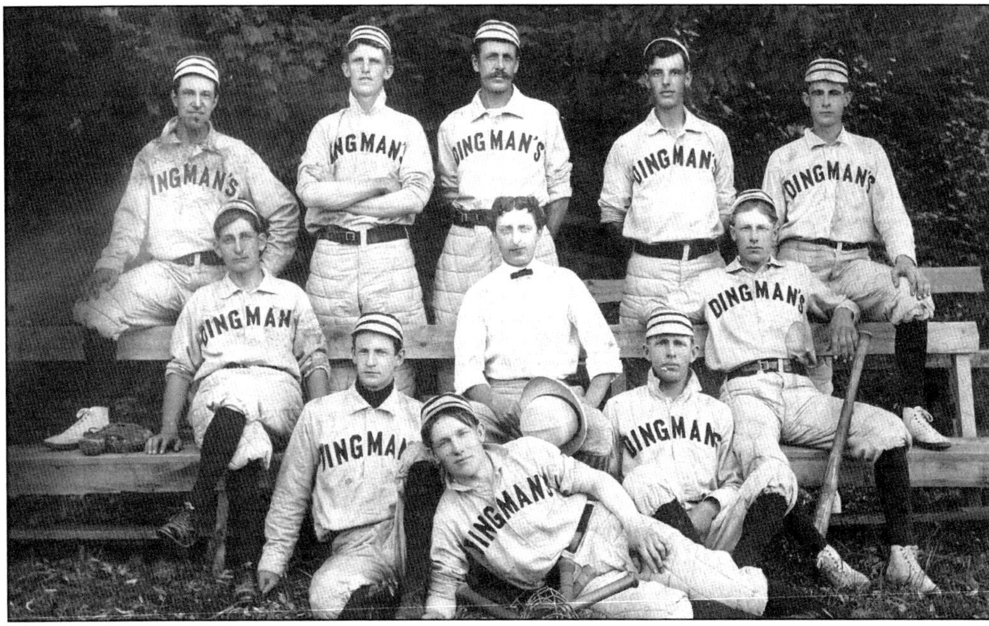

Like many small towns and villages, Dingmans Ferry promoted its own baseball team. The team headquartered at the Delaware House played in the fenced-in field behind the bar. The only entrance to the field was through the hotel's bar. Pictured here, from left to right, are the following: (first row) William Truax, Andrew Middaugh, and Gus Middaugh; (second row) Warren VanGorden, James Barry, and Charles Middaugh; (third row) William Richards, George Darragh, John Hornbeck, Royal Lakin, and Anson Kinter. (Courtesy Roberta and Leroy Cron.)

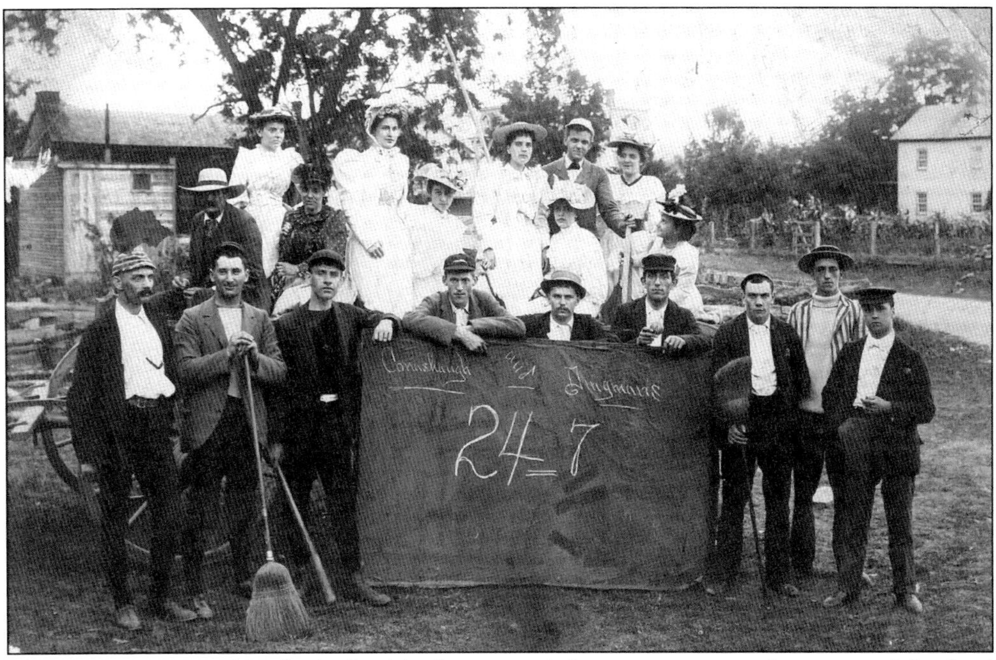

The game is over, and by the look of the broom and the score, it was a clean sweep. The final tally was Conashaugh 24 and Dingmans 7. (Courtesy Roberta and Leroy Cron.)

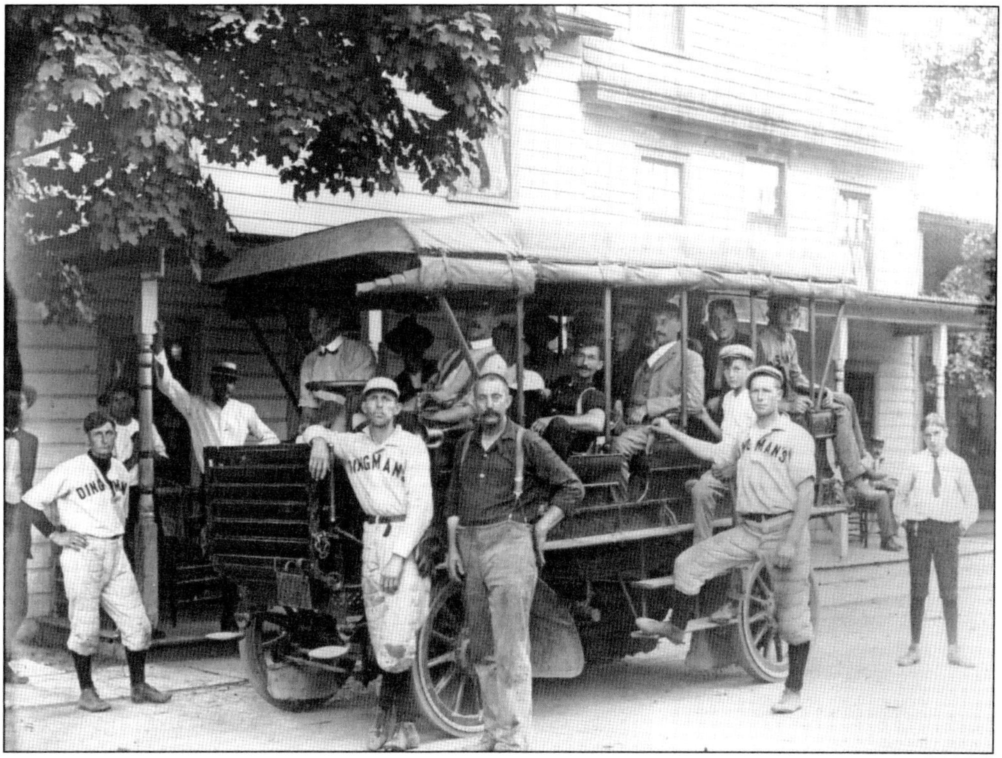

In the early 20th century, town ball teams traveled to other area games. Here, the Dingmans Ferry team loads up in front of the Delaware House, perhaps to play its arch rival in nearby Port Jervis, New York. (Courtesy DF/DTHS.)

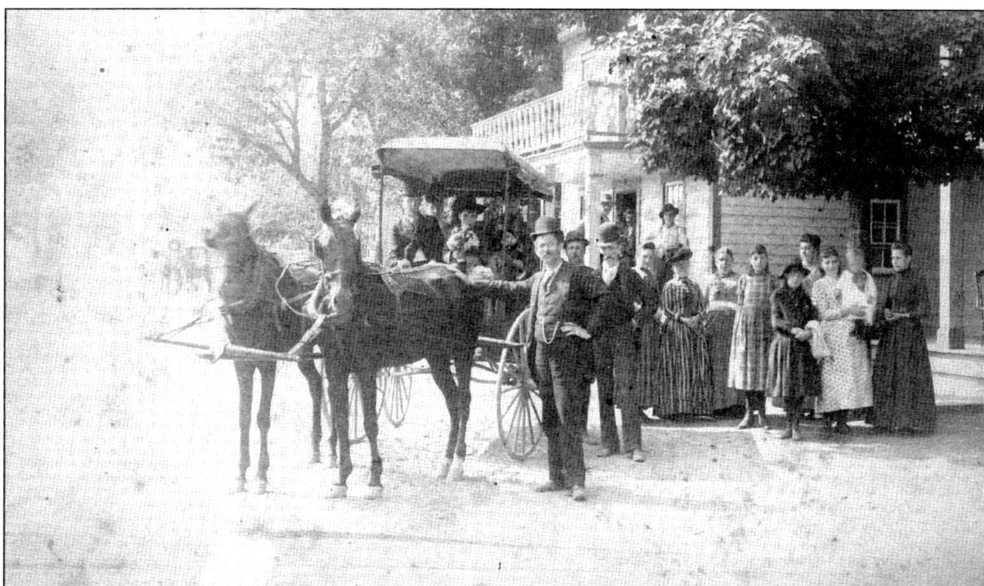

Dingmans Ferry was a favorite vacation spot of the 1890s. Visitors from New York City would travel to Port Jervis by train and then by coach the 18 miles to Dingmans Ferry. This photograph was taken in front of the Delaware House about 1890. (Courtesy Roberta and Leroy Cron.)

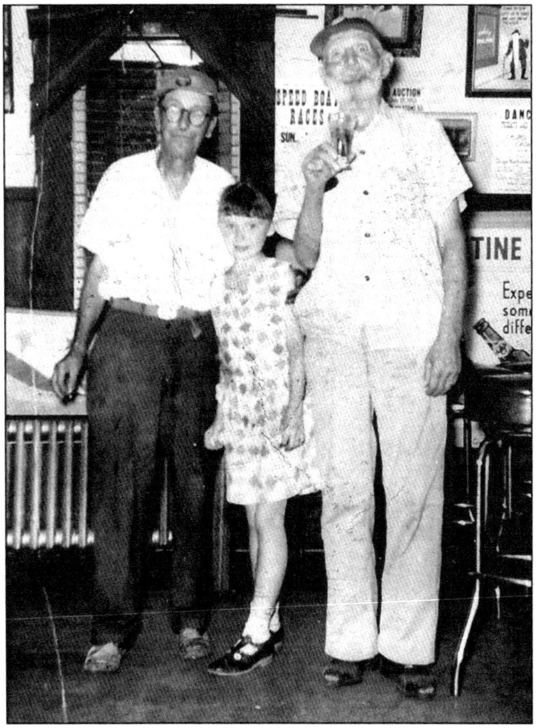

Gus Middaugh (right) enjoys an ice-cold beer at the Delaware House. Fred Hotalen (left) and Terry Hoffman pose with him in this 1950s photograph. (Courtesy George Hotalen.)

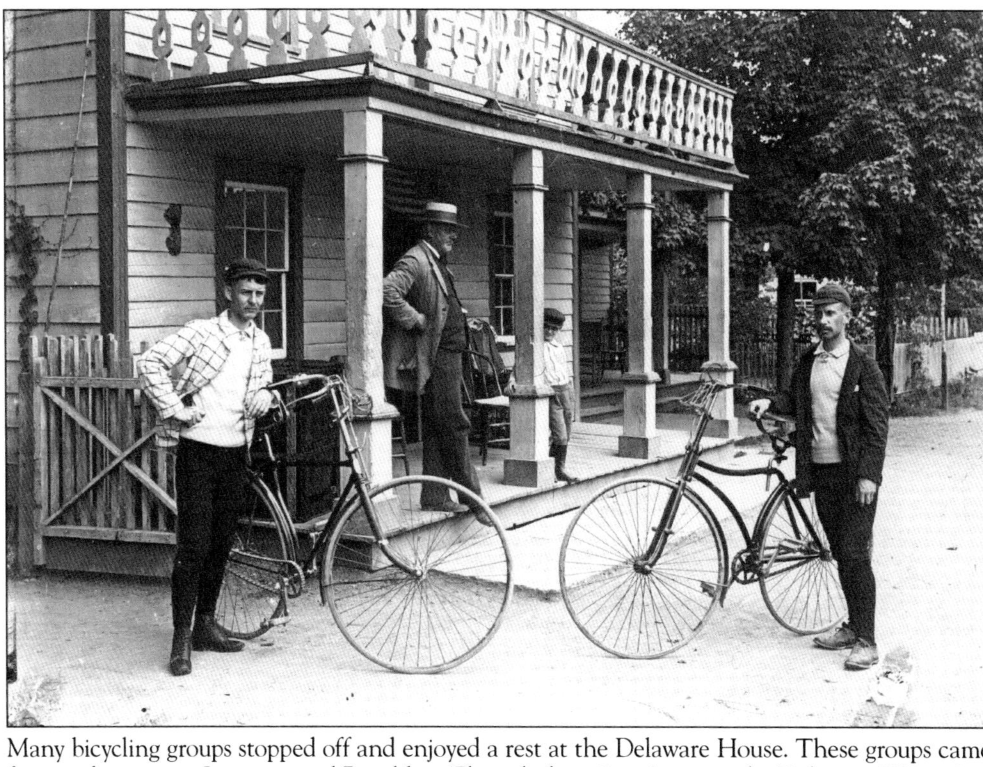

Many bicycling groups stopped off and enjoyed a rest at the Delaware House. These groups came from as far away as Scranton and Brooklyn. The ride from Port Jervis to the Delaware Water Gap was considered to be the most beautiful in the region. (Courtesy Pike County Historical Society.)

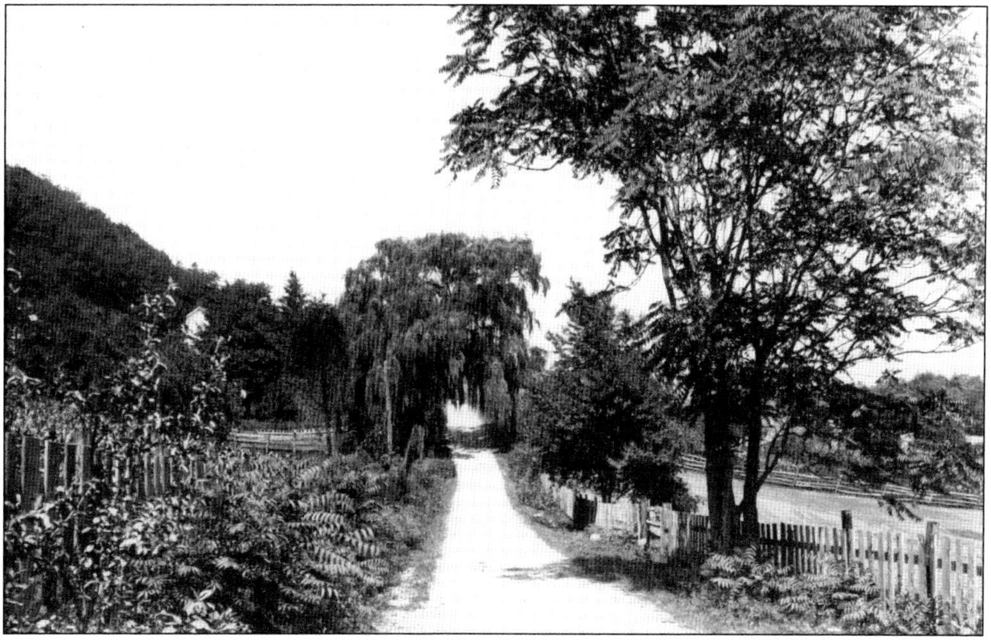

This image highlights a section of road between Milford and Dingmans Ferry. According to the June 9, 1878, edition of the *Milford Dispatch*, the area near the Courtright Farm "was one of the many coasting places for bicycles on the River Road." (Courtesy Pike County Historical Society.)

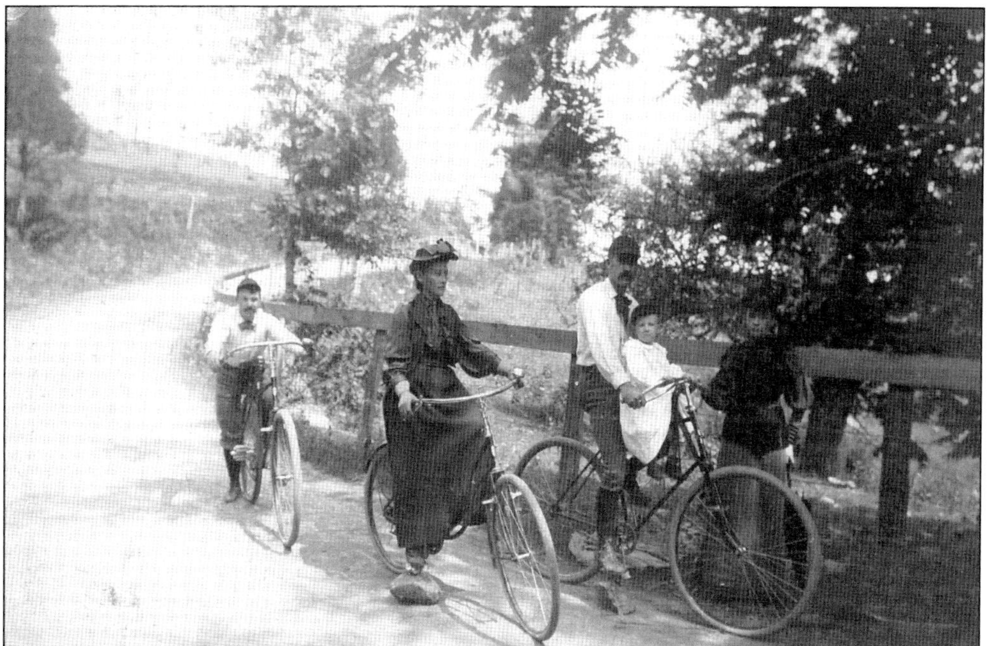

Bicyclists pedal along the River Road, near the Conashaugh Creek, in the 1890s. (Courtesy Roberta and Leroy Cron.)

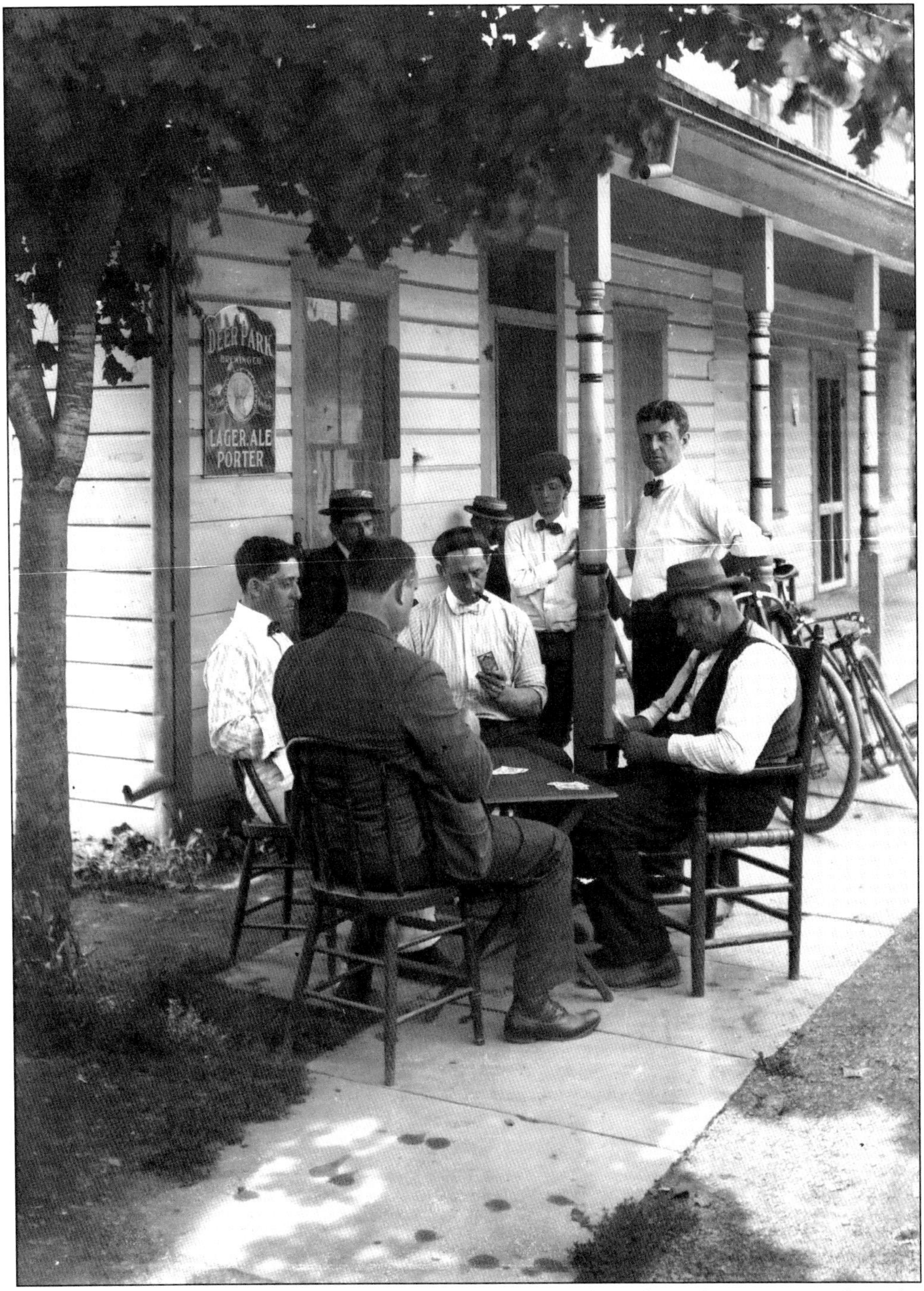

Dingmans Ferry was one of numerous popular resort towns along the Delaware River, where the beauty and remoteness afforded a peaceful setting away from New York City and Philadelphia. In this c. 1890 photograph, Delaware House guests play open-air card games and drink refreshing draft beer from Port Jervis's Deerpark Brewery. (Courtesy DF/DTHS.)

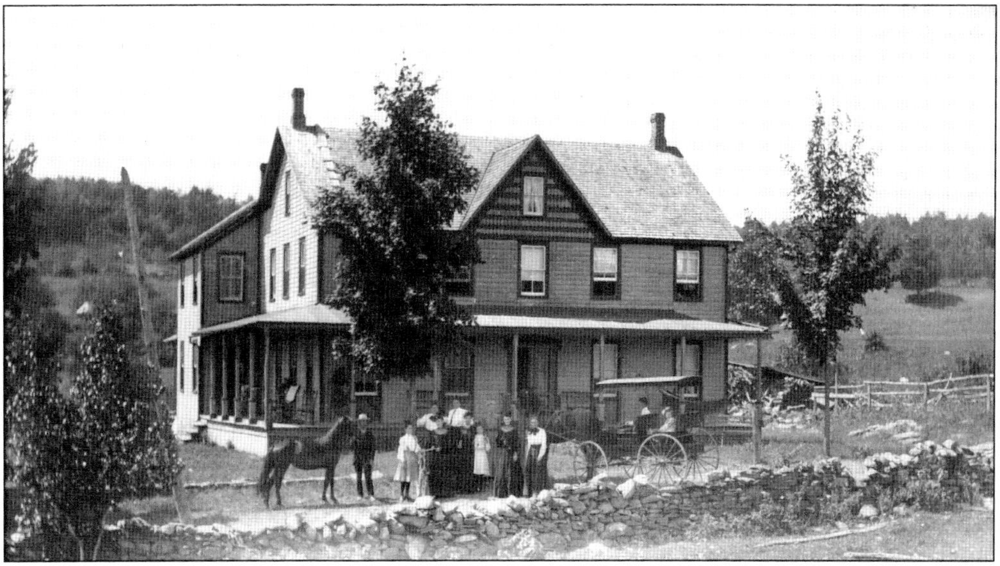

The Hergert family operated a boardinghouse on Bethany Turnpike (Route 739) in this lovely farmhouse, which today is the main building of the Delaware Run complex. (Courtesy Pike County Historical Society.)

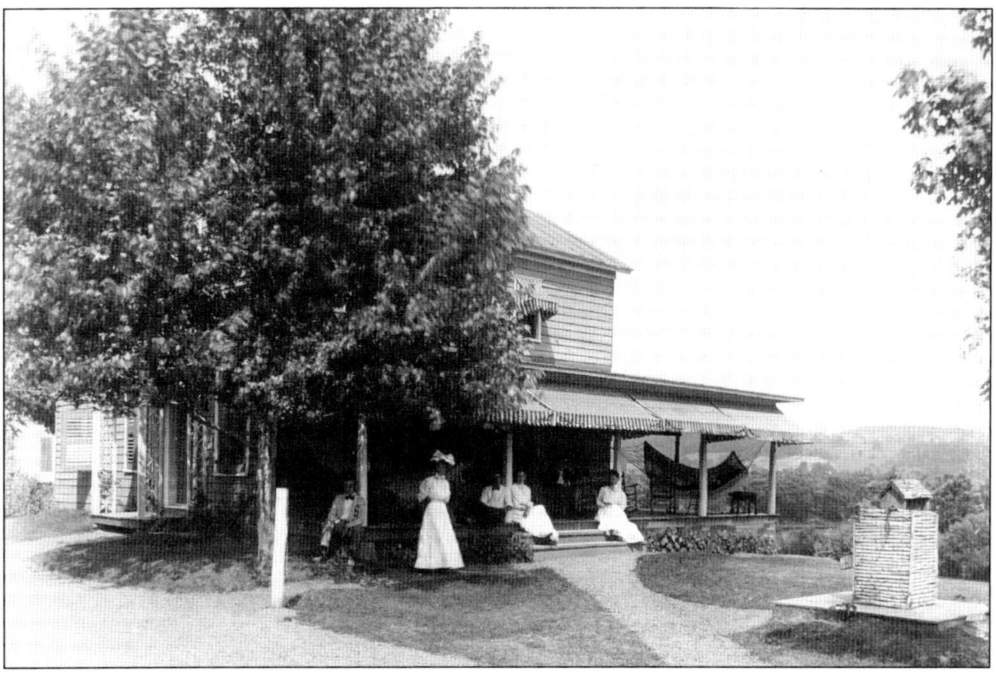

This 1890s photograph brings to life the building replacing the original Dingman Homestead. On this site, Andrew Dingman built a stone house sited diagonally from the present-day cemetery on Main Street (Route 209). In later years, this stately home became a boardinghouse known as Stellwagon and Nostrand's Cottage and was considered the most historic location in the village. (Courtesy Pike County Historical Society.)

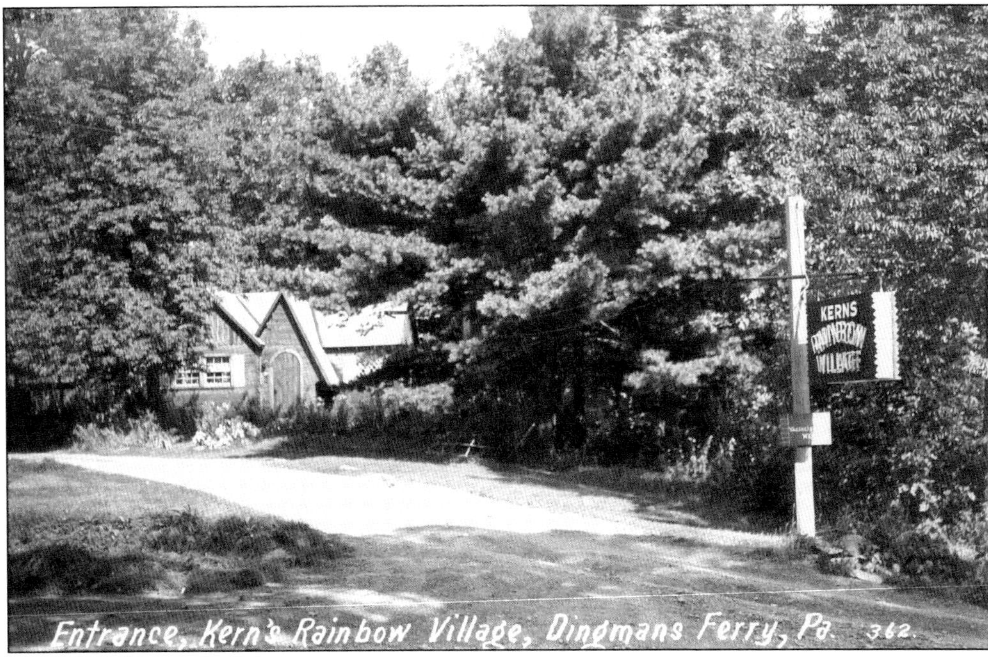

Kern's Rainbow Village was a summer resort built by Francis and Ethel Kern in the 1940s. The weekend getaway was located on Silver Lake Road, across from today's Red Lion Inn. Here, the Kerns built a colony of storybook-like buildings. (Courtesy Viola Kern Canouse.)

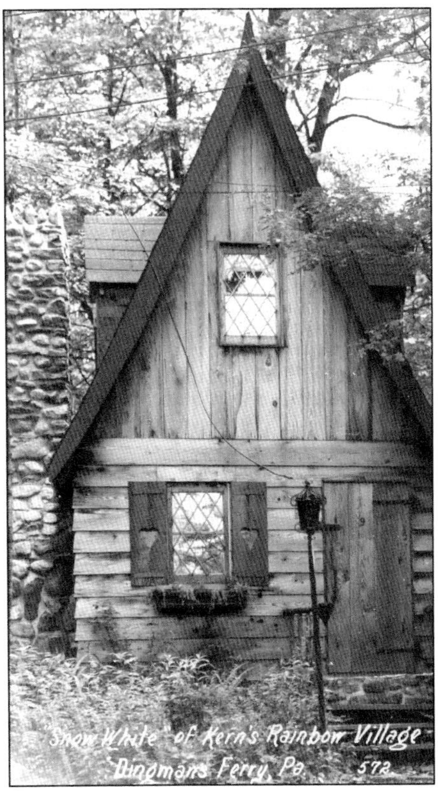

One of the charming buildings of Kern's Rainbow Village was the Snow White. All of the structures had appealing names, including Goldfinch, Cardinal, Meadowlark, Whipporwill, Peacock, Stardust, Blue Jay, and Rainbow House. (Courtesy Viola Kern Canouse.)

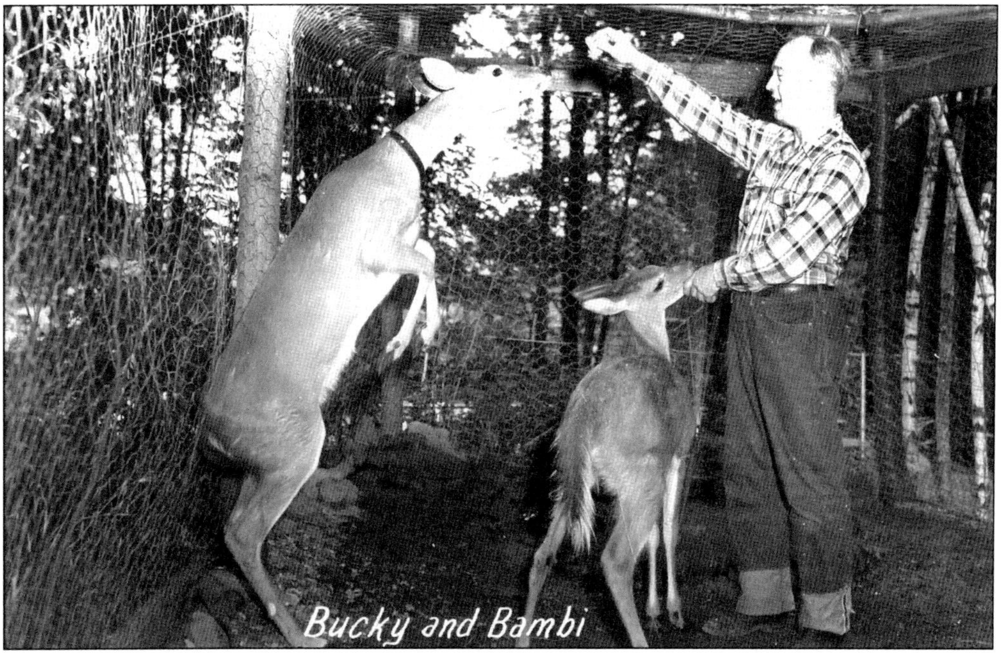

The Kerns loved the country life and the animals that called Dingmans Ferry home. Over the years, they would adopt various orphaned animals, including these two deer. Here, Francis Kern plays with Bucky and Bambi, who later became the center of the Moon Valley Park petting zoo he opened in the 1950s on the outskirts of Milford. (Courtesy Viola Kern Canouse.)

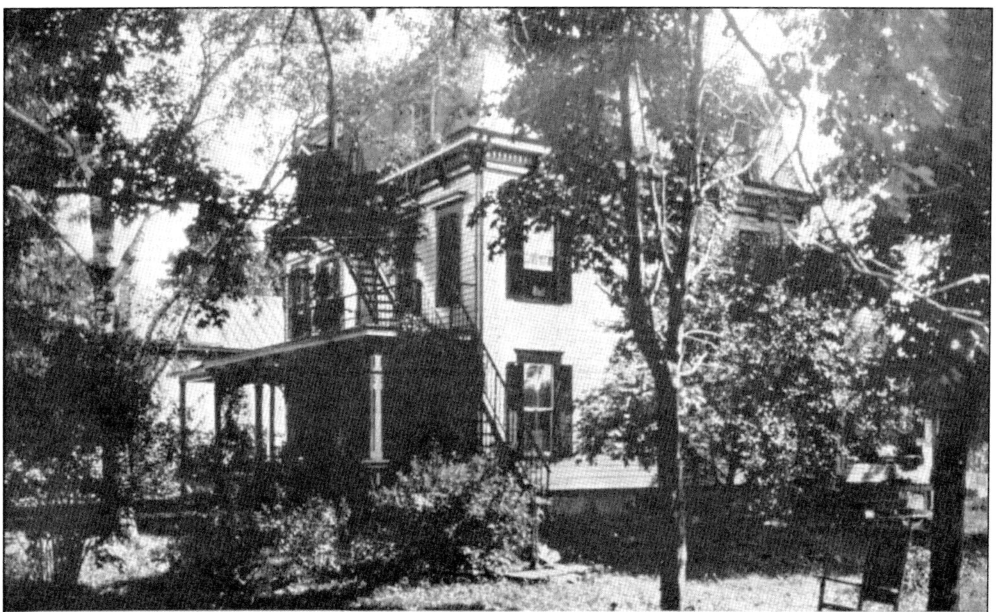

In the early 1900s, J. B. Westbrook built the Mansion House as a private residence. In 1903, A. Albright purchased the property and operated it as a hotel. Located on Main Street opposite Johnny B. Road, this stately building was lost to fire in 1950. (Courtesy Harry Arnold.)

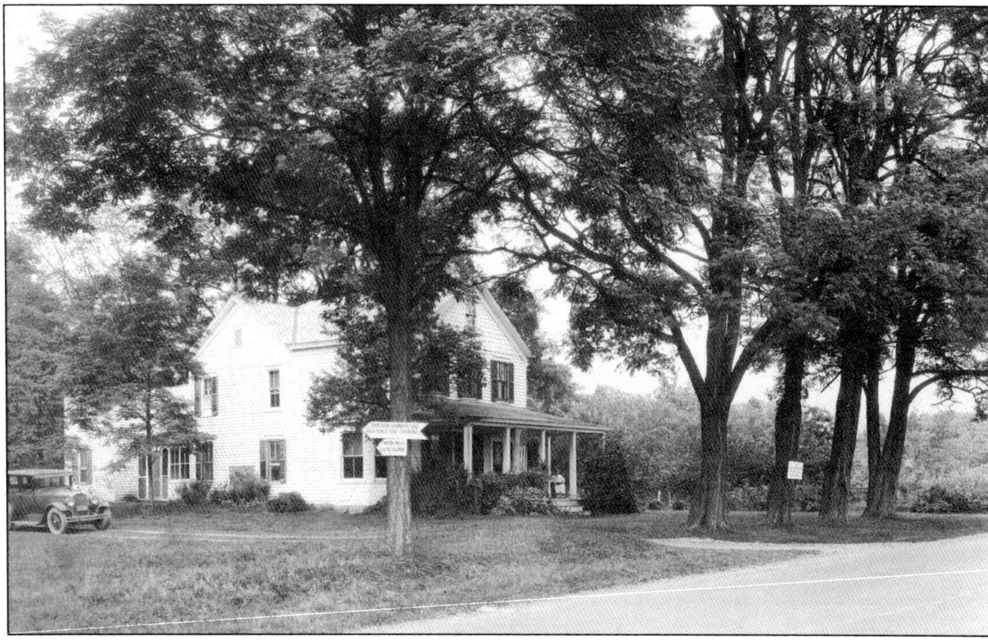

The Brumbaugh Homestead, located on Main Street (Route 209) just south of Chestnut Ridge Road, was originally the Hornbeck Farm, an elegant home dating back to the mid-1800s. In the first half of the 20th century, it was known as the Indian Ladder House and was owned by Harry Briscoe. (Courtesy DF/DTHS.)

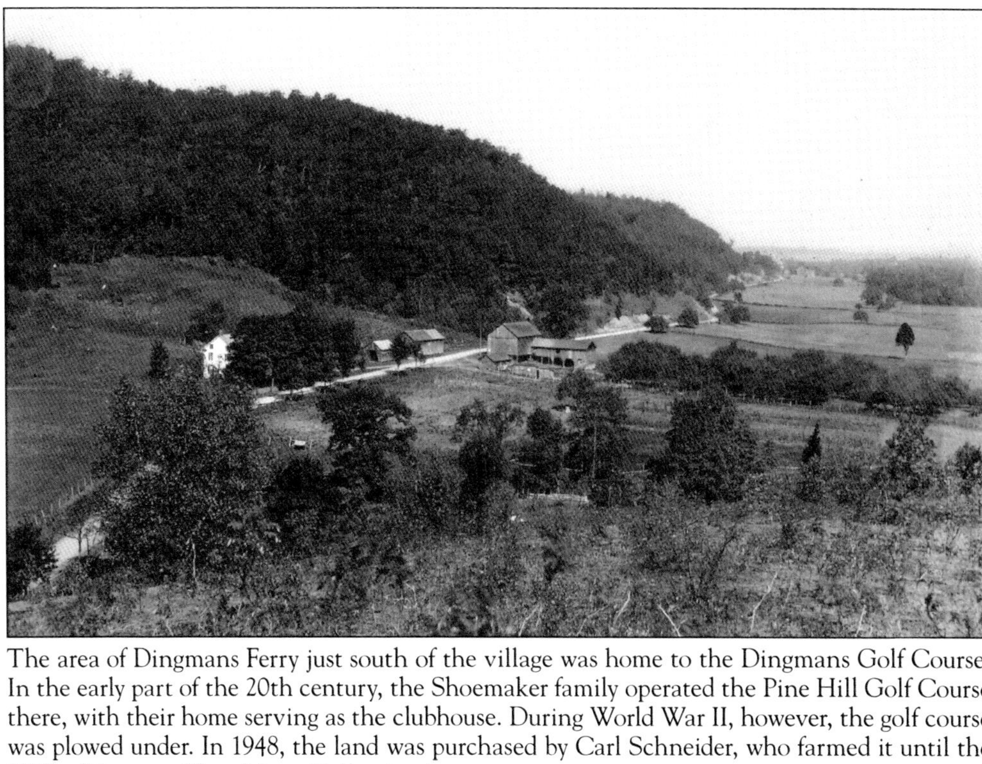

The area of Dingmans Ferry just south of the village was home to the Dingmans Golf Course. In the early part of the 20th century, the Shoemaker family operated the Pine Hill Golf Course there, with their home serving as the clubhouse. During World War II, however, the golf course was plowed under. In 1948, the land was purchased by Carl Schneider, who farmed it until the 1970s. (Courtesy Flora Myers Collection.)

Two

RIVERS AND STREAMS

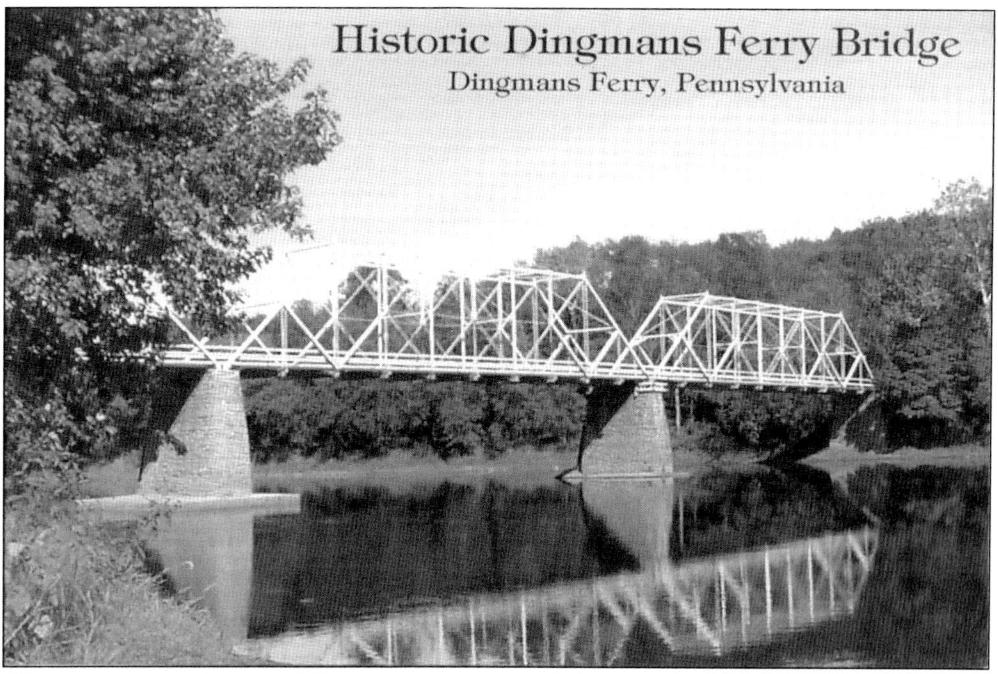

This postcard, produced in 2000, recognized the 100th anniversary of the current Dingmans Bridge. In 1900, a log listed the tolls as horseless carriage 40¢, two-horse wagon 25¢, one-horse wagon 18¢, horse and rider 10¢, horse led 6¢, bicycle 5¢, cattle 3¢, and footman 2¢. Always a convenient and popular Delaware crossing, the bridge collected tolls in excess of $15,000 in 1922. (Courtesy DF/DTHS.)

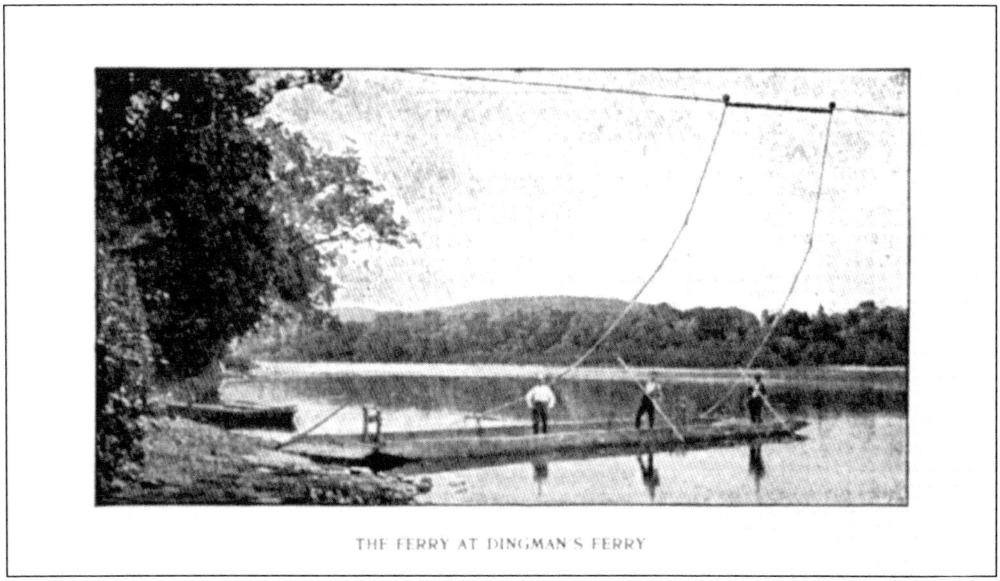

The Dingman family operated the bridge and ferry service for over 150 years. The last ferry service ran from 1860 to 1900. The Perkins brothers then purchased the rights to the bridge at sheriff's sale and constructed the present span. In this postcard, the cables guiding the raft across the Delaware are visible. (Courtesy Dorothy Schouppe Collection.)

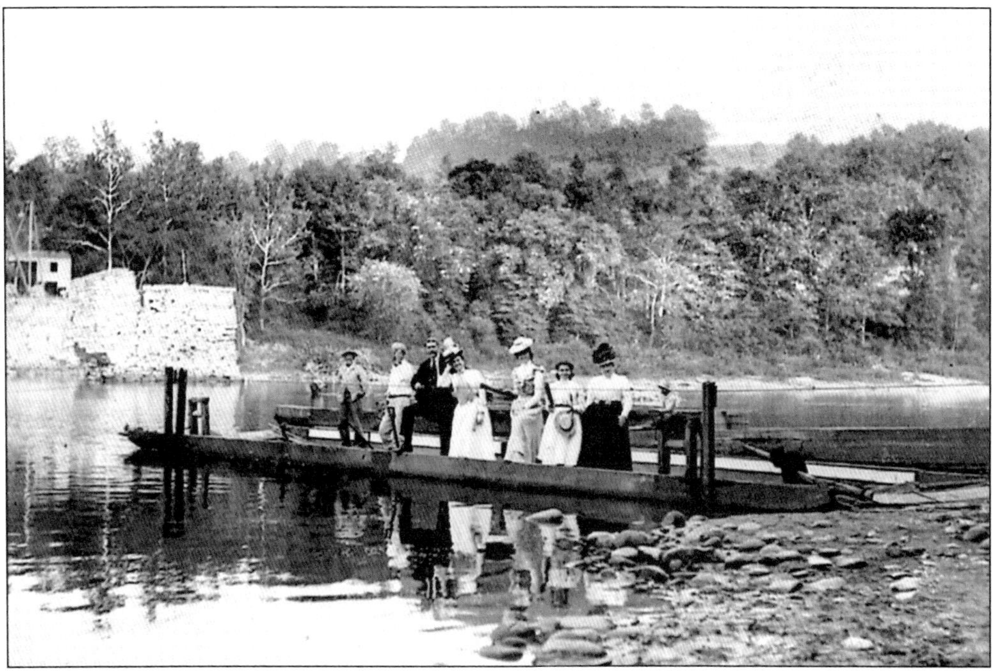

Andrew Dingman, founder of Dingmans Ferry, began the first ferry service in 1735. It operated continually for 100 years, and in 1835, the first bridge was built at this location. When the bridges failed, the ferry was reestablished and travel continued. Here, in the 1890s, a Victorian family prepares to cross. (Courtesy DF/DTHS.)

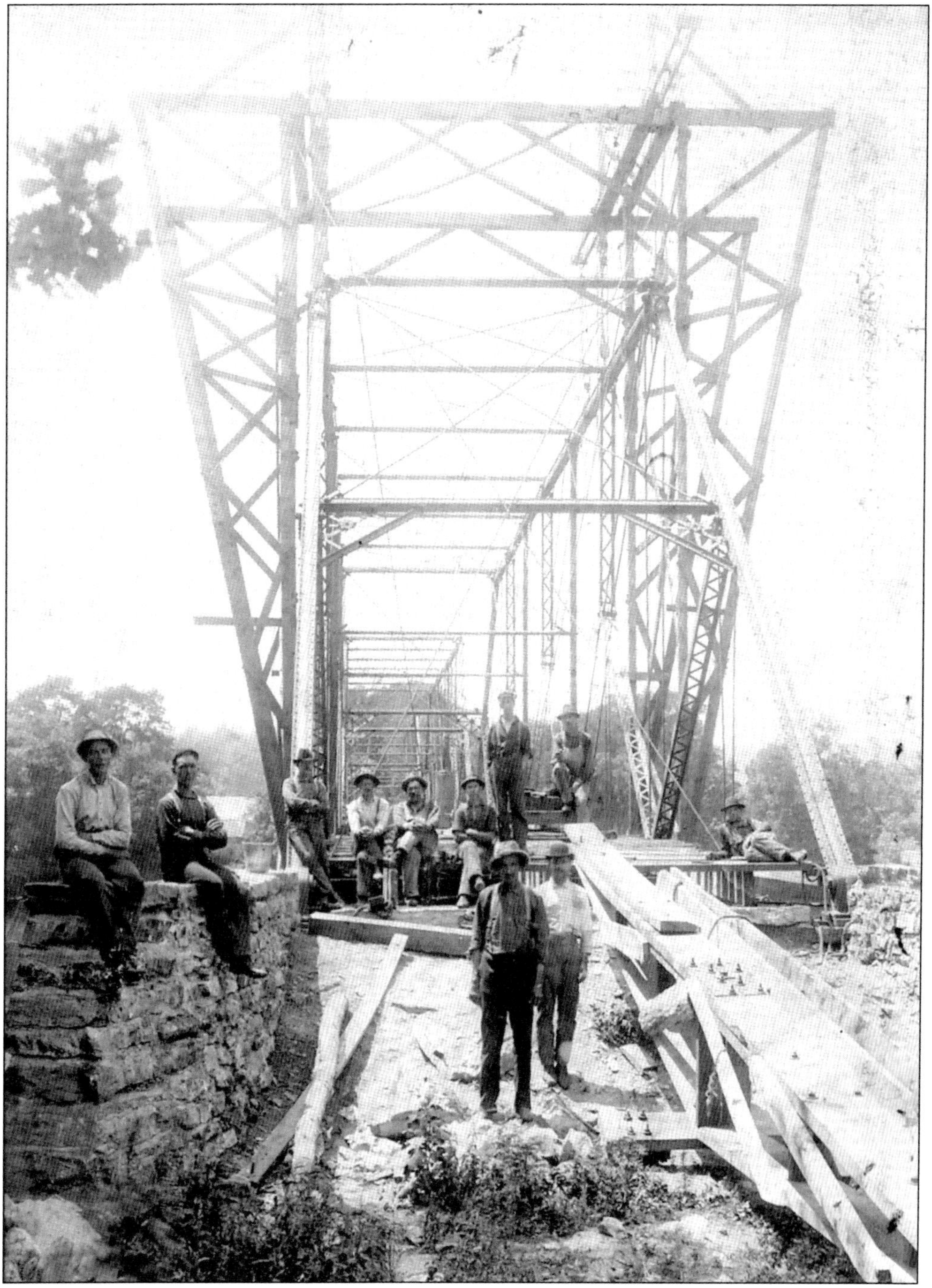

Dingmans Ferry has seen four bridges spanning this section of the Delaware River. The first, built in 1836, lasted until 1847, when high water swept the Milford Bridge downstream into the Dingmans Bridge. A new one was erected in 1850, but only lasted five years, when high winds blew the structure down. After a year, another bridge was built, but very poorly, literally falling apart in 1862. This 1900 photograph shows the current bridge under construction. (Courtesy DF/DTHS.)

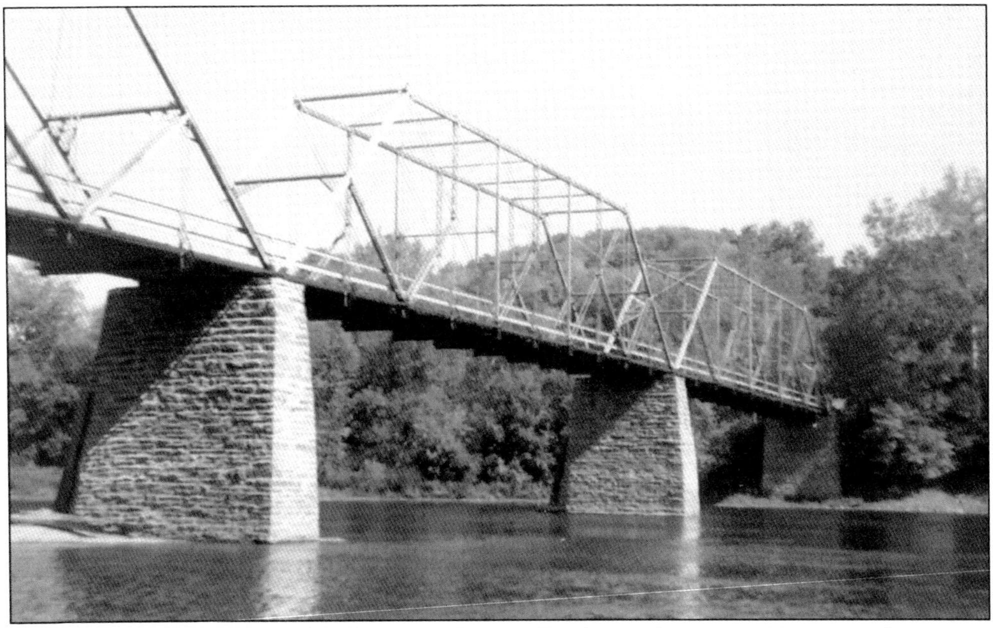

The Dingmans Bridge is one of the last privately owned bridges in the country. Serving as the gateway to Pike County for over 100 years, it stands as a monument to the past. (Courtesy DF/DTHS.)

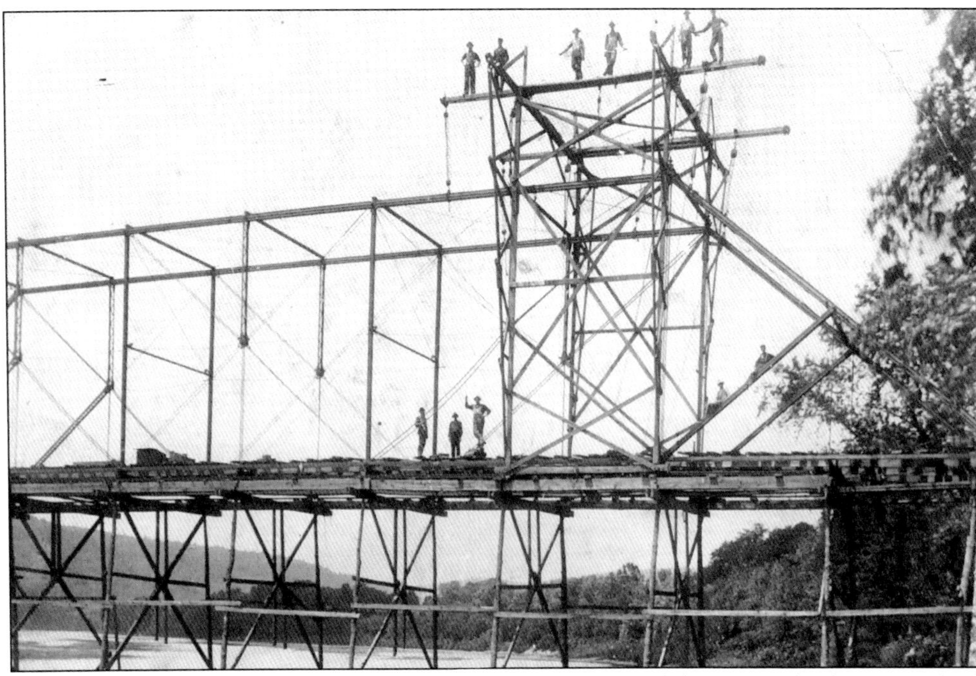

Bridge workers stop to pose in 1900, during the construction of the current bridge. It was built mainly from the remains of an old iron bridge from Muncie, which had spanned the Susquehanna River. Its construction six feet higher than the previous bridge has proved beneficial, as it has withstood the floods of 1903, 1955, 1981, and 2005. (Courtesy DF/DTHS.)

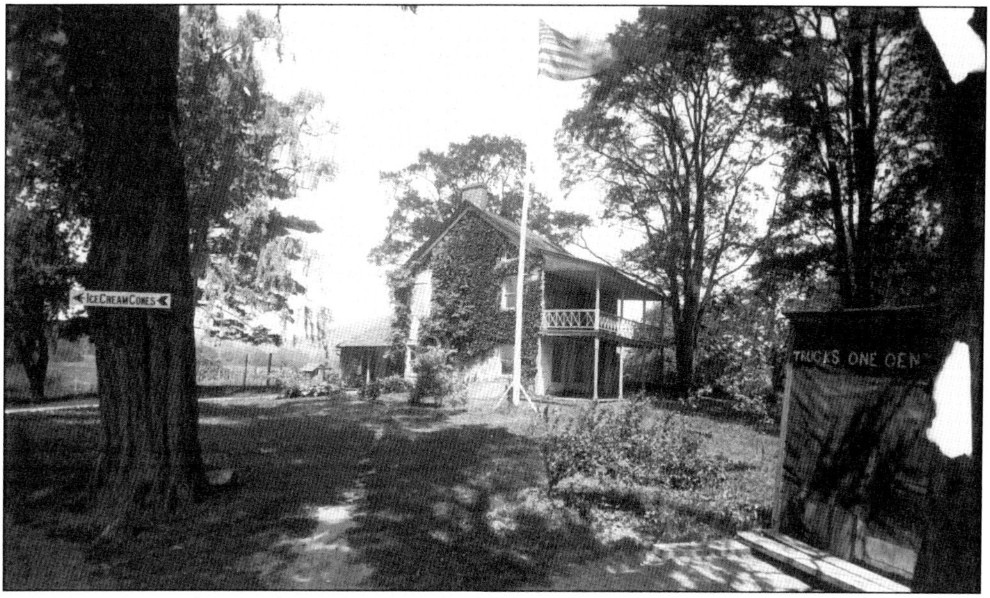

Daniel Dingman, the grandson of Andrew, built the Dingman Ferry River House in 1804. Daniel exerted the most critical impact on the village's early development. He served 10 years as state representative and used his influence to construct the Bethany Turnpike (Route 739), connecting Dingmans Ferry to New Jersey and Wayne County. His foresight resulted in the establishment of the first Dingman School. For 25 years, as an associate judge for this region, he rendered decisions in a legendary style. In local history, Daniel Dingman is remembered as a strong individual and a witty character not easily forgotten. (Courtesy Pike County Historical Society.)

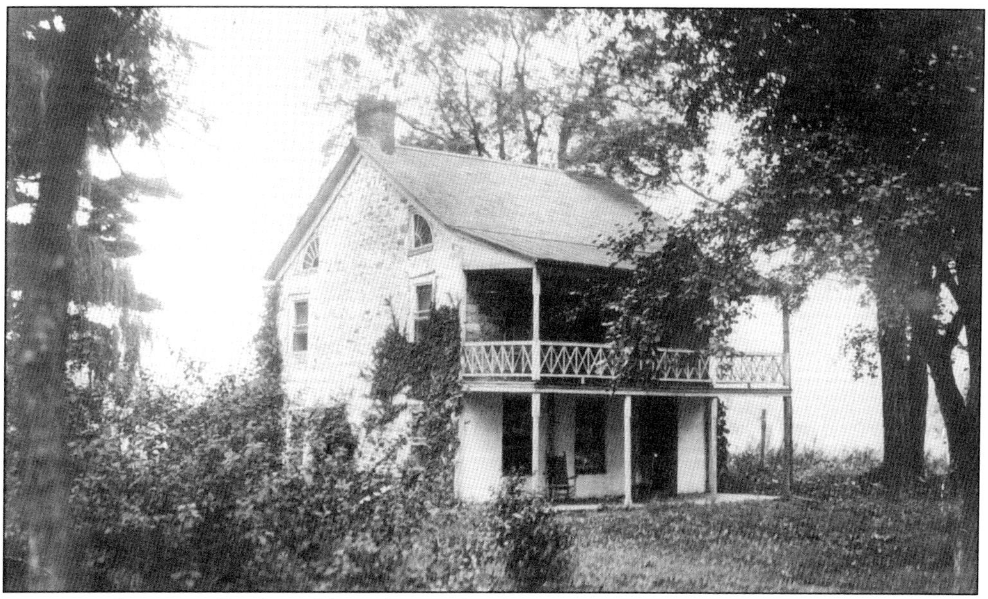

Numerous dangerous floods could not destroy the elegant, centuries-old river home of the renowned Dingman family. Still standing in the 21st century, it is a vital landmark, serving as the Dingmans Ferry Bridge's office and headquarters. (Courtesy Pike County Historical Society.)

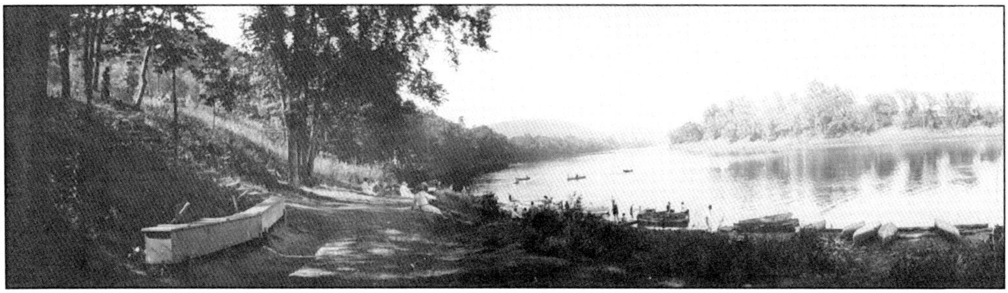

This serene panoramic view shows the Dingman Eddy, originally owned by Harry Garretson and later by Ike Andrews. Due to Garretson and Andrews' foresight, the eddy was transformed into a recreation area in the mid-1900s. (Courtesy Inez Dickison.)

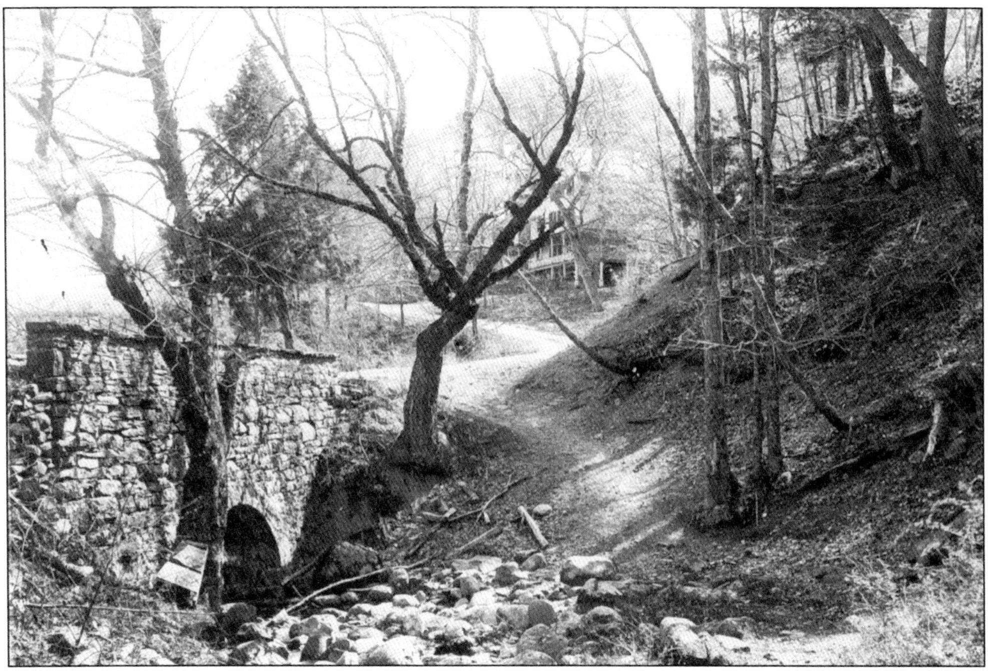

Seen here around 1893 is the Conashaugh Creek, with its beautiful stone arch bridge, constructed in 1858. The River Road is meandering up the hill to the Conashaugh Spring. (Courtesy Pike County Historical Society.)

Major Dingmans Ferry tourist attractions are the falls—Silver Thread and High—the highest in the Poconos, with Silver Thread even higher than Niagara Falls. Operated for many years by the Ogden family, the falls offer breathtaking views, which are enjoyed by thousands of visitors each year. (Courtesy Roberta and Leroy Cron.)

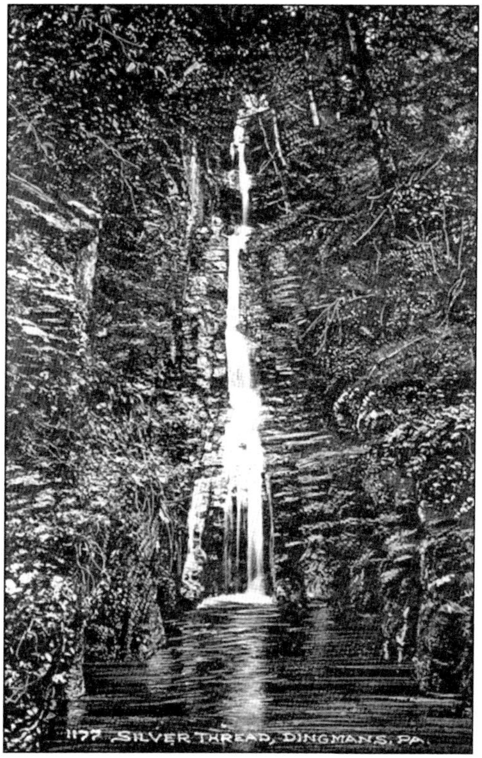

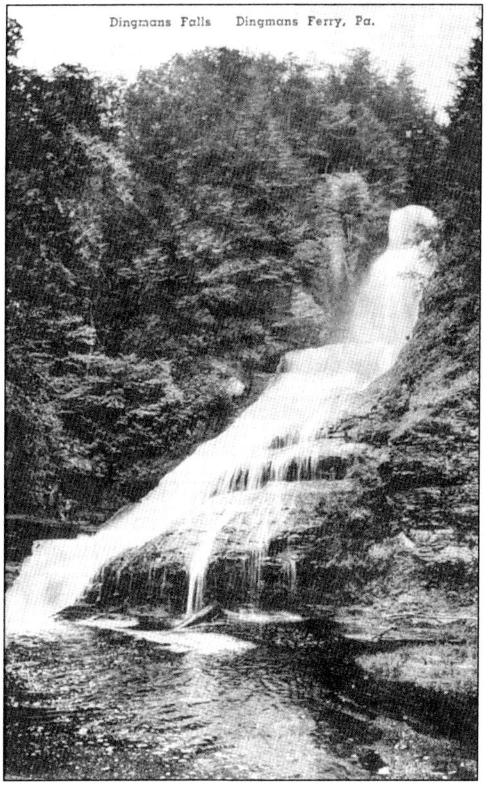

High Falls, shown cascading in this view, continues to be a tourist attraction for visitors and the local population throughout the vacation season. These falls are now owned by the National Park Service. (Courtesy DF/DTHS.)

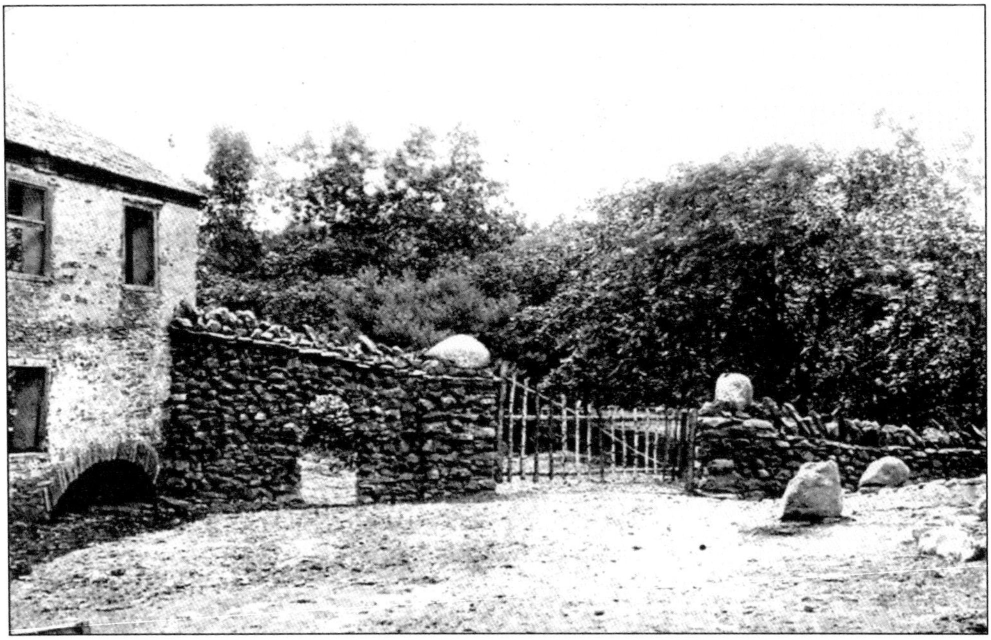

In 1893, George W. Childs, the famous editor and publisher of the *Philadelphia Public Ledger*, purchased the old Woolen Factory and property. Childs was a philanthropist who loved nature; as an enduring tribute to his qualities and a gift to future generations, his widow deeded this breathtaking property of cascading waterfalls and varied wildlife to the state in 1912. Since 1983, the National Park Service has maintained this popular park, which as Child stipulated, shall always remain accessible to the public. (Courtesy DF/DTHS.)

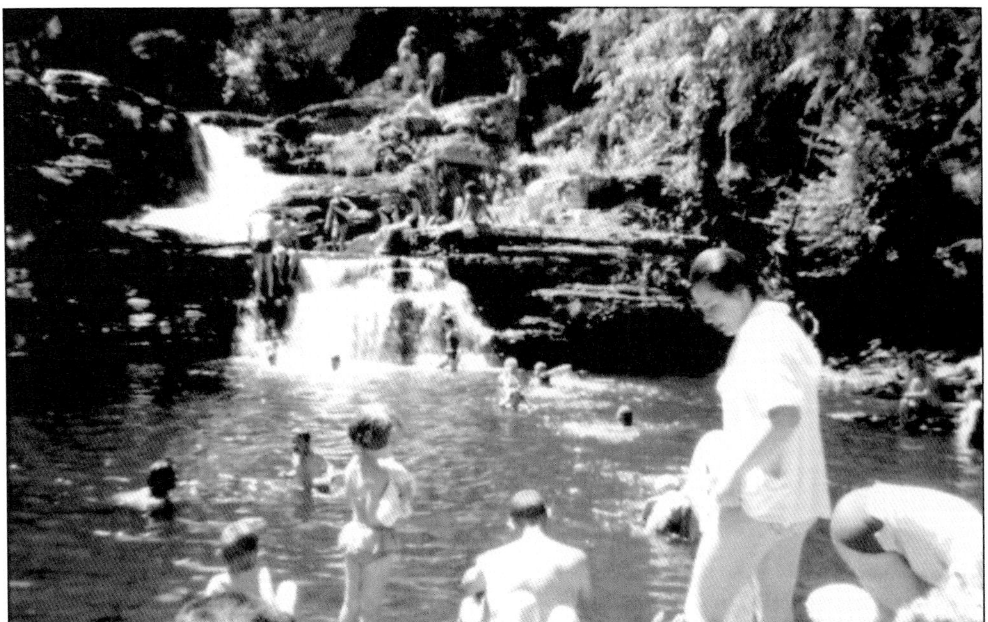

Mountains and lakes of Pike County have attracted visitors to this northeast corner of Pennsylvania for over 150 years. Here, summer tourists and local residents enjoy a cool and shady Childs Park. (Courtesy Pike County Historical Society.)

A roaring Dingmans Creek powered as many as 10 mills during the mid-to-late 1800s, boosting the local economy. Shown here is Factory Falls, so named for the Woolen Factory that operated here from 1826 to 1832. (Courtesy DF/DTHS.)

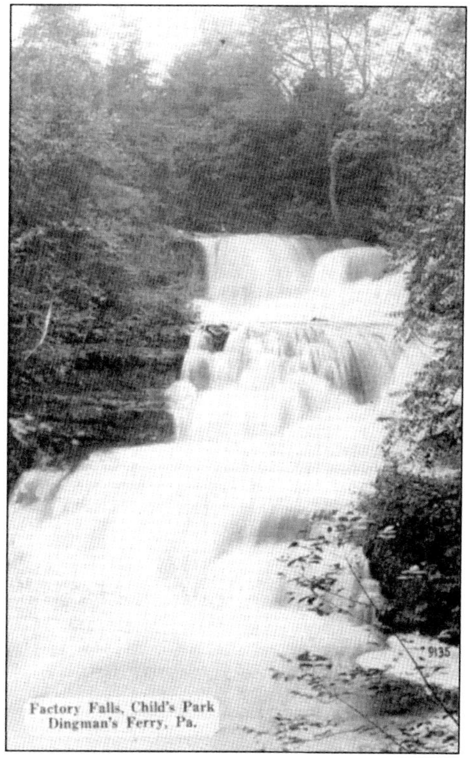

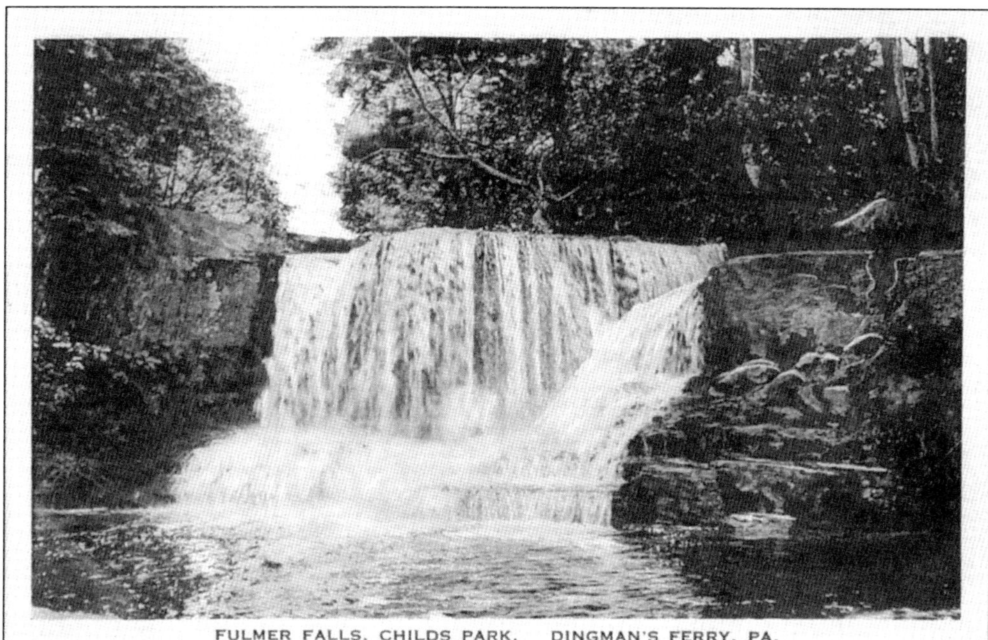

The power of the Dingmans Creek is evident in this photograph. These falls were named after Fulmerville, an area just above today's Childs Park. In the 1850s, a very successful tannery operated under the proprietorship of John Fulmer and his son Phillip, owners of the High Falls Hotel. (Courtesy DF/DTHS.)

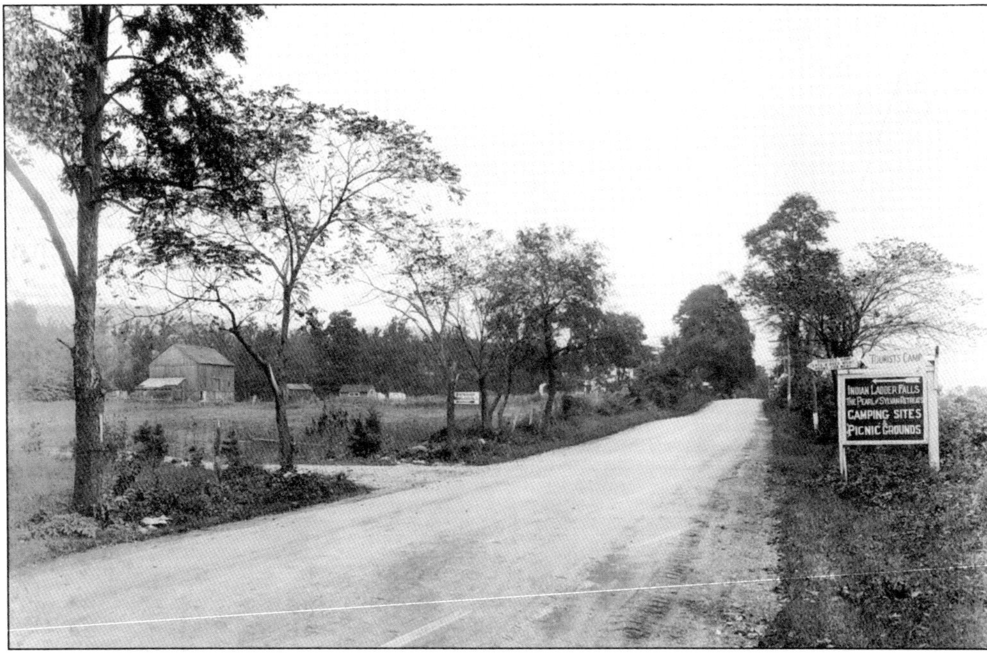

The Falls at Indian Ladder was a popular tourist destination in the 1920s. This view, looking north on Route 209, reveals a billboard proclaiming the falls "The Pearl of Sylvan Retreats." (Courtesy DF/DTHS.)

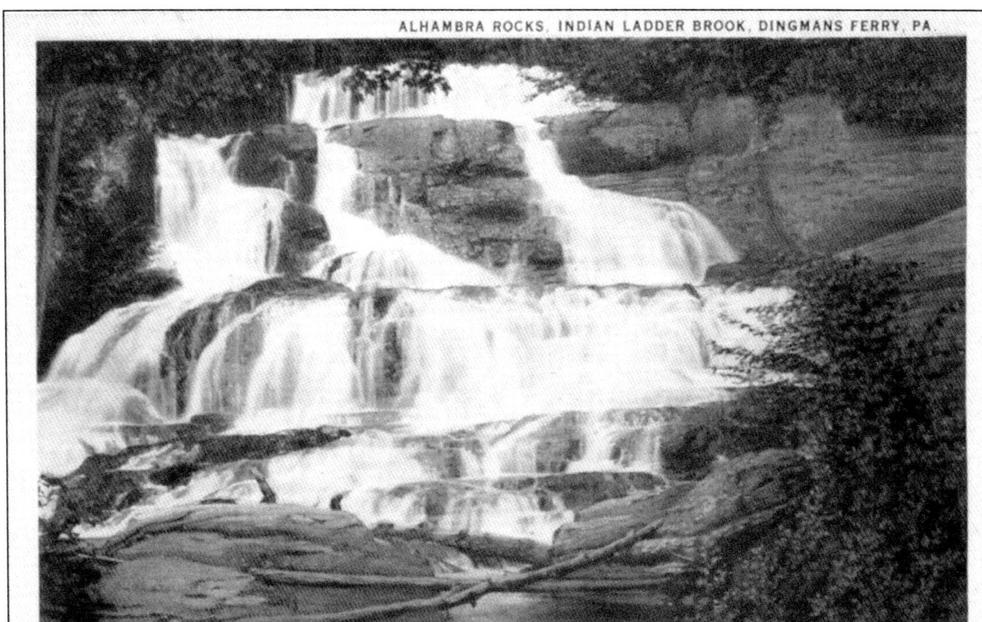

This postcard shows Alhambra Rocks on Indian Ladder Brook. Originally called Deckers Creek or Hornbeck Creek, this picturesque brook is just south of Chestnut Ridge Road. (Courtesy Roberta and Leroy Cron.)

Three

MAIN STREET

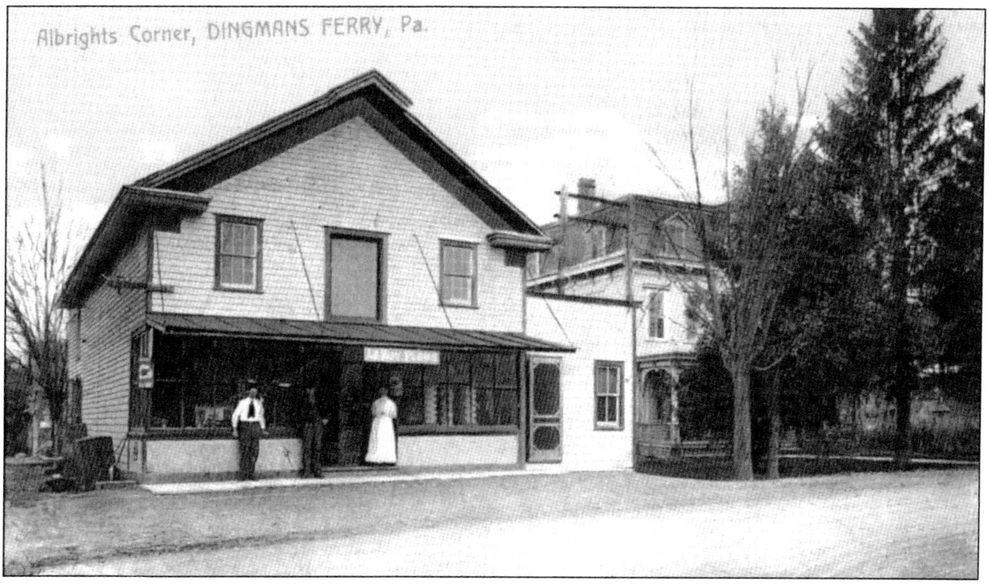

The village of Dingmans Ferry was a thriving community of popular hotels, enterprising gas stations, restaurants, and small grocery stores. This postcard shows the Albright Store, located on the corner of Tie Alley and Main Street. The small building to the right, the original telephone company, opened in 1904, and the large building to the right was the Mansion House Inn. (Courtesy DF/DTHS.)

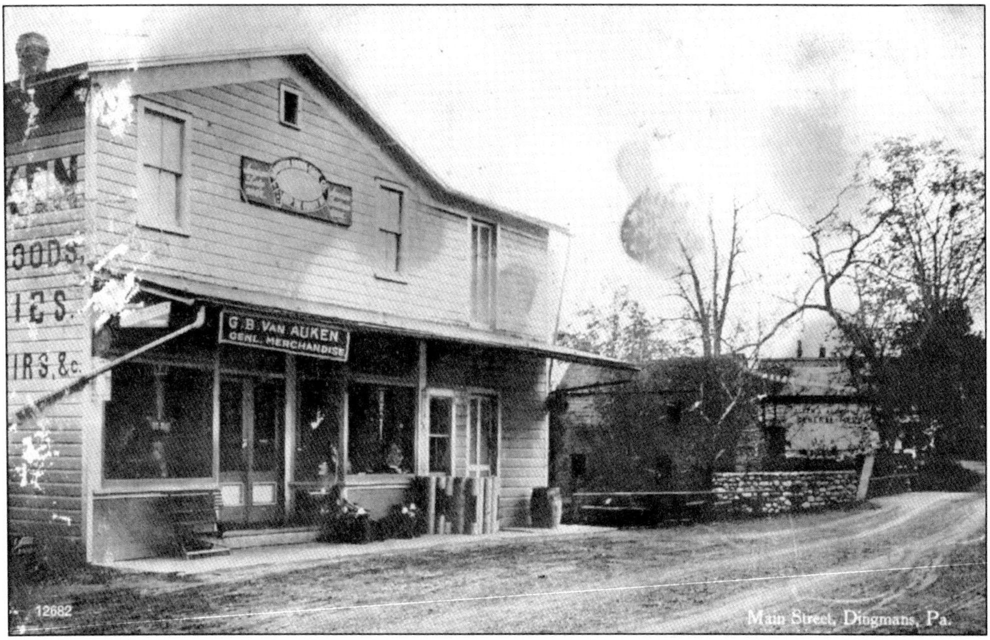

This Main Street general store is situated where the Dingman Garage would later be built. The shop was operated by Gen. George B. VanAuken, who resided on Mill Street. (Courtesy Kathleen and Stephen Bumball.)

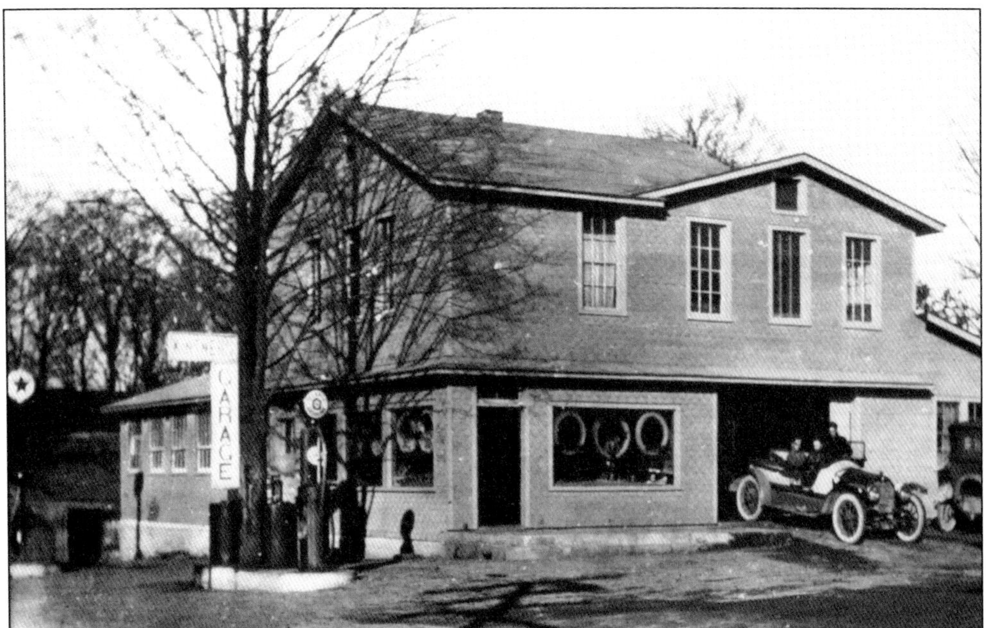

Kinter's Garage was built in 1925 on the same corner as Frank Gunn's blacksmith shop. The service station business had become a vital part of Dingmans Ferry, as more people were beginning to visit this community by automobile. (Courtesy Pike County Historical Society.)

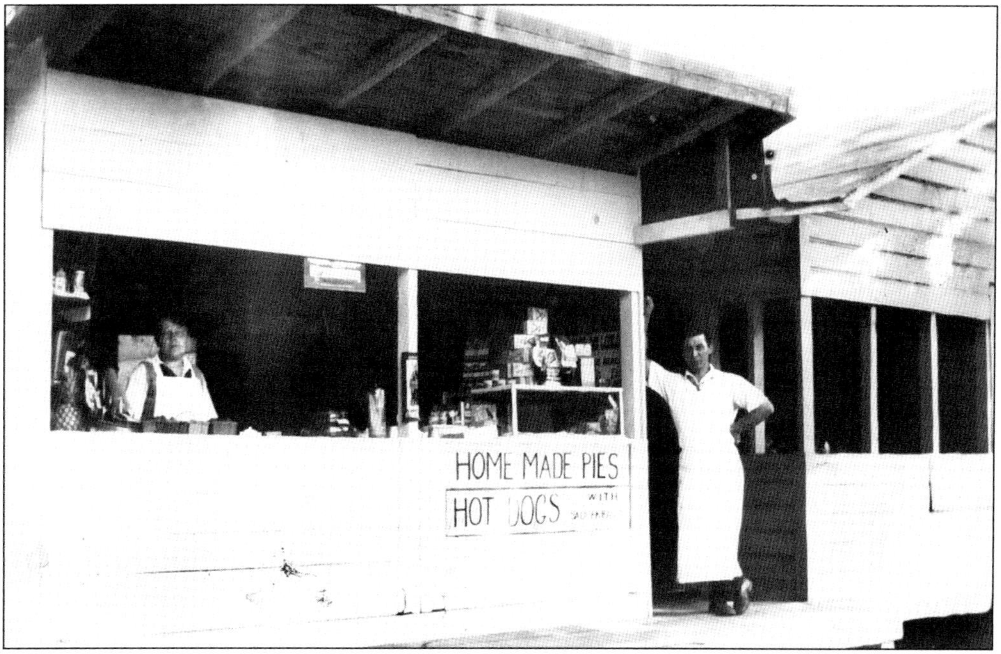

In 1929, Otto and Emma Kittel took over the Maple Rest, renaming it Kittel's Koffee Kettle. Tourists often purchased homemade baked goods, and locals enjoyed Saturday night square dancing in the large hall. (Courtesy Elsie Bensley.)

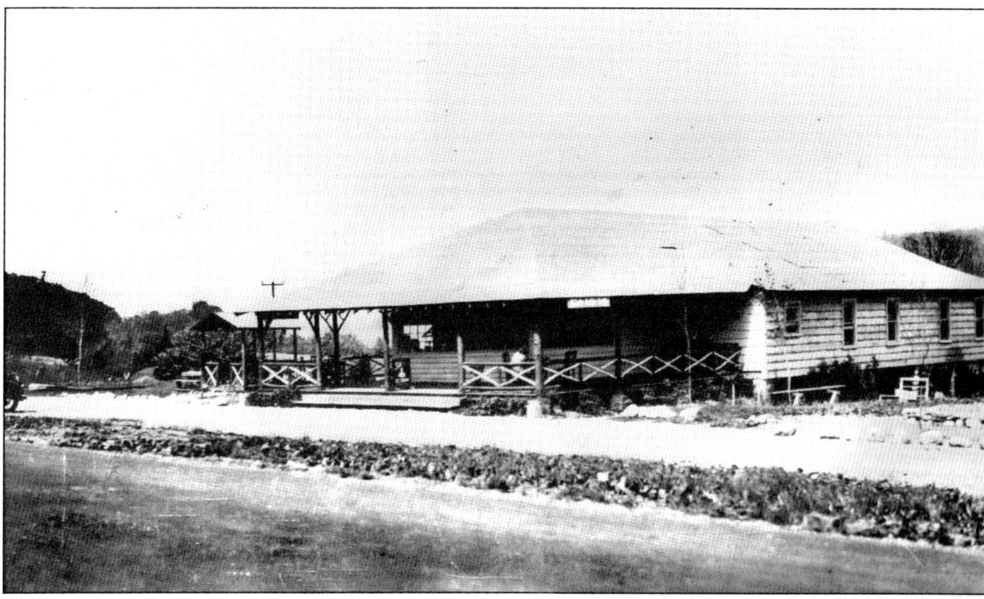

In later years, Kittel's, located on Route 209 just north of Chestnut Ridge Road on the left, prospered into a full restaurant and bar. Always a favorite and fondly remembered by longtime residents, the restaurant was sold in the 1940s. Until its destruction in the 1970s, it was known as the Wayside Inn. (Courtesy Elsie Bensley.)

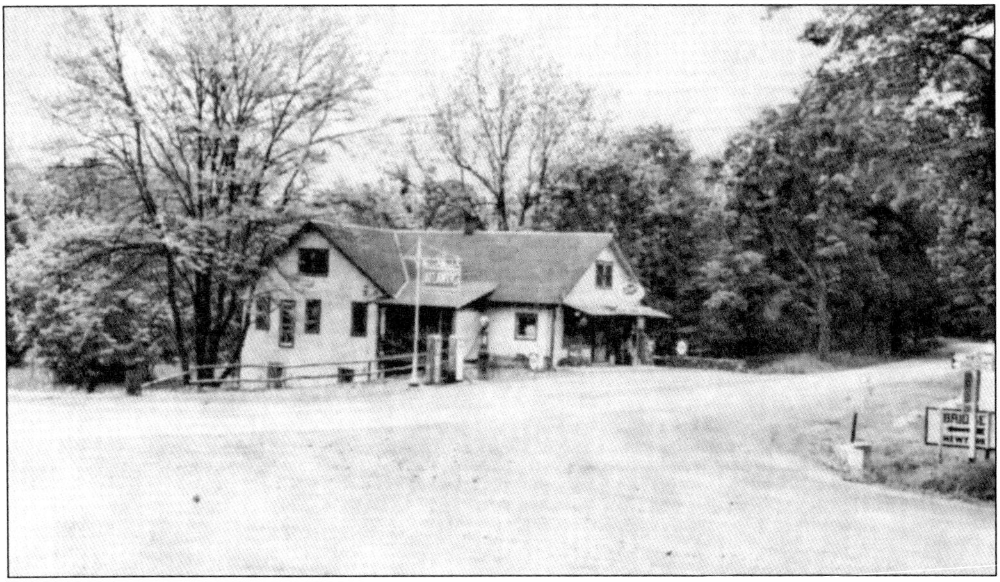

Adams General Store, on the corner of Main Street (Route 209) and Bethany Turnpike (Route 739), was constructed in the 1890s and operated as a grocery store for many years. (Courtesy Pike County Historical Society.)

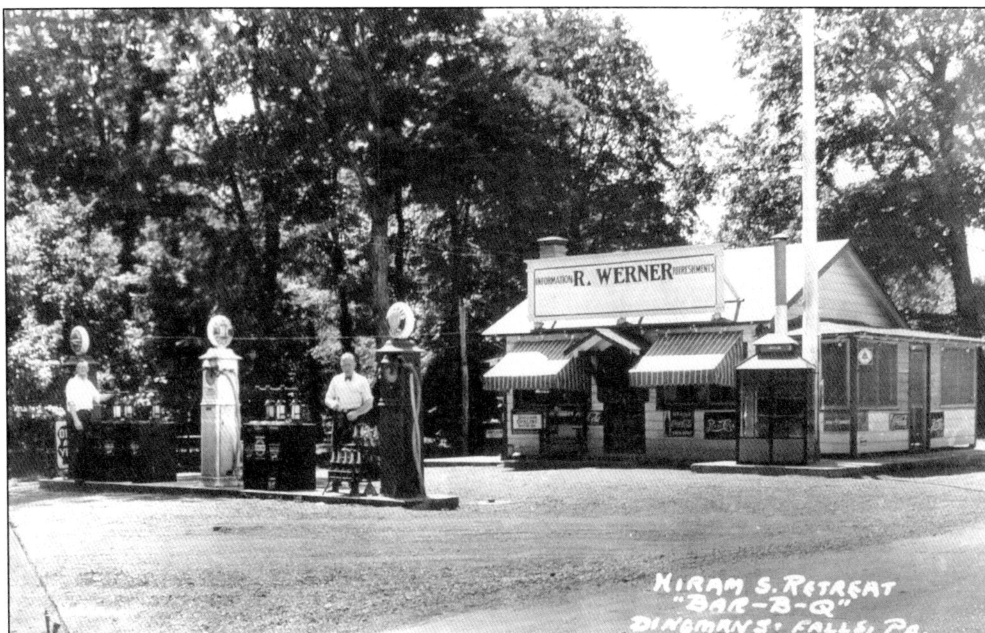

Robert Werner, pictured with Allen Albright, is ready to serve his customers at the Hiram S. Retreat, where he offered travelers a place to pull over and enjoy a delicious barbecue meal. Located on Route 739 just north of the bridge, it was the former Albright refreshment stand. By the 1930s, the store had expanded to include gas pumps. (Courtesy Mildred Jagger.)

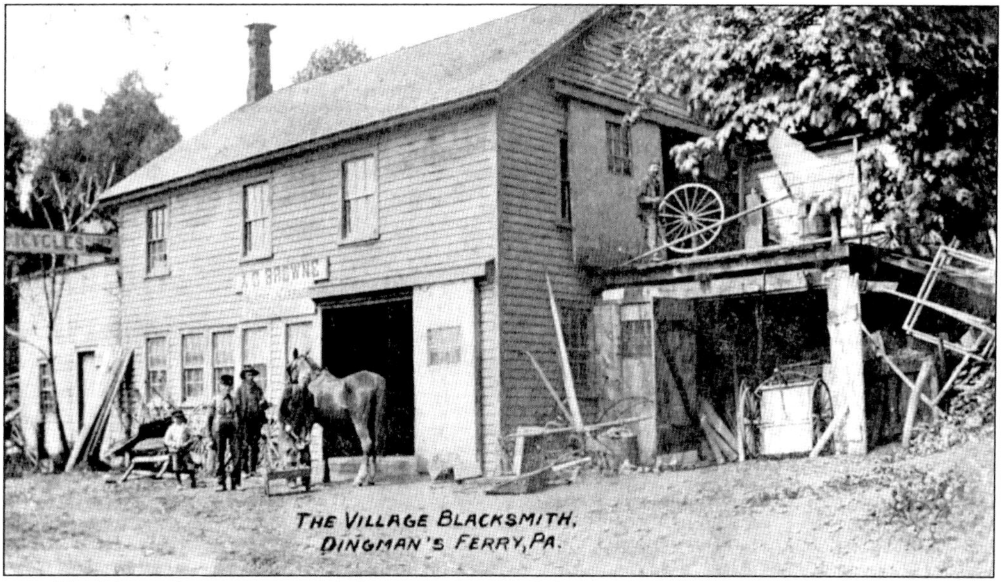

Local builder and entrepreneur A. D. Browne owned the last blacksmith shop in Dingmans Ferry, located on Main Street next to the Methodist church. He also operated the Browne Building in Milford and the Homestead, a large boardinghouse on the Vandermark Brook. Along with this blacksmith shop, he opened a bicycle shop to accommodate the popular tourist sport. Here, a boarder made the first brake for a bicycle and sold the patent for $25,000. (Courtesy DF/DTHS.)

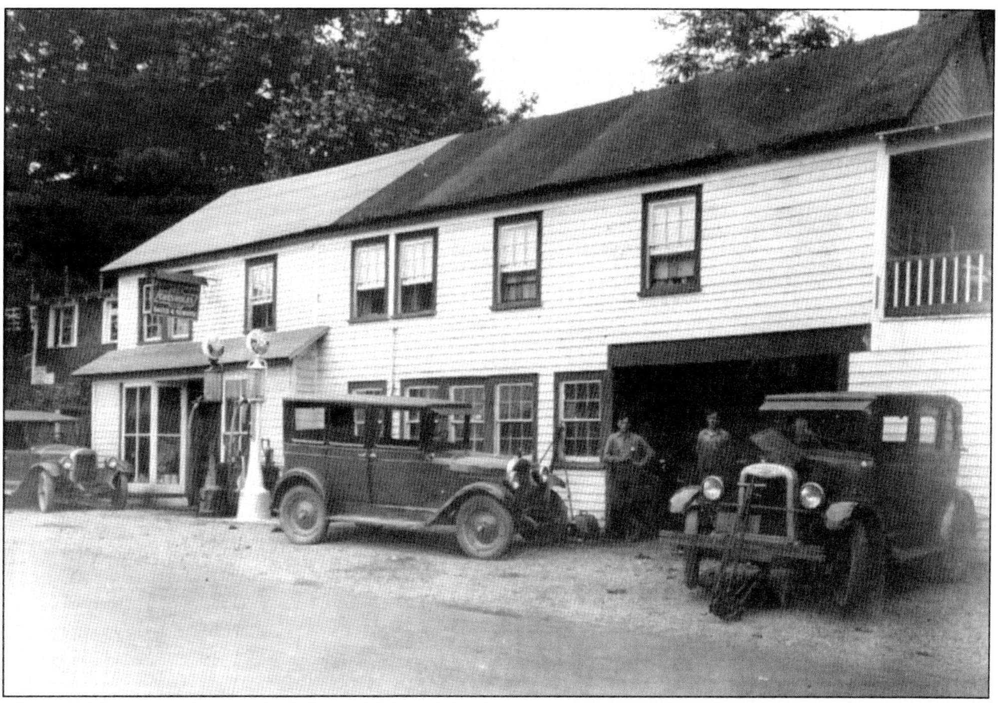

This 1930s view depicts Ralph and Nina Ford's garage. Located in the old Browne blacksmith shop, the building was used as a service station until 1944, when it was razed for the Methodist church parking lot. (Courtesy Pike County Historical Society.)

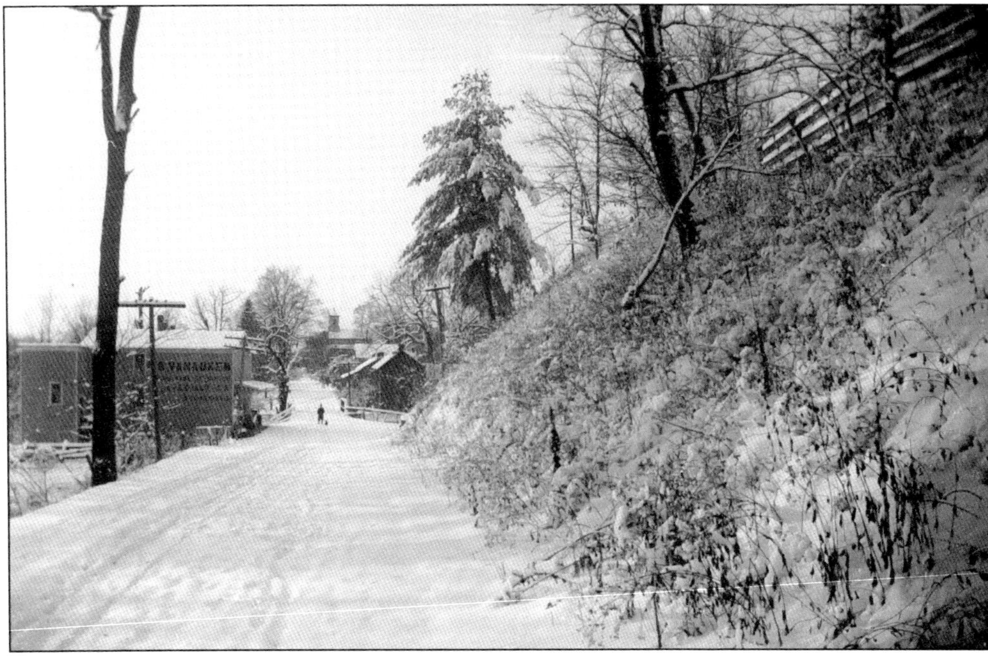

A solitary walker crosses the Dingmans Creek in this Main Street winter scene, looking south. On the left is the store of Gen. George B. VanAuken, and in the distance is the Methodist church steeple. (Courtesy Pike County Historical Society.)

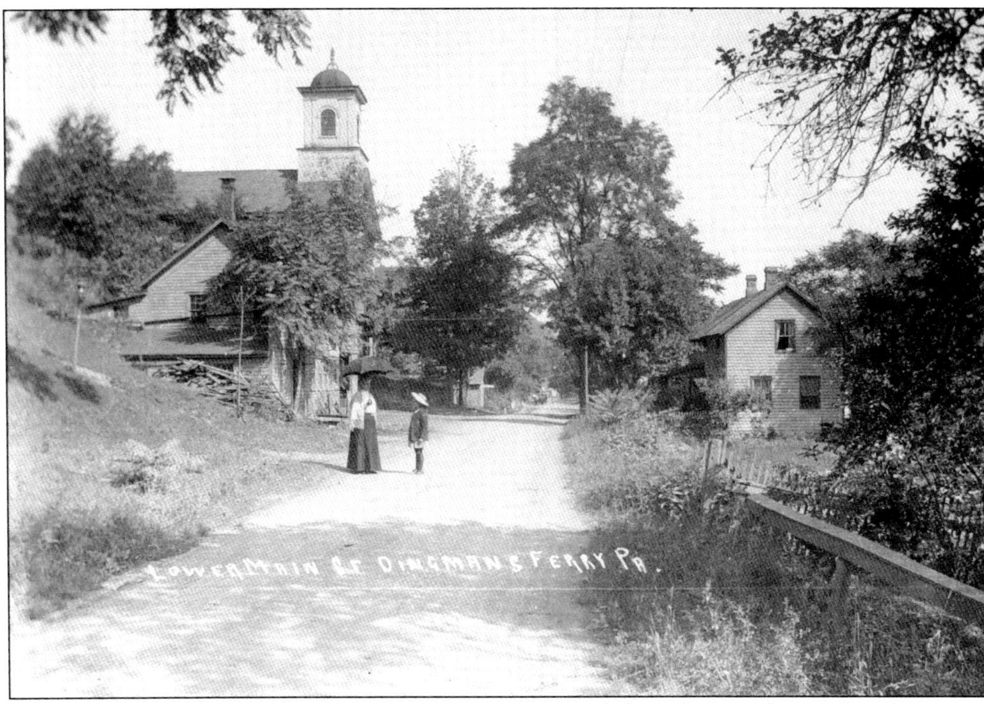

In the late 1800s, this section of lower Main Street graced the village's edge, with rich pastures and farm fields further south. This view looks north, with A. D. Browne's blacksmith shop and the Methodist church in the distance. (Courtesy Pike County Historical Society.)

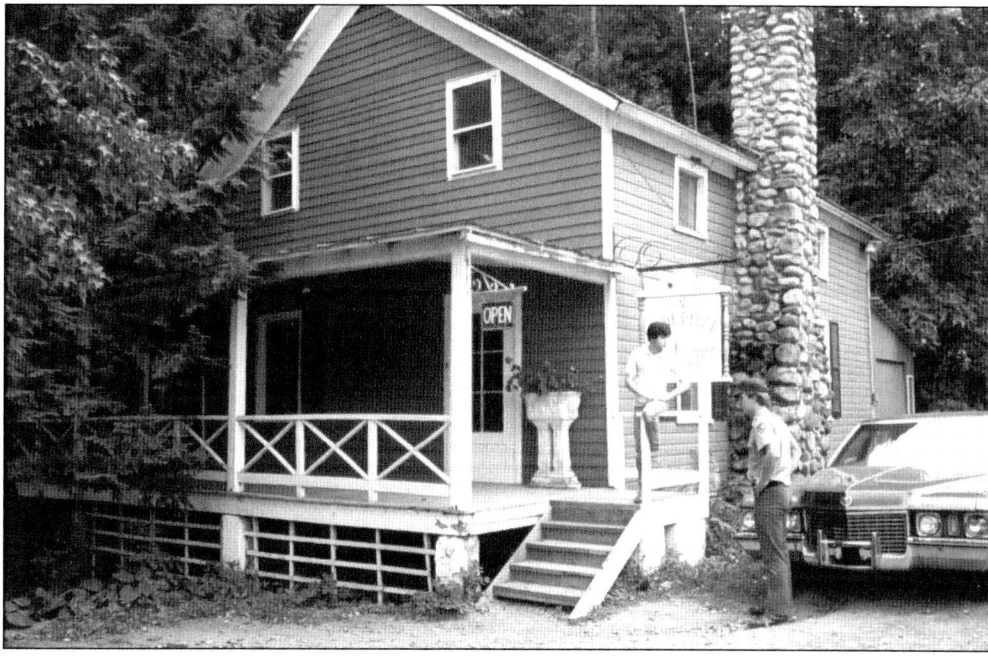

The Blue Delft Antique Store, seen here around 1970, conducted business on the corner of Routes 739 and 209. This building was originally part of the Dingman House. (Courtesy Delaware Water Gap National Recreation Area.)

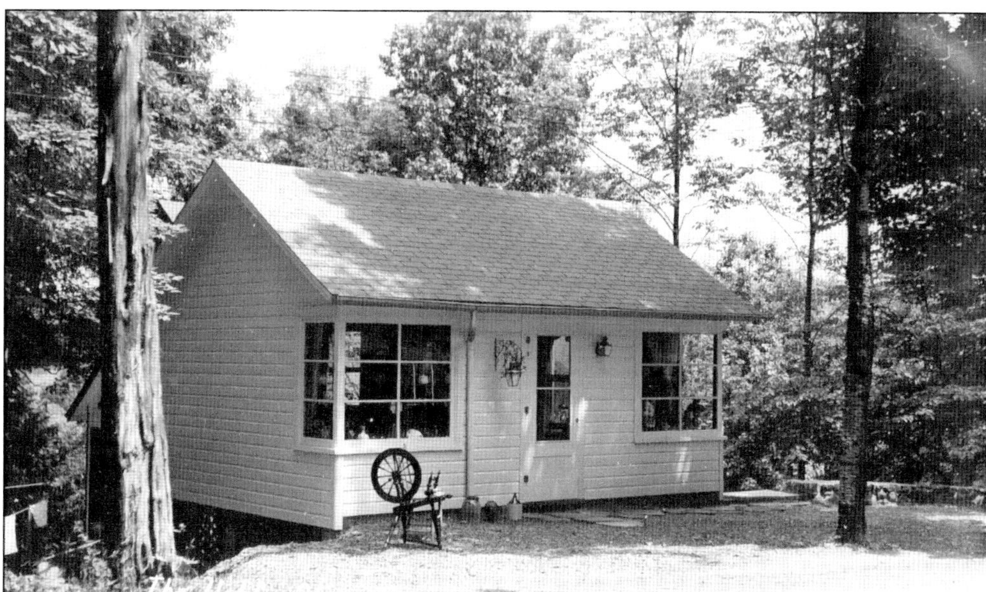

The little antique store known as the Hobby Shop, just north of the Dutch Reformed church, was constructed by Charles Cron and operated by the Hibbs family. (Courtesy Roberta and Leroy Cron.)

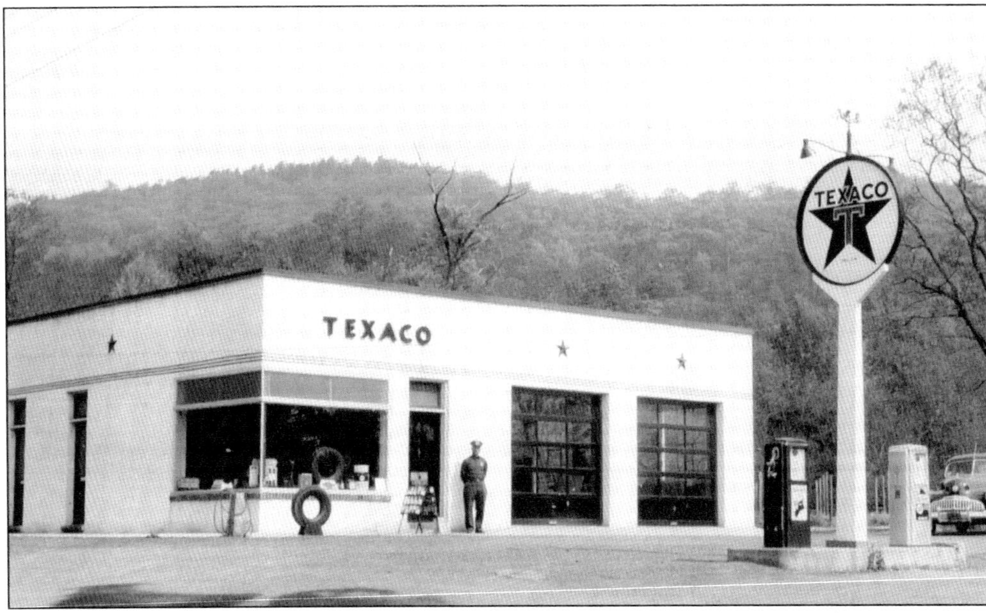

For many years, residents and visitors relied on the service station on the corner of Routes 739 and 209. After the High Falls Hotel burned in 1946, Paul Snearley built this modern station, replacing his previous one on Mill Street and Route 209, and operated the business for many years. Here, Snearley stands proudly in front of his Texaco station in the 1950s. (Courtesy DF/DTHS.)

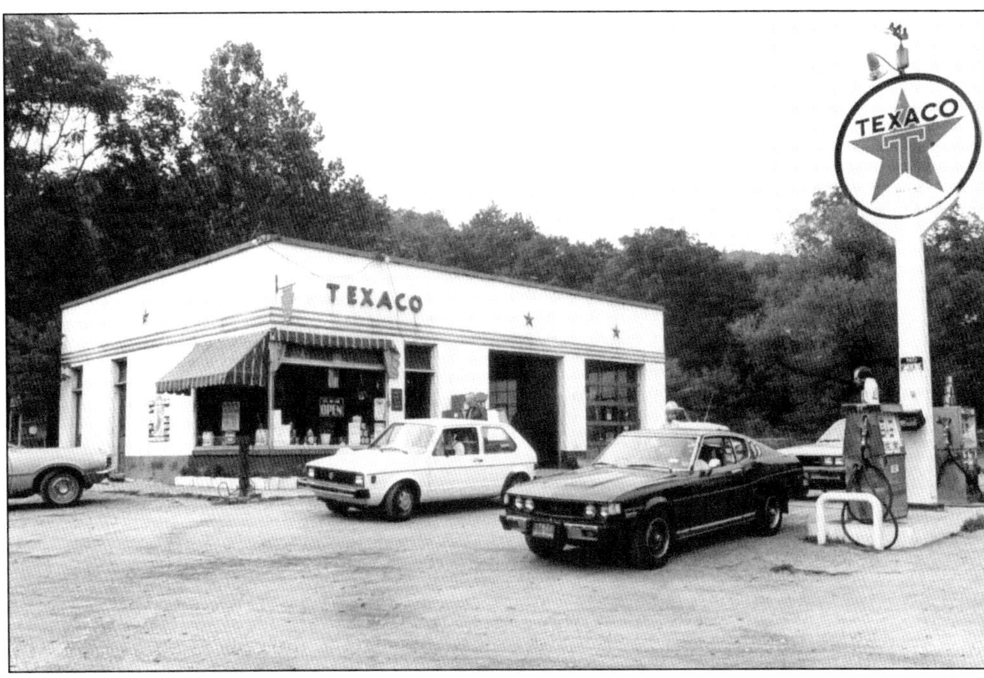

This is a later view of Snearley's Texaco station on Route 209. When this photograph was taken, Romain Whittaker was "the man who wore the star" and rented this building from the National Park Service. (Courtesy Delaware Water Gap National Recreation Area.)

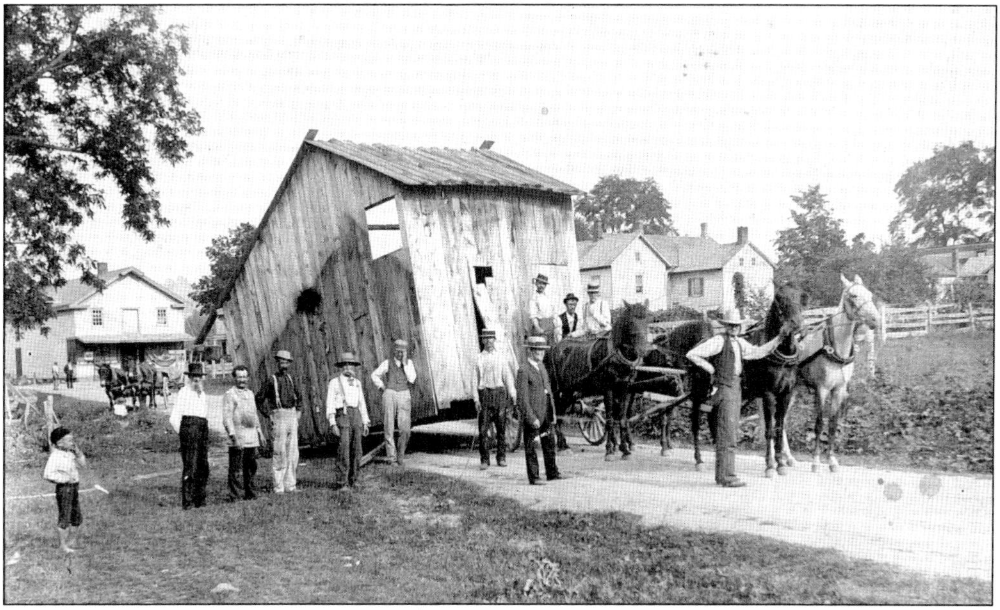

It took a village to move a barn back in the 1890s. Young Levi Jagger, the small boy to the far left, watches as a group of local men drag a barn up Mill Street. The buildings in the distance are the Albright Store (left) and the Hood home. (Courtesy Barbara Snyder Herman.)

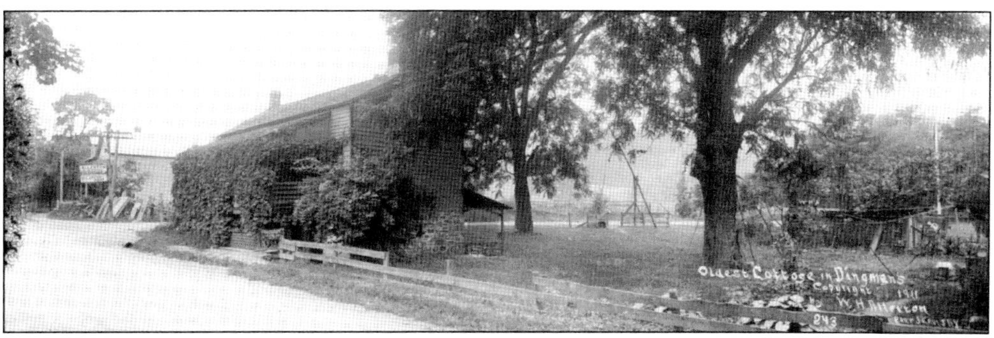

Judge Dingman built this "Long House," as it was called, on the corner of Mill and Main Streets. It was considered to be the oldest building in Dingmans Ferry. In later years, it became the site of Paul Snearley's first service station and finally the Green Dolphin Restaurant. (Courtesy Pike County Historical Society.)

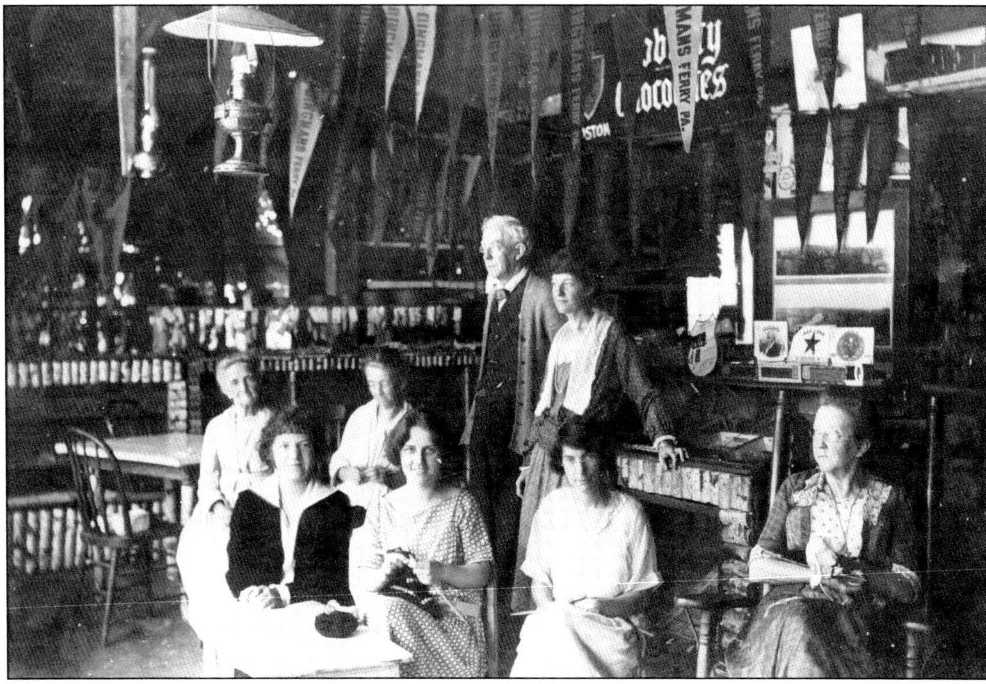

This is a rare photograph of the inside of William H. Allerton's refreshment pavilion and photography studio. Posing among the many Dingmans Ferry pennants in the summer of 1922 are the following, from left to right: (first row) Dot DePue, unidentified, Ethel Allerton, and Aunt Mamie Allerton; (second row) Kate Angle, Mrs. Allerton, W. H. Allerton, and unidentified. (Courtesy Laura and Jan de Graaf.)

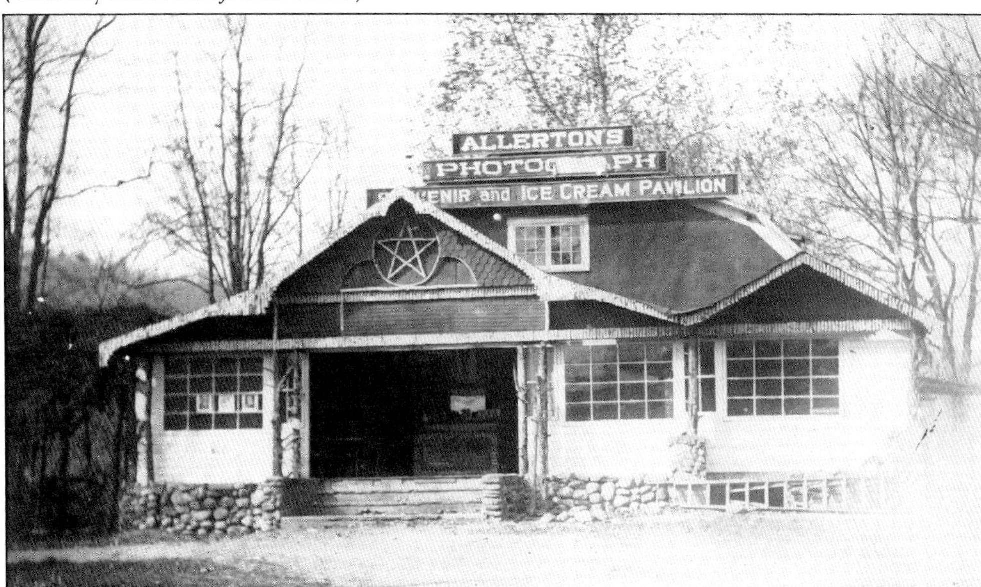

The photography studio of William Allerton was located on Mill Street (Johnny B. Road) just up from the Old Oaken Bucket. Allerton, a well-known photographer, had two studios in the area—one in Dingmans Ferry and the other in Port Jervis, New York. (Courtesy Laura and Jan de Graaf.)

Originally named Dingmans Choice, and later changed to Dingmans Ferry in the 1860s, the village had a few different post offices. This building, on Main Street next to the Mansion House, served residents in the early 20th century. (Courtesy DF/DTHS.)

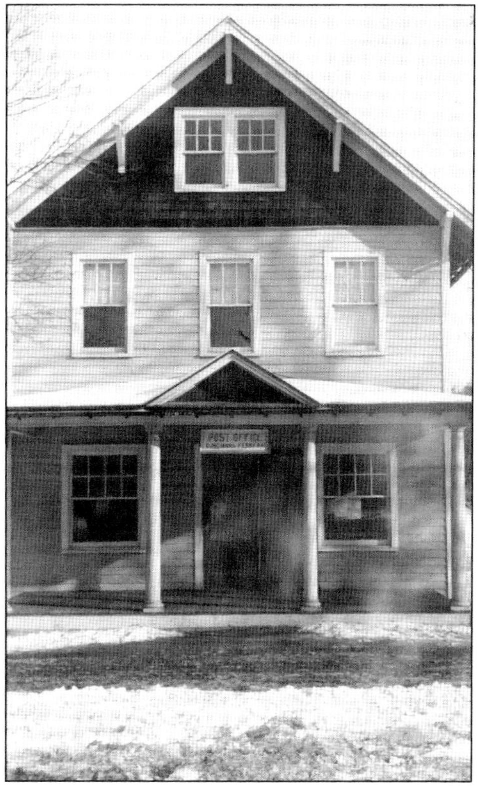

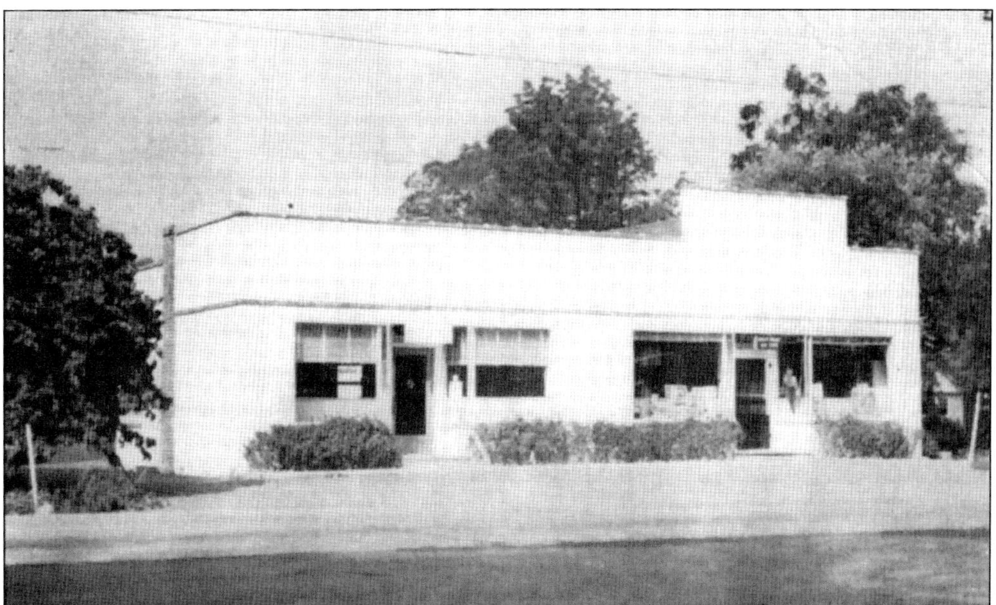

In 1973, residents mailed their letters at the Dingmans Ferry Post Office and purchased goods at Grace Drake's store in this building, located on the southern corner of Johnny B. Road and Route 209. (Courtesy Roberta and Leroy Cron.)

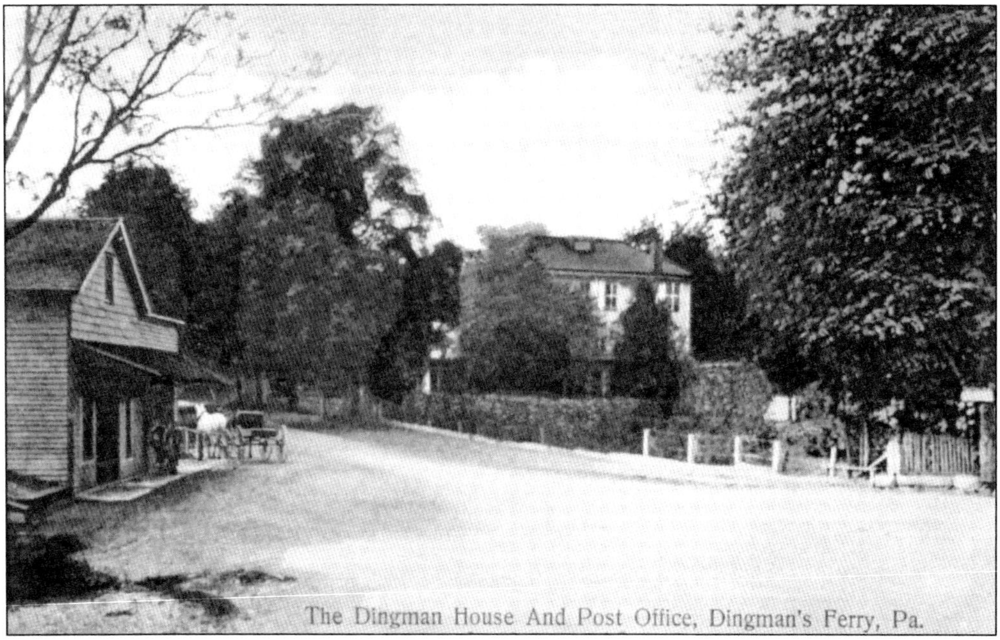

When this postcard was produced in the late 19th century, the general store on the corner of Route 739 and Route 209 was used as the post office. Years later, the business became known as the Adams General Store. The Dingman House can be seen in the distance. (Courtesy Harry Arnold.)

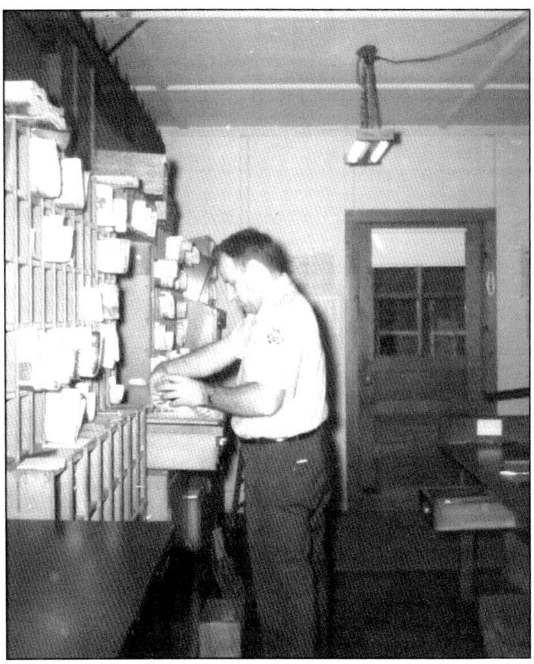

The mail was always on time when Harold Dickison was postmaster. This photograph was taken inside the post office in 1972, when it was located next to Grace Drake's store on Main Street (Route 209). Dickison served as postmaster from 1962 to 1982. (Courtesy Inez Dickison.)

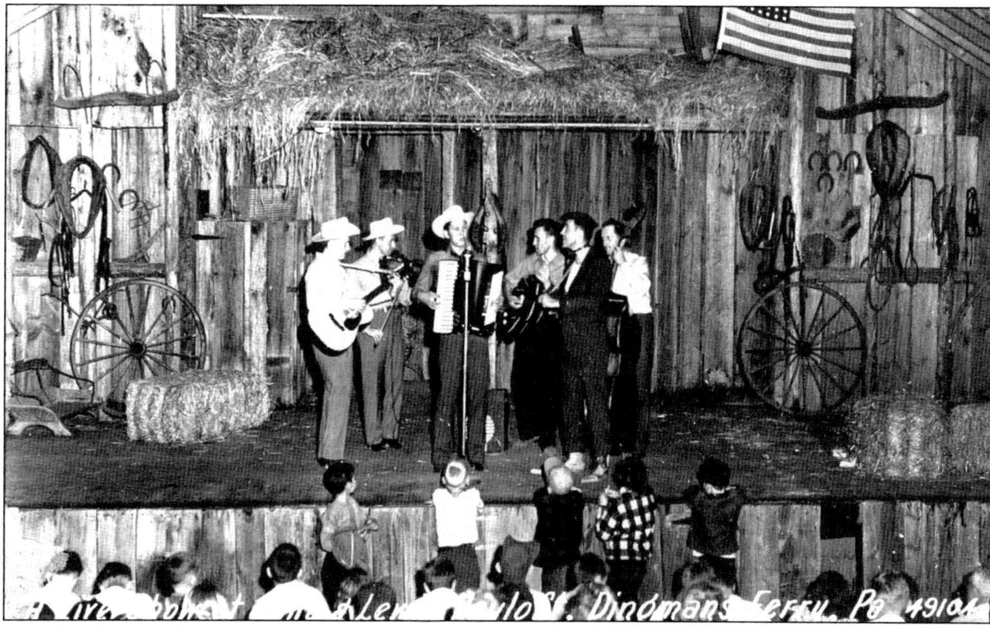

The band played many weekends at Sally and Lew's. This popular night spot was originally Sheperds Bar in the 1920s and 1930s, but by the 1950s, it was known as Sally and Lew's Hayloft. The business entertained the locals with dances and movies and was the place to be in 1950s Dingmans Ferry. (Courtesy Kathleen and Stephen Bumball.)

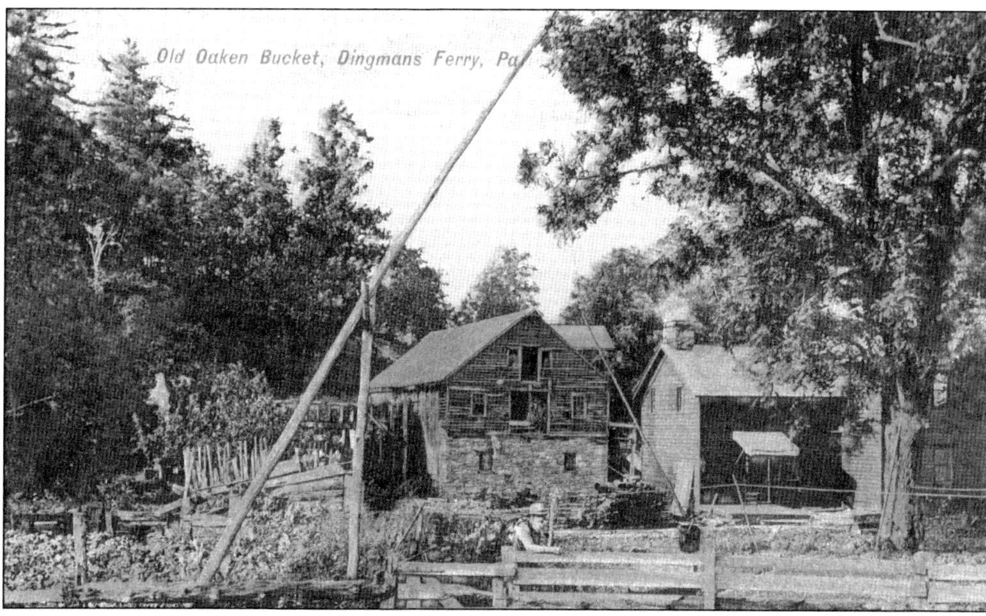

The Old Oaken Bucket was the public well on Mill Street. In the background of this view is the Darragh Mill. This area of Dingmans Ferry thrived as a center of activity along the scenic River Road (Route 209) for more than 65 years. In the 1830s, Judge Daniel Dingman constructed the successful gristmill on Dingmans Creek, just as it flows under Main Street (Route 209). Different operators ran the mill, and in 1903, it closed as the Darragh Mill. (Courtesy Roberta and Leroy Cron.)

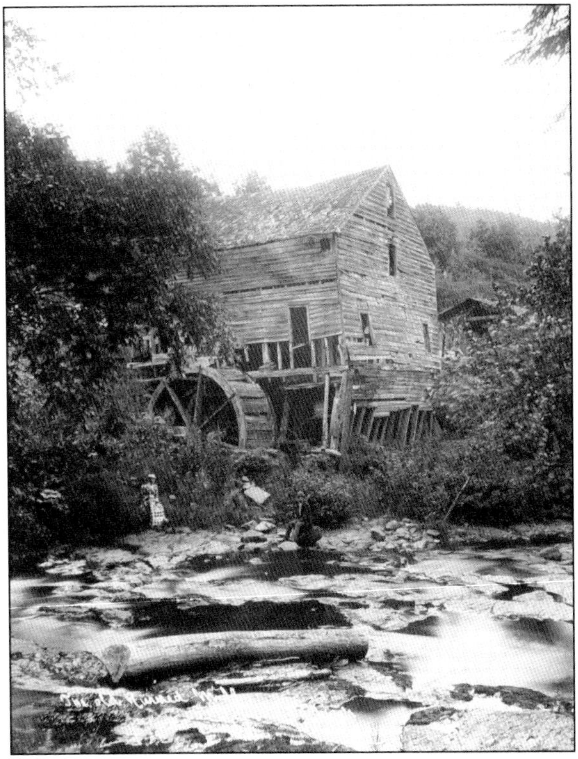

The Mollineaux Mill, considered to be the first gristmill in the village, was constructed in 1827 on Mill Street (Johnny B. Road), where the road veers to the right toward Dingmans Falls. Begun by James Mollineaux, it ceased operation in the 1880s, and in later years, the Silver Thread Cottages occupied the property. (Courtesy Pike County Historical Society.)

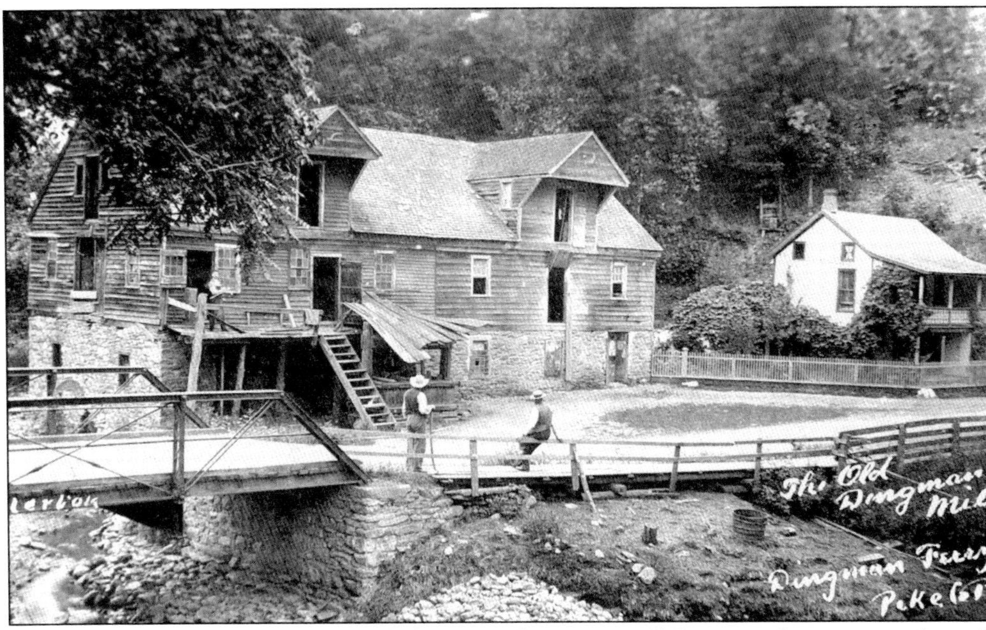

The Dingman-Darragh Mill originally functioned as a gristmill, but over the years, a cider mill and wheelwright shop were added to it. After the mill was dismantled, the house to the right was moved over to the creek's edge. (Courtesy Roberta and Leroy Cron.)

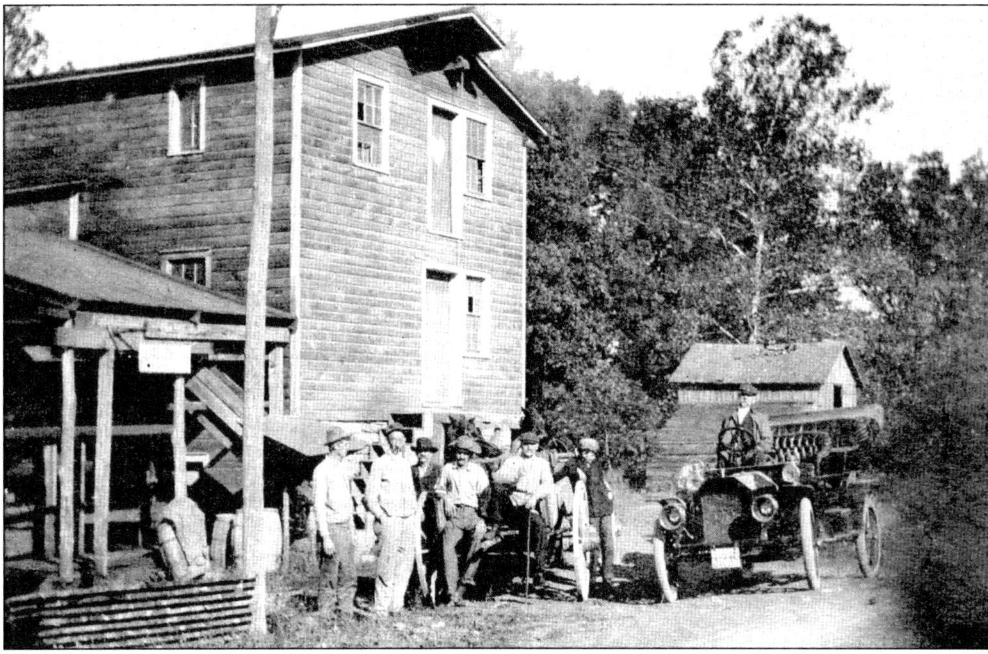

The mills in the area were the mainstay of the community, as they employed many locals and provided a much-needed service to the region's farms. A group of workers takes a break to pose in front of the Darragh Mill. Located on Mill Street, the business was in operation until about 1915. (Courtesy Roberta and Leroy Cron.)

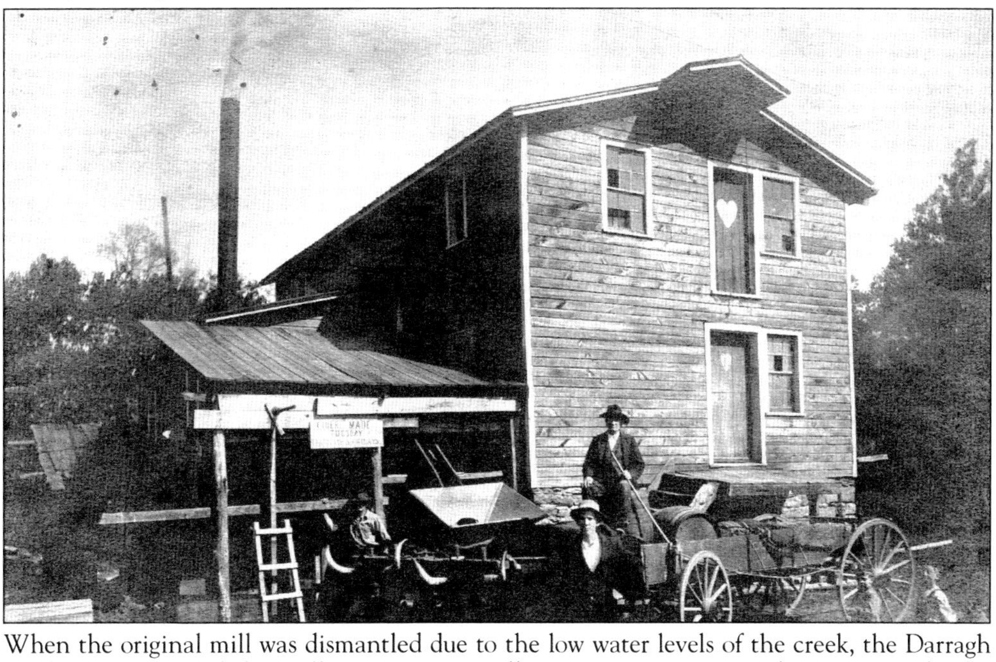

When the original mill was dismantled due to the low water levels of the creek, the Darragh brothers constructed this mill upstream on Mill Street. It was a steam-driven saw and cider mill, with cider only made on Tuesdays, Thursdays, and Fridays, according to the sign. In this photograph, Ed Darragh is beneath the sign, Levi Jagger is by the oxen, and Oliver Bensley is on the wagon. The two children are unidentified. (Courtesy Roberta and Leroy Cron.)

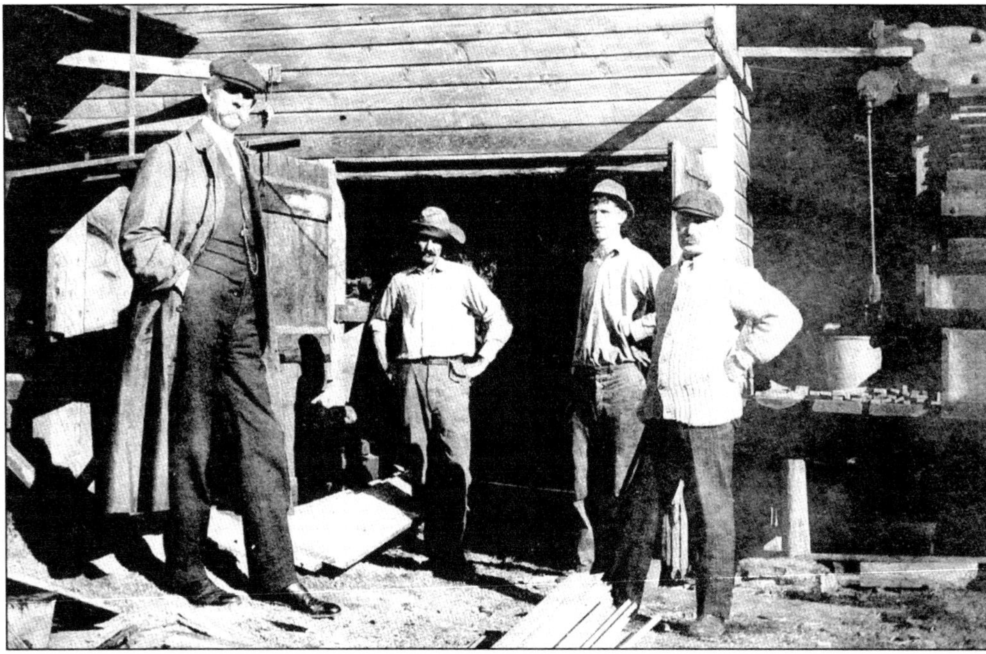

The milling of lumber was a very prosperous venture for local mills. As the area was developed and hotels and homes were constructed, the need for building wood increased. Pictured here in the center, from left to right, are owners Ed and George Darragh of the Darragh Mill. (Courtesy Roberta and Leroy Cron.)

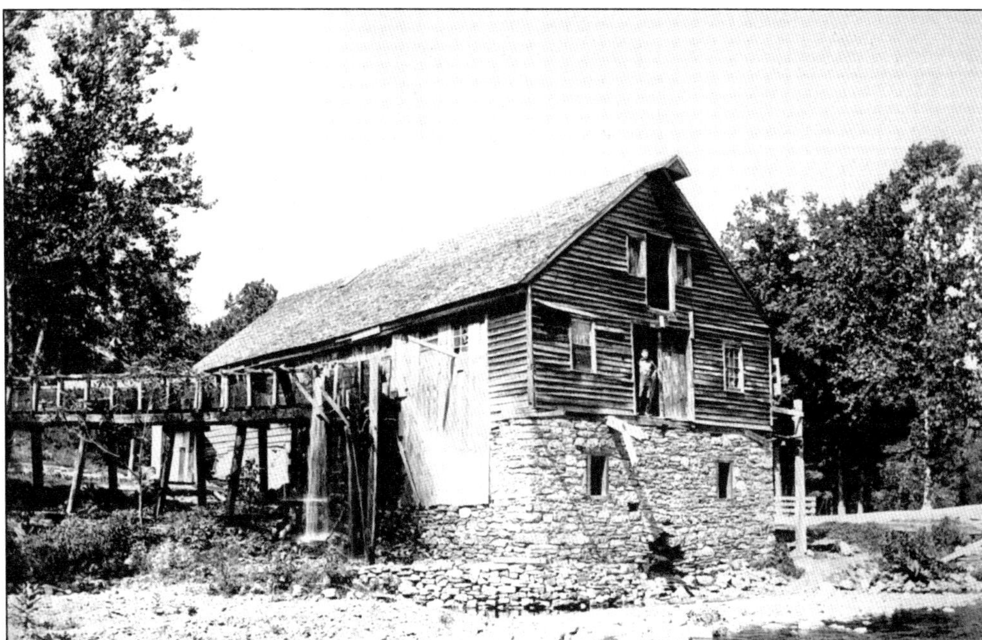

In this c. 1880 rear view of the original Darragh Mill, the flume brings the creek's power to the mill. Note the stone wall built precariously close to the surging stream, and visualize the structure at jeopardy during high waters. The water visibly splashes out as the water turns the wheel. (Courtesy Pike County Historical Society.)

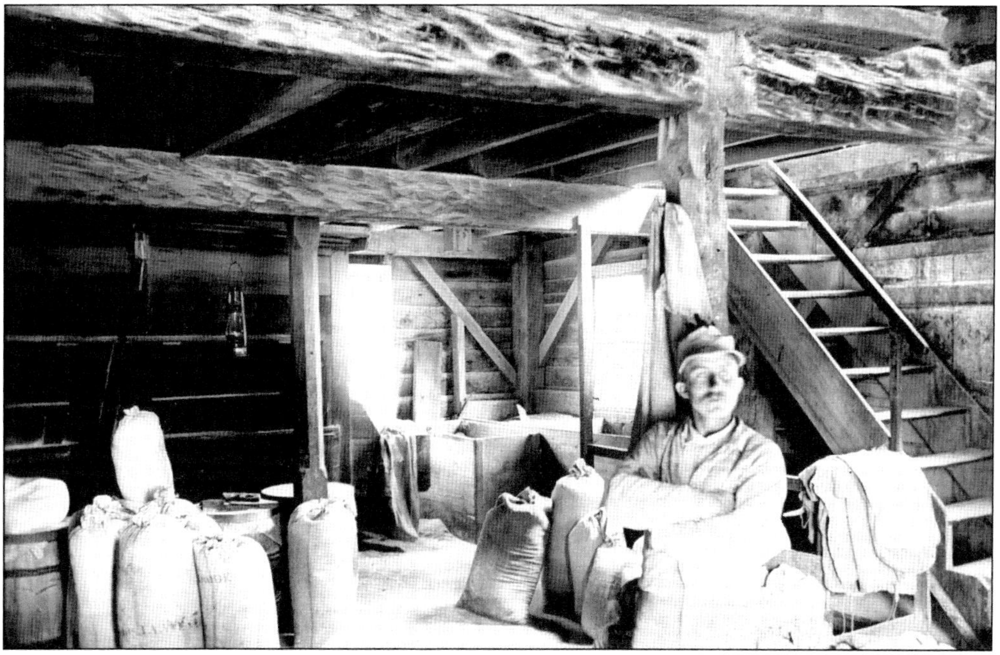

This early view shows the interior of the Darragh Mill, which had a 24-foot waterwheel powered by the Dingmans Creek. The miller, shown here in 1880, rests among the bags of grain. (Courtesy Pike County Historical Society.)

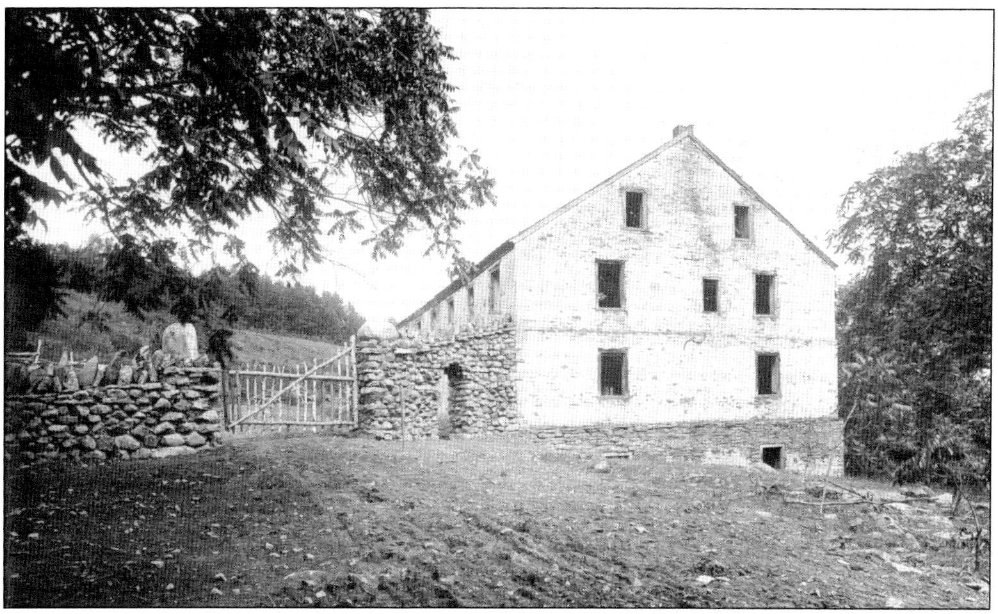

In the area surrounding Dingmans Ferry, many mills were constructed. In Doodle Hollow, just above Dingmans Falls, was the Angle Saw Mill. Further up the road was Theodore Howey's Cider and Saw Mill. Pictured is the Woolen Mill at Child's Park. Constructed in 1826 by John Brooks, this was an operation with over 50 employees. A large building housing three and a half floors, the factory manufactured wool products for only six years before it was abandoned. (Courtesy Pike County Historical Society.)

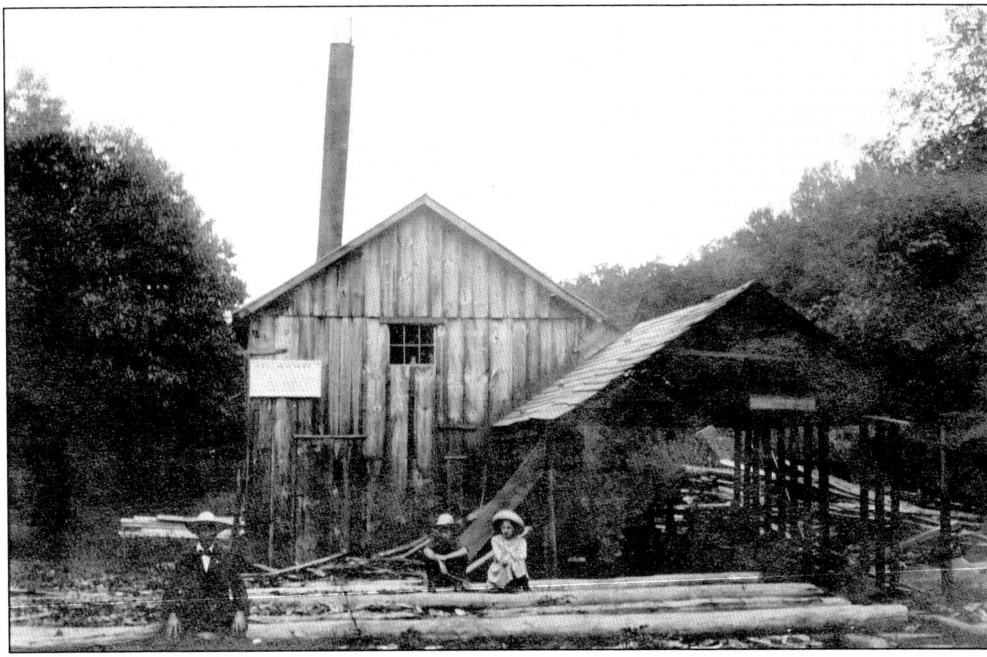

The Howey Cider and Saw Mill was located in Deep Hollow off of Milford Road. Operated by Theodore Howey and later his son Henry, this engine-driven mill ran into the early 1900s. (Courtesy Raitt family.)

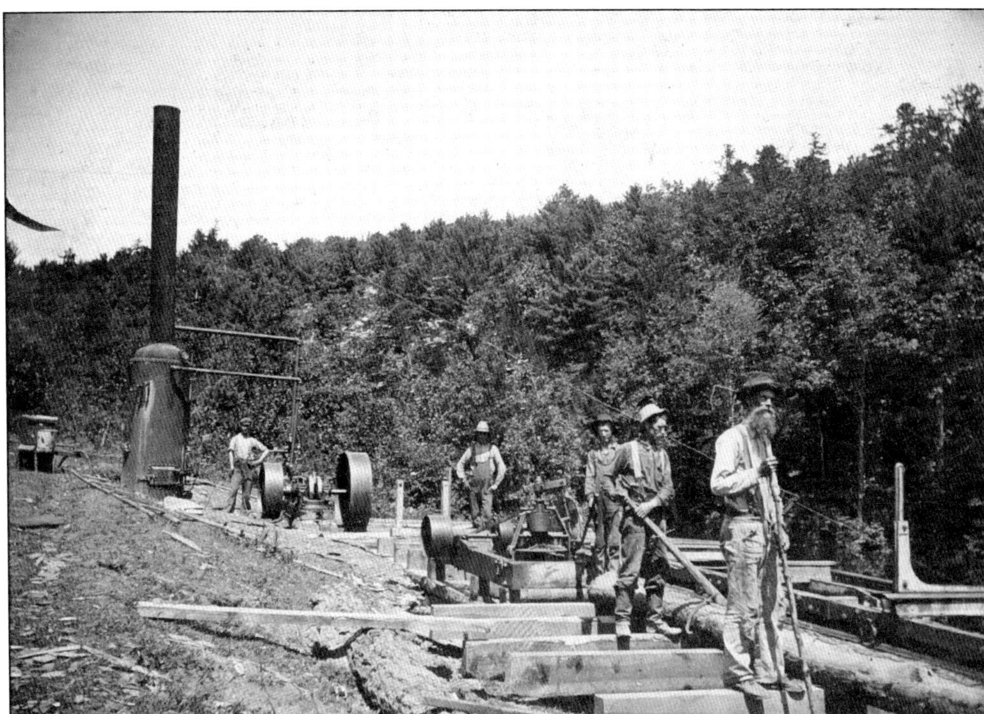

In this 1900 photograph, the workers of the Howey Mill prepare to cut lumber. In the distance, the steam-driven engine is visible. (Courtesy Dorthann and Joe White.)

Four

EDUCATION AND RELIGION

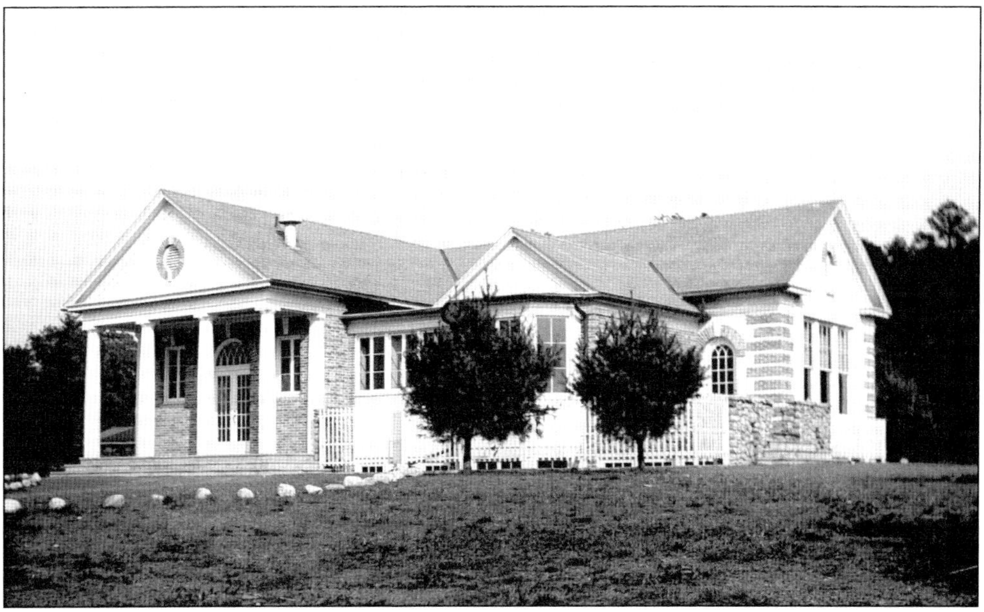

In April 1933, the Delaware Township Consolidated School was located on School House Road. This modern building replaced the Academy School, and when it opened, students walked their books and belongings from the Academy here. The Delaware Township School housed pupils from grades one through eight and operated for nearly 50 years. Hilda Stroyan taught grades one through four, and Letita Ryder taught grades five through eight. The school is now the National Park Offices. (Courtesy DF/DTHS.)

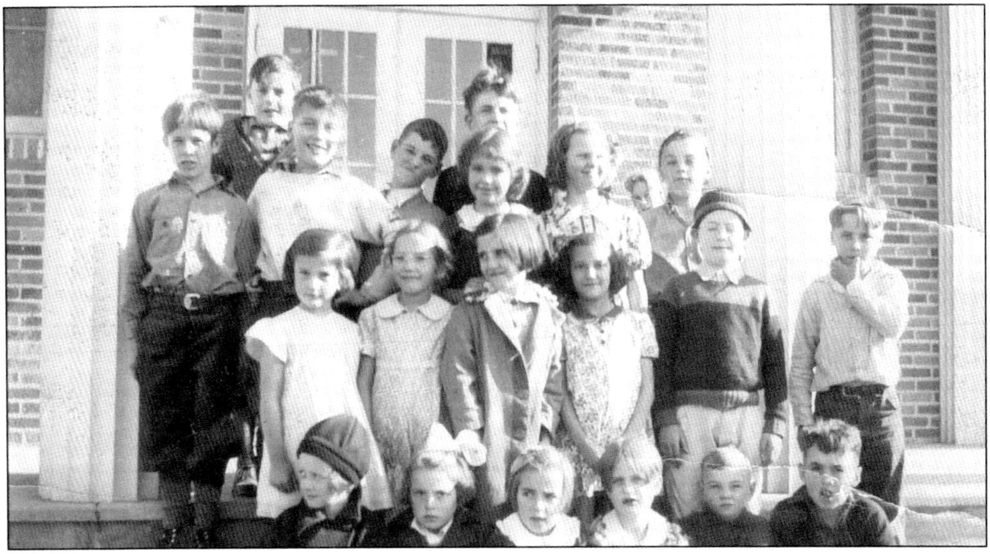

Posing for a class portrait at the Delaware Township School in the 1930s are the following, from left to right: (first row) June Stuart, Joan Ryder Mervine, Frances MacGregor Franzin, Irene Howey, Russell Brown, and Jack Emery; (second row) Frances Jagger Myck, Doris Cron, Marie Smith, Grace Jagger Bradley, Kenneth Howey, and Gerald Ryder; (third row) Donald Smith, Lawrence Plante, Mary Lou Richards, unidentified, and Junior Stewart; (fourth row) Jack Kemp, Donald Brown, Clarence Ladlee, and Jack MacGregor. (Courtesy Roberta and Leroy Cron.)

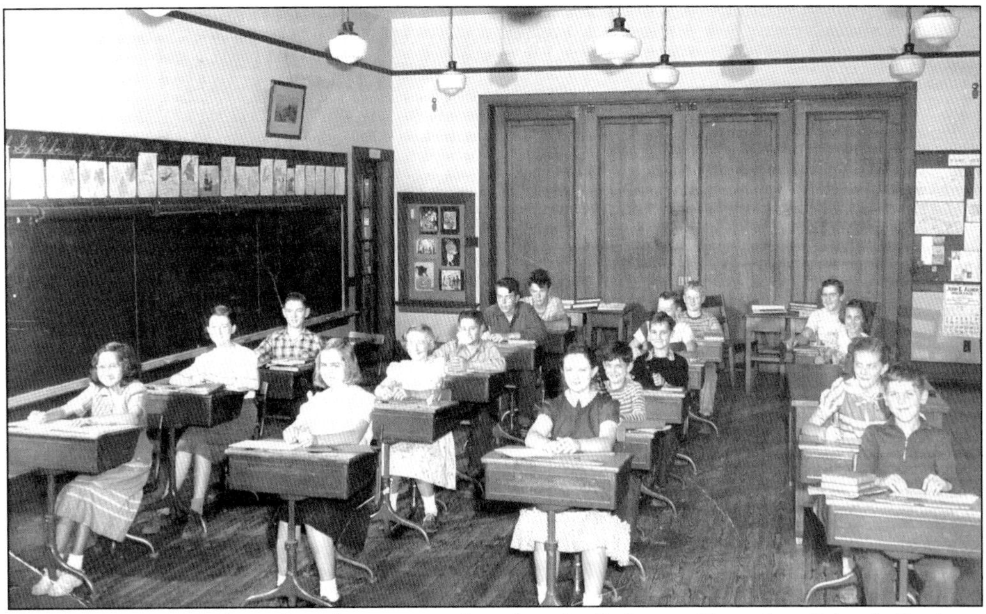

In 1949, grades five through eight were combined at the Delaware Township School. Students in the mixed class are, from front to back, as follows: (first row) Beverly Myers, Evelyn Herr, and John Stasa; (second row) Betty Sebring, Nancy Findlay, Louie Myers, Leonard Coddington, and John Kloetzer; (third row) Barbara Snyder, George Hotalen, Charlie Sebring, Kenny Snyder, and Bruce Irvine; (fourth row) Jimmie Snyder, Amy Howey, Marilyn Smith, and Harold Gross. (Courtesy Barbara Snyder Herman.)

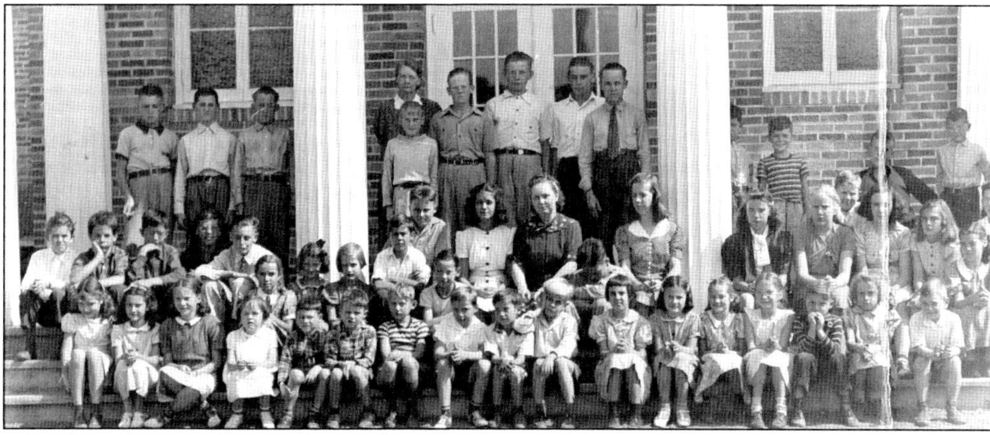

This class photograph was taken at the Delaware Township School in 1941. Pictured here, from left to right, are the following: (first row) Mary Lou Richards, Grace Jagger, Evelyn Cron, Barbara Bensley, Brian Kloetzer, John Kloetzer, Clouse Wojack, Robert Brumbaugh, Donald Cron, Arthur MacGregor, Marie Smith, Frances Jagger, Beatrice Cron, Doris Cron, Franklin Ryder, Joan Ryder, and Russell Brown; (second row) Kenneth Howey, Donald Smith, Frank Hotalen, Junior Stewart, Jack Kemp, Frances MacGregor, June Stuart, Irene Howey, Edward Gross, Harold Cron, and Jack Emery; (third row) Gerald Ryder, Inez Hotalen, teacher Letita Ryder, Betty Smith, Myrtle Bensley, Edna Jagger, Jeanie Smith, Vivian Sumners, Betty Gross, and Doris Gross; (fourth row) Lawrence Plante, Donald Brown, Russell Ladley, Madeline Slater, Jack Myck, Lester Jagger, Carl Frosse, Jack MacGregor, Clarence Ladley, Tom Hotalen, Leroy Cron, Lawrence Jagger, Robert Drake, and Blace Hotalen. (Courtesy Roberta and Leroy Cron.)

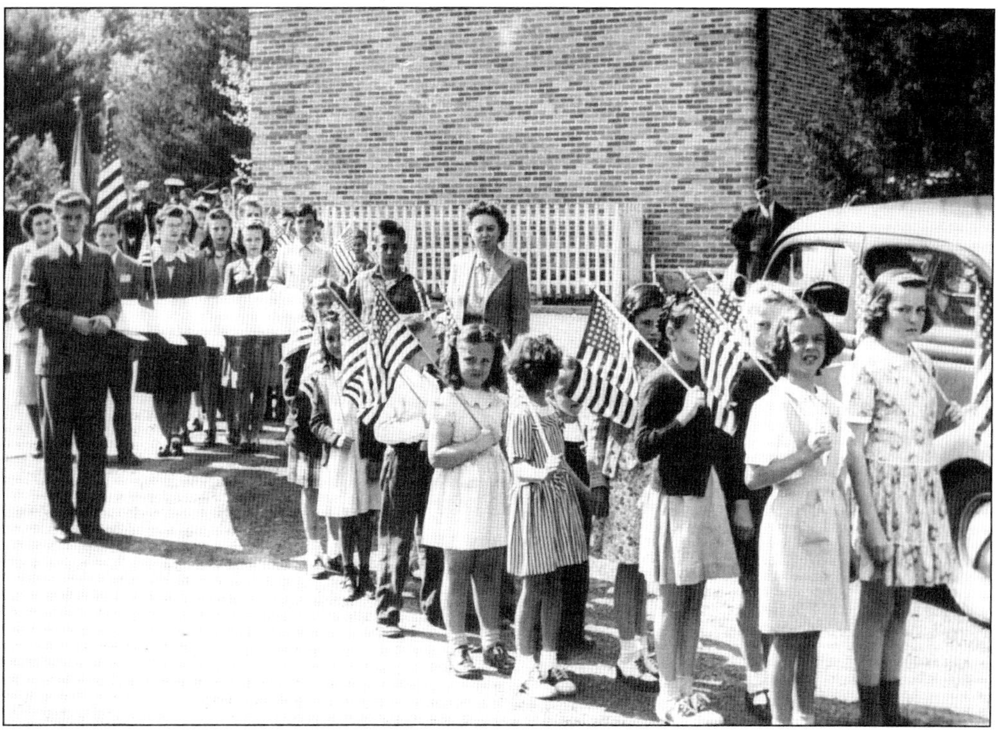

In this 1950s photograph, Delaware Township Consolidated School students prepare to march in the Memorial Day parade. (Courtesy Pike County Historical Society.)

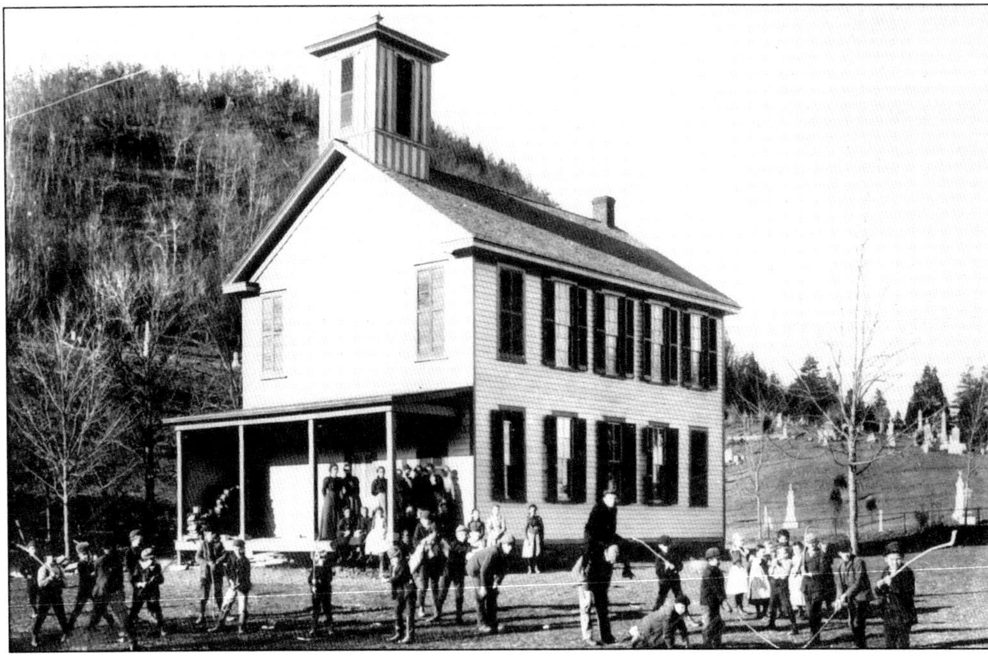

Dingmans Ferry's first school, the Academy, was established in 1815 after Judge Daniel Dingman accepted a proposal giving Dingmans Ferry $1,000 toward the construction of a school. The Academy school educated youth until 1933, when the new Delaware Township Consolidated School was opened. (Courtesy DF/DTHS.)

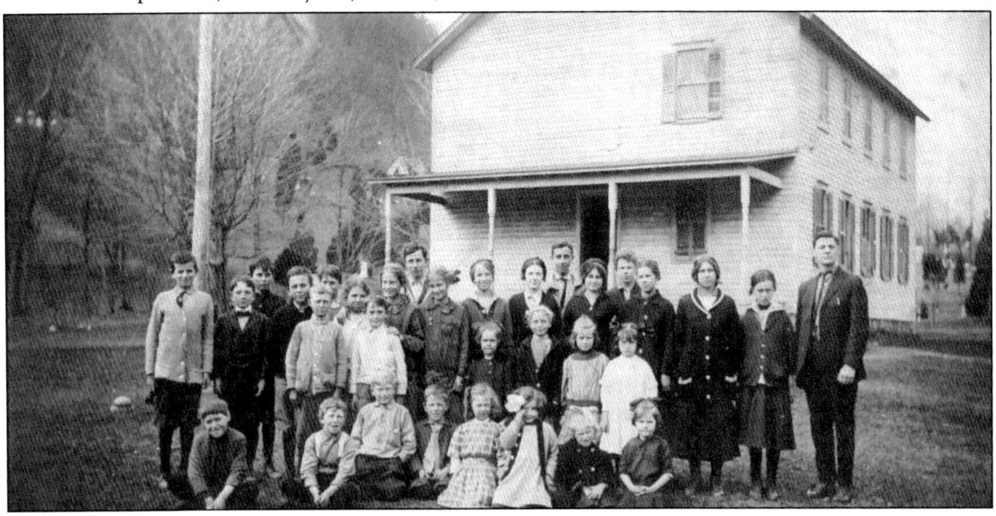

In 1914, the pupils and teacher of the Academy school pose for a school photograph. Identified students, with teacher Edward Schalffer, are Clarence Brown, Russell Brown, Daniel Middaugh, Earl Retallick, Ruth Brown, Zelda Kneiper, Florance Brown, Virginia Kinter, Roy Retallick, Paul Snearley, William Crone, Carl Hood, Estelle Kintner, Lucy Smith, Marion Crone, Helen Smith, Raymond Hood, Carlyle Hood, Clarence Snyder, Ruth Shoemaker, Rena Shoemaker, Edith Smith, Ellen Crone, Helen Lynch, Edna Gunn, Symantha Snyder, Verna Brown, Howard Smith, Irving Smith, and Lawrence Hietzman. Located next to the cemetery on Route 209, the school was rebuilt three different times—in 1870, 1898, and 1901—after being destroyed by fire. Unfortunately, the building has since been demolished. (Courtesy George and Carolyn Hotalen.)

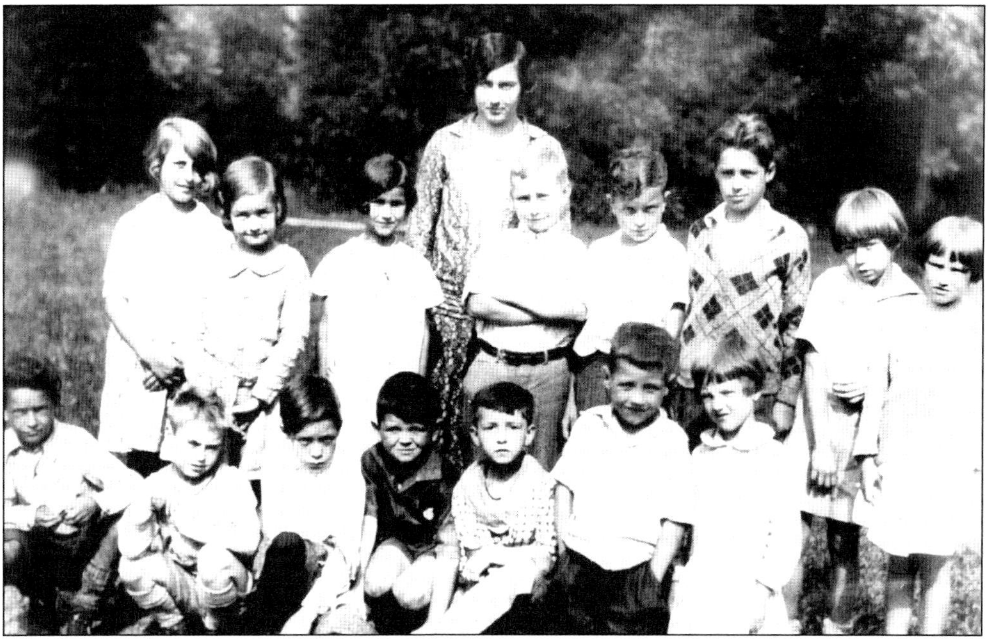

Academy students pose with their teacher around 1930. Pictured here, from left to right, are the following: (first row) Norman Hotalen, Lawrence Plante, Charles Howey, Tommy Parkinson, Dick Plante, Richard Smith, and Betty Smith; (second row) Natalie Ryder, Rosamond Littlefield, Josephine Hotalen, teacher Anna Hinkel, Eddie Theurich, Olin Personeus, Bud Ryder, Dotty Theurich, and Marion Bensley. (Courtesy George and Carolyn Hotalen.)

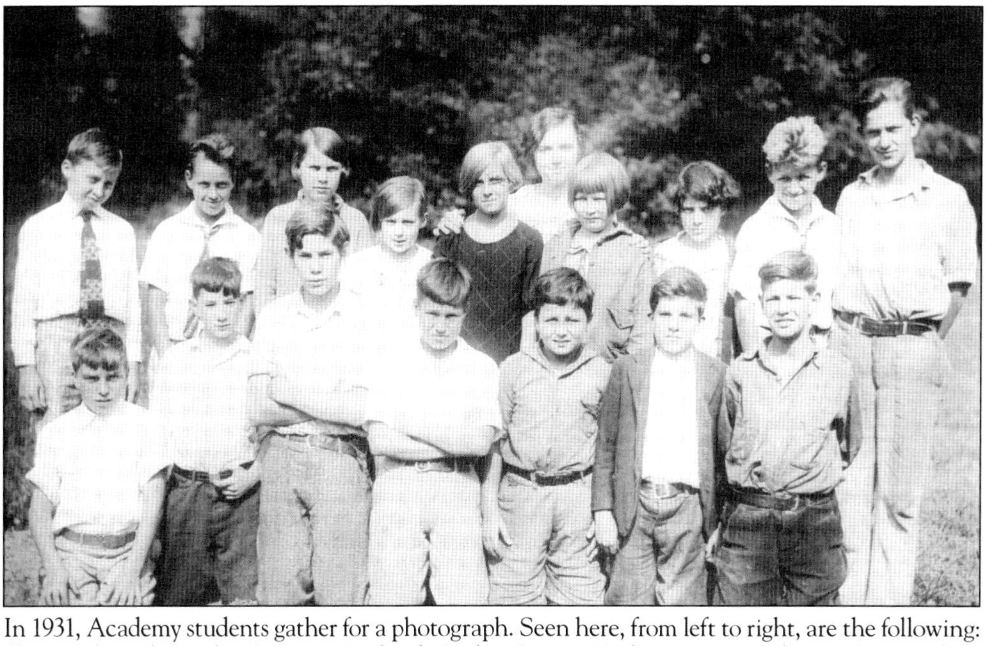

In 1931, Academy students gather for a photograph. Seen here, from left to right, are the following: (first row) Carl Bensley, Jimmie Newland, Arthur Jagger, Herbert Martin, Thomas Bie, Carlton Shepherd, and Floyd Hotalen; (second row) Otto Kittel, Carlyle Carhuff, Bertha (Jagger) Lindsley, Ada (Howey) Grygo, Lillian (Ryder) Treible, teacher Letita M. Ryder, Elsie (Kittel) Bensley, Margaret (Shepherd) Herr, John Kurz, and William Hotalen. (Courtesy Pike County Historical Society.)

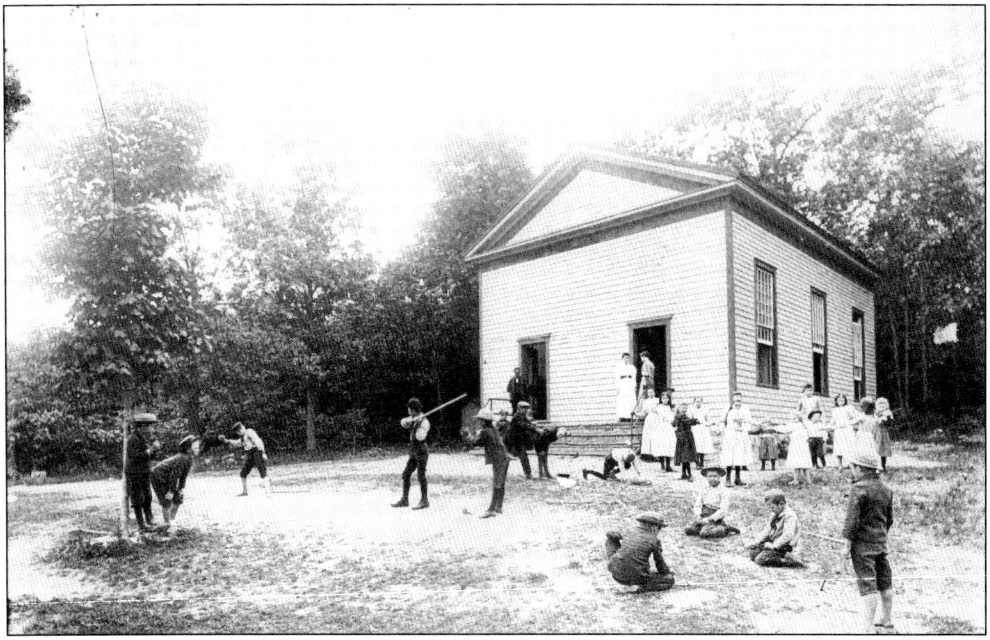

This 1800s photograph shows the Dutch Reformed church, though lacking its four columns prior to the construction of the front façade. The church was used as a school from 1870 to 1872, after the Academy was destroyed by fire. These children enjoy the spring day by playing baseball and ring around the rosy. (Courtesy DF/DTHS.)

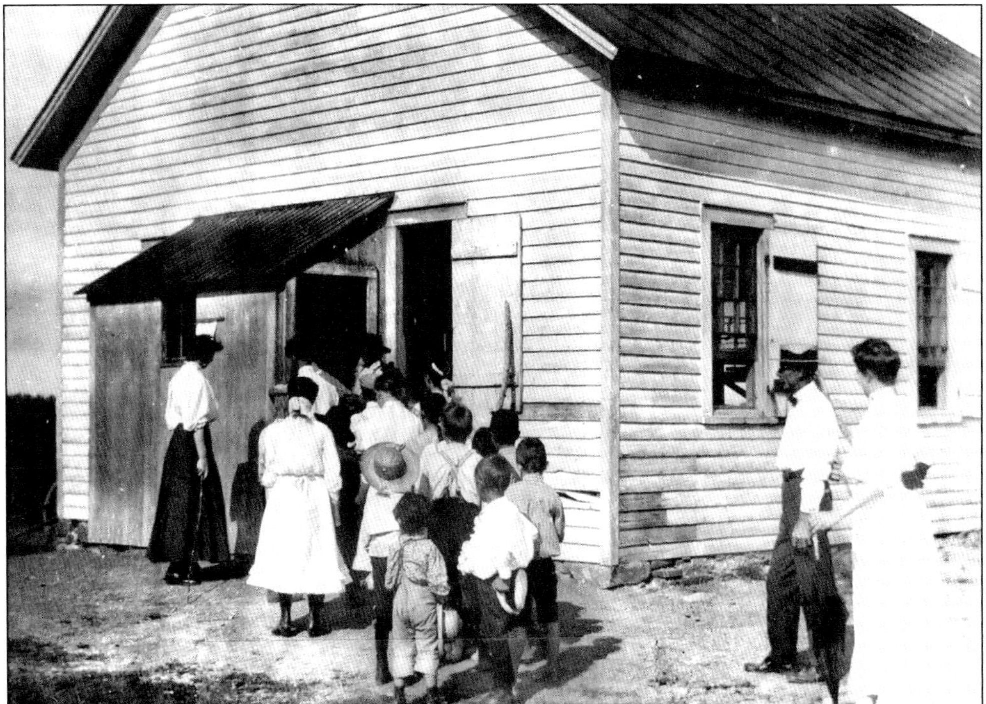

The Center School was built in 1895 on the corner of Wilson Hill and Milford Roads. The area children were educated there until 1924. (Courtesy DF/DTHS.)

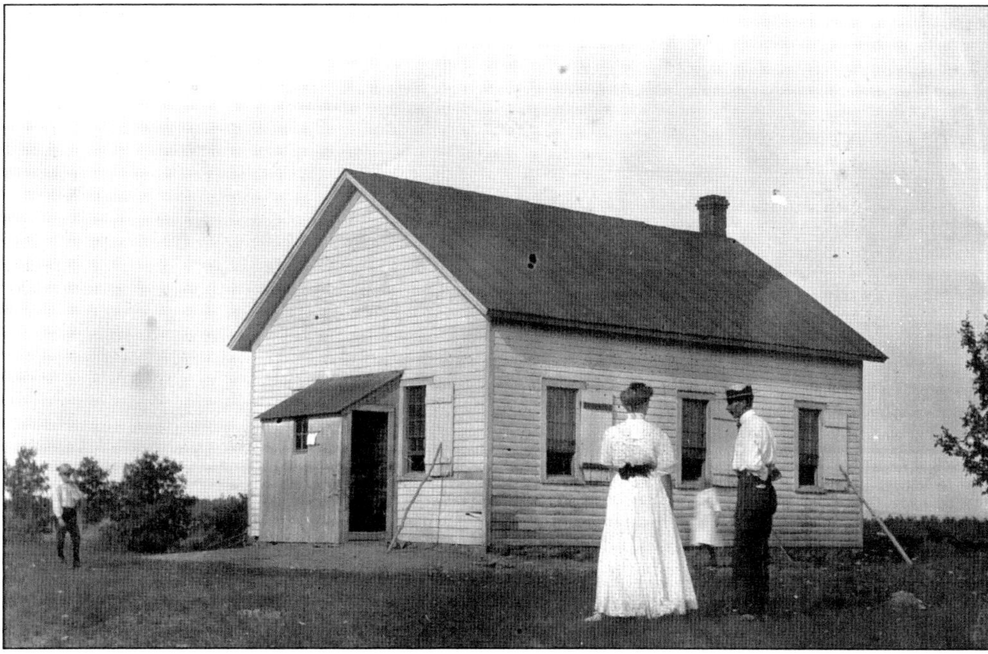

The original Center School was consumed by fire in 1901 and rebuilt soon after. It accommodated 50 pupils in grades one through eight. Pete Doty and Jeanette Gilmore Mitchell are pictured. (Courtesy DF/DTHS.)

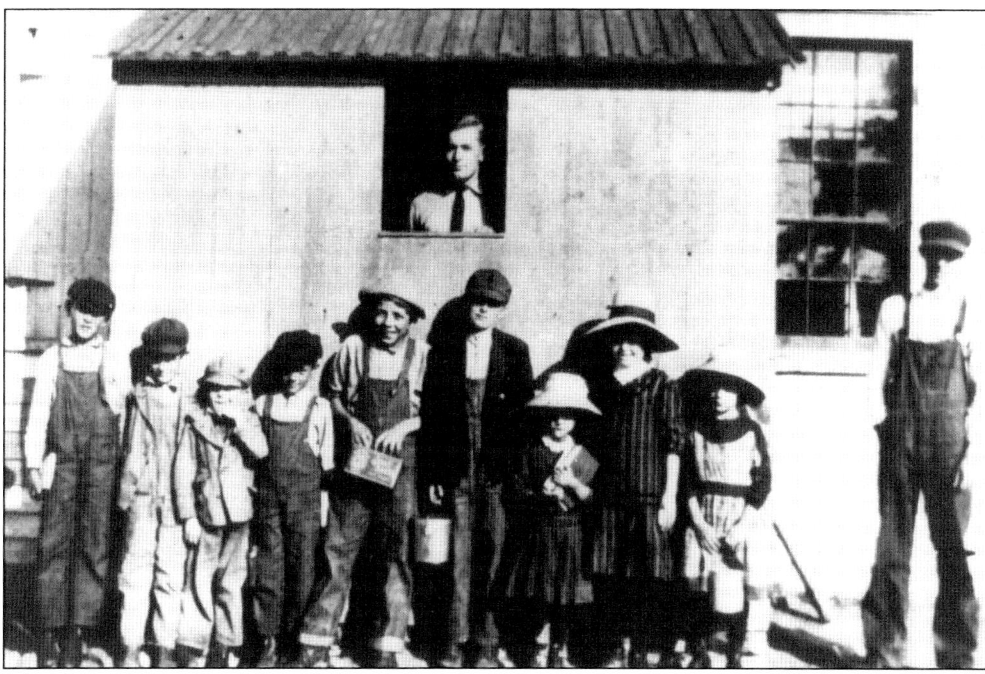

The three Cron girls show off their Easter bonnets, along with their classmates at the Center School, around 1910. Seen here, from left to right, are Charles Cron, William Brodhead, Haynes Brodhead, Harold Cron, John "Bike" Smith, August Cron, Blanche Cron, Anna Cron, Cornelia Cron, and Ira Jagger. Their teacher is Fred Middaugh. (Courtesy Roberta and Leroy Cron.)

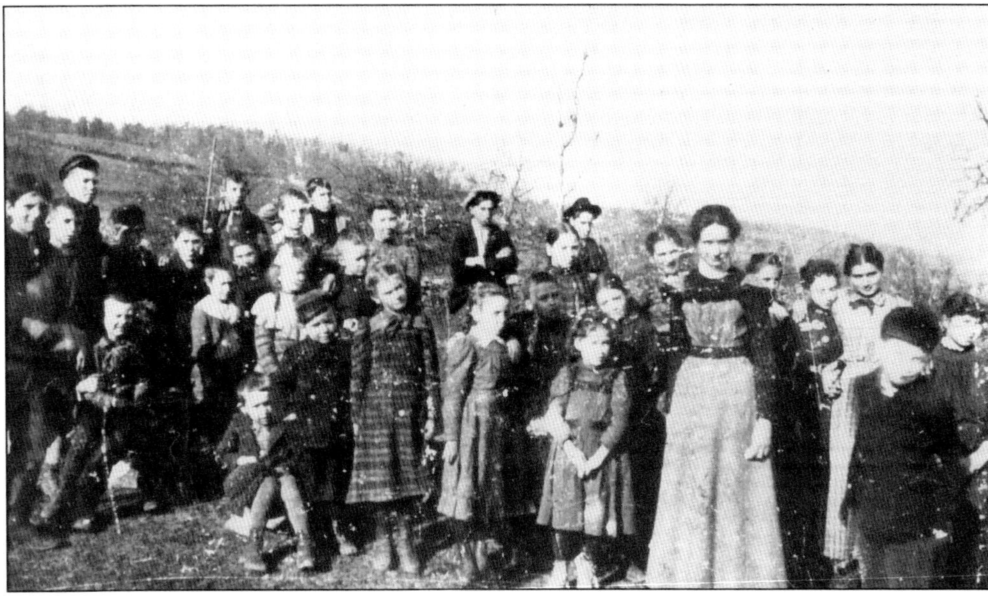

Sara Oldfield's students pose at the Center School about 1900. Many of the families represented in this photograph have called Pike County home for over 150 years. Identified here are Clarence Smith, Ben Courtright, Fred Martin, Henry Smith, Walton Jagger, Albert Smith, Jake Howey, George Martin, Edward Smith, Amsey Smith, Amy Cron Vallerchamp, Myrtle Jagger, John Snyder, Nora Smith Meade, Frank N. Downs, Maude Cron Treible, Millie Snyder Shields, Ruth Brodhead Seilheimer, Betty Heater Chidester, Hattie Cron Downs, Harry Jagger, Chrissie Smith Vandermark, Katie Martin Cron, Lizzie Howey, Della Martin Crone, Grace Snyder VanSickle, and Harold Smith. (Courtesy Roberta and Leroy Cron.)

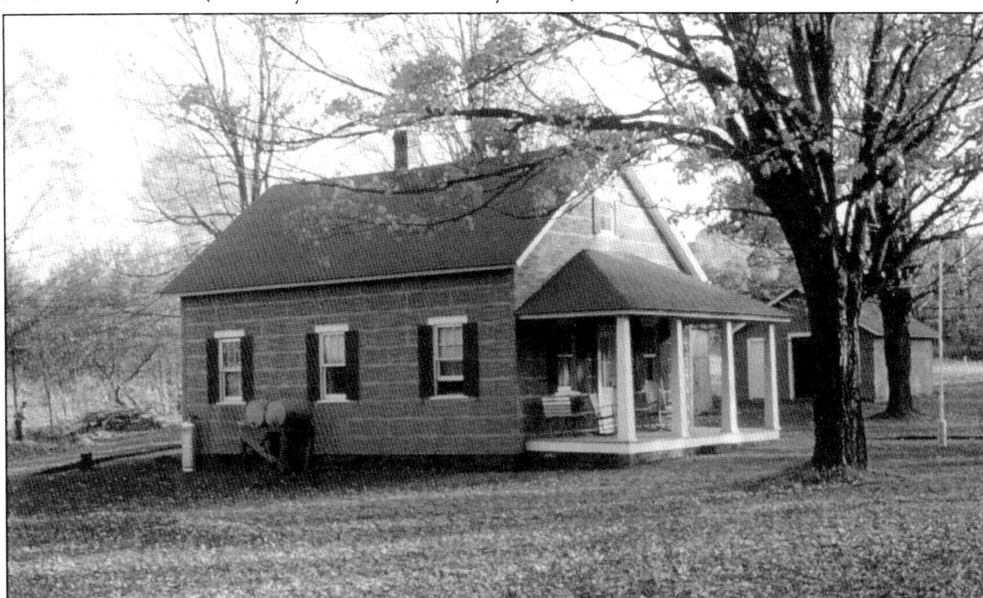

In the 1960s, John and Anna Whalen renovated the Center School and used it as a residence for many years. Today, the building still stands and is the home to Sunshine Station, a daycare center. (Courtesy DF/DTHS.)

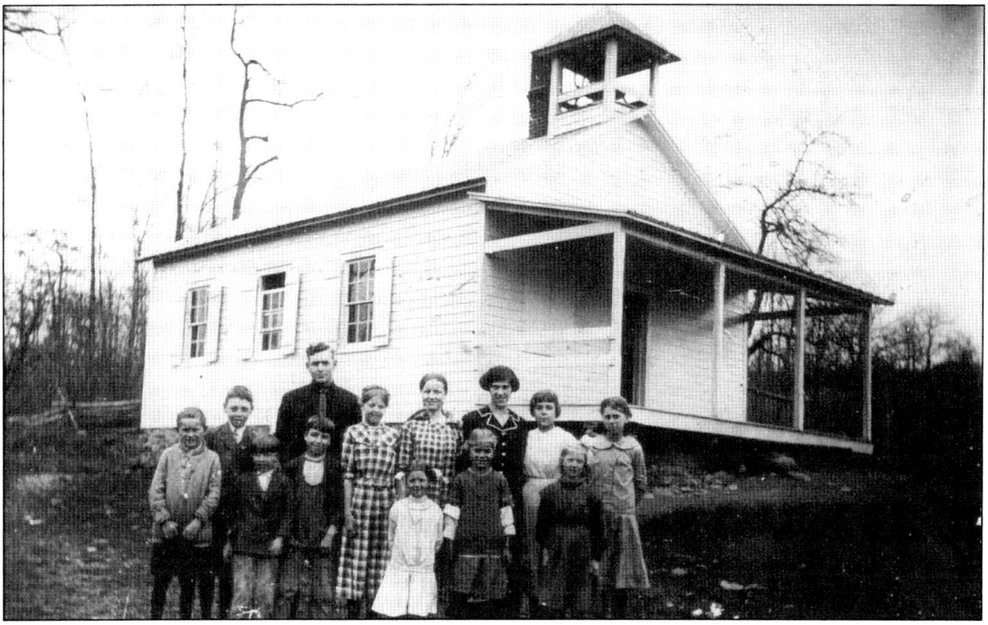

The Cole School, located at Shepherd's Corner, where Silver Lake Road intersects Milford Road, was constructed in 1867 and rebuilt in 1908 after a fire. This one-room schoolhouse was in use until 1933, when all area schools consolidated. Shown here around 1914, are Arthur Albright, Stanley Emery, Ed Angle, Phil Angle, Phyllis Dotey Edwards, Clarissa Snearley, Elsie Emery, Cora Angle, Mary Albright, Helen Greening, and Lura Albright. Fred Middaugh was their teacher. (Courtesy DT/DFHS.)

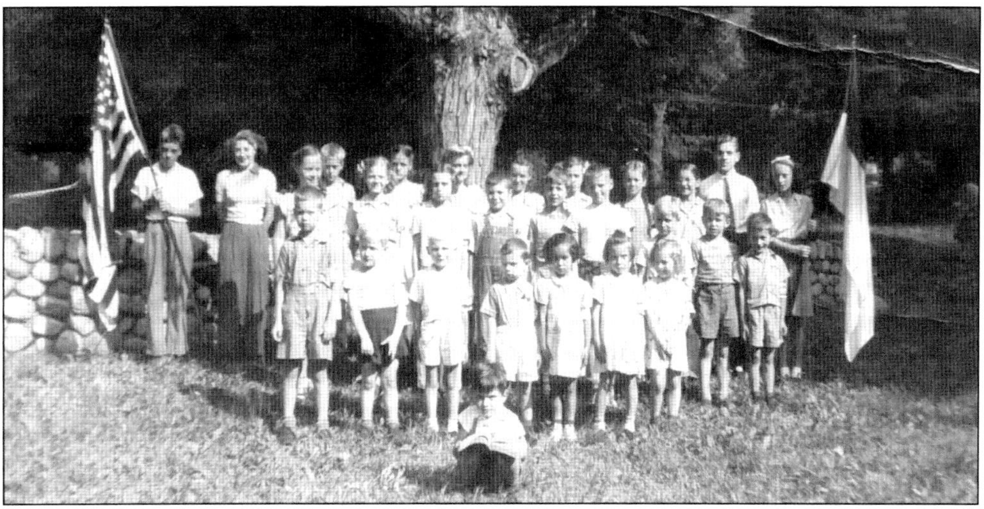

Bible school at the Dutch Reformed church was a favorite for local children. On this summer day in 1942, students posed at Delaware Cemetery. Pictured here, from left to right, are the following: (first row) Brian Hunt, Bruce Irvine, Perry Irvine, Roger Hunt, Beverly Myers Eagle, Marilyn Smith Morris, and Nancy Findlay O'Brien; (second row) two unidentified children, Joan Ryder Mervine, Leroy Cron, Mary Lou Richards, A. Proven, two unidentified children, and Louie Myers; (third row) Junior Stewart, ? Corbett, four unidentified children, Viola Kern Canouse, Doris M. Cron, Reverend Moke, and unidentified. George Hotalen appears in the foreground. (Courtesy George and Carolyn Hotalen.)

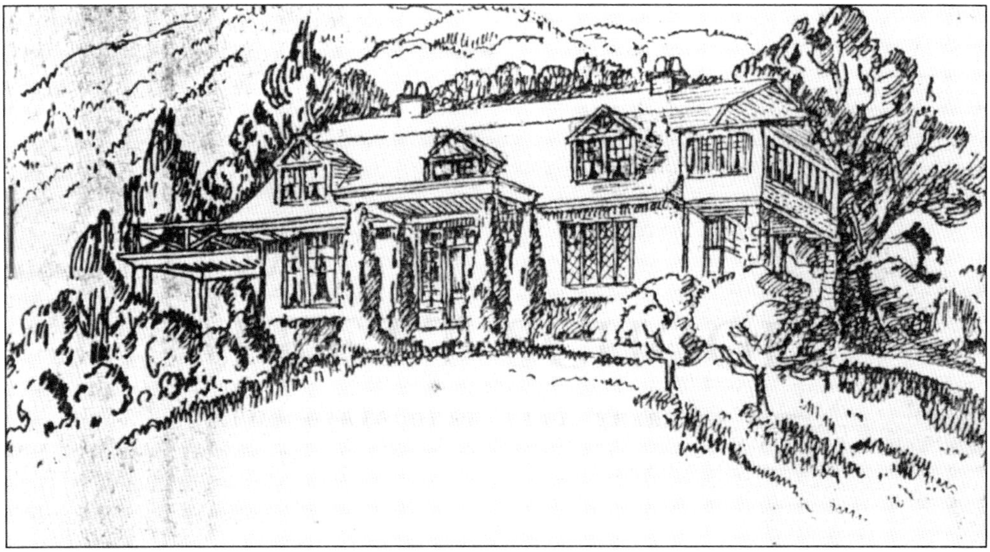

Standing on the mountainside of Route 209, between the Delaware Cemetery and the Marie Zimmermann Farm, the Brett School was a special needs school for girls over five years of age. Established in 1931, it operated until 1967; the building then became a residence, with Lee Rosbach as caretaker. It was demolished in 1972 for the Tocks Island Project. (Courtesy DF/DTHS.)

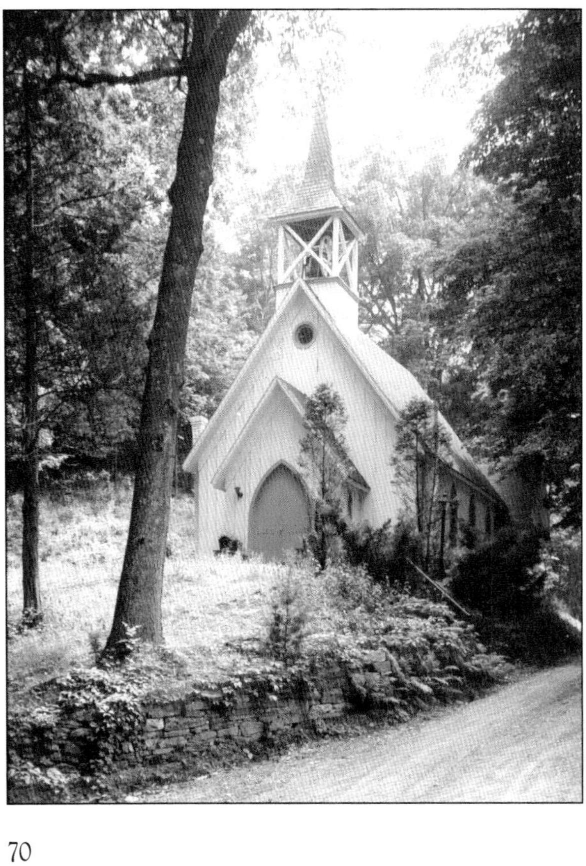

The Episcopal Church of St. John's the Evangelist was built on Bethany Turnpike (Route 739) in 1887. This beautiful Gothic-style structure stood just north of the Dingmans Bridge. (Courtesy Delaware Water Gap National Recreation Area.)

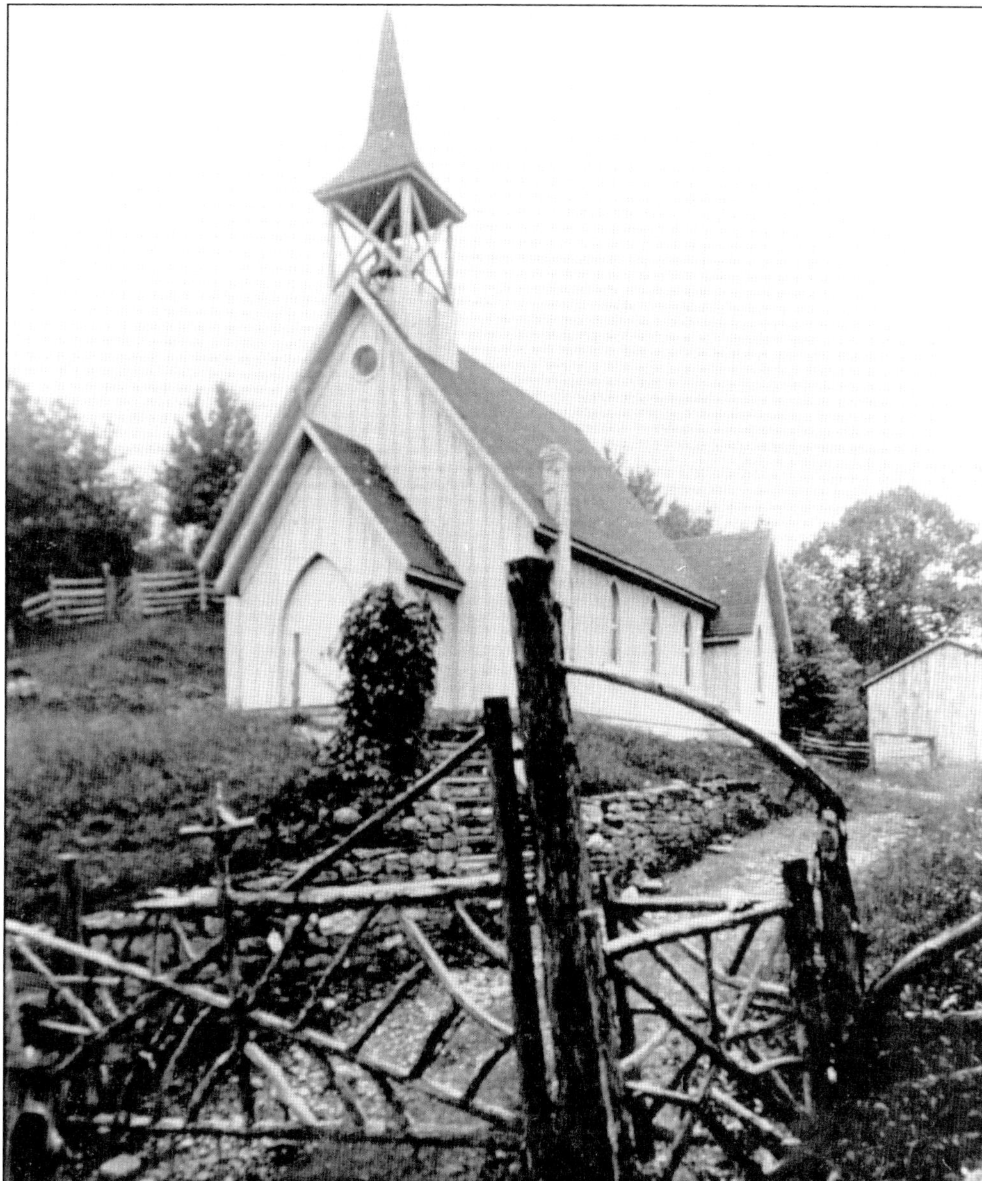

Episcopal Church--1896

This early-20th-century photograph preserves and personifies the quaint St. John's Episcopal Church, which stood on a hill. Built on lands donated by John Kilsby, its construction was a labor of love for both the local residents and summer guests who gave time and money to see its completion. Note the simple cross on the gate. (Courtesy DF/DTHS.)

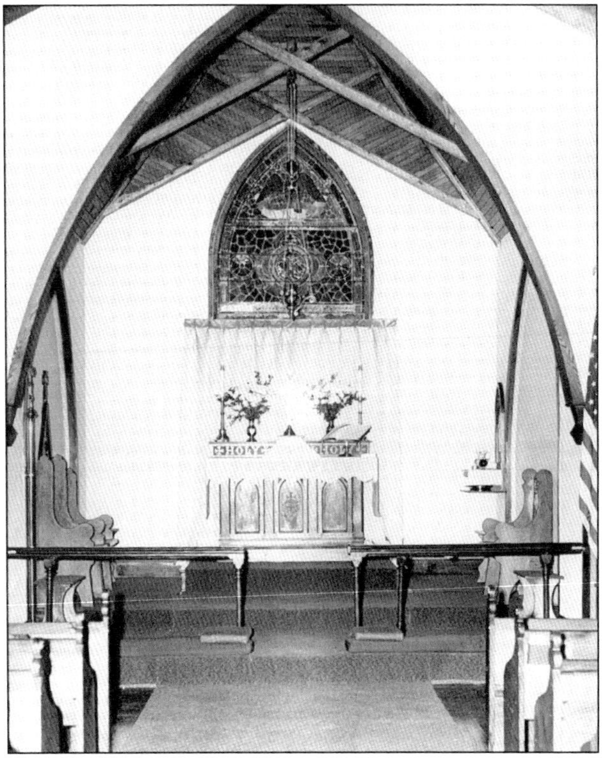

This inspirational interior view of St. John's reveals a simple design of Gothic arches over the windows and a beautiful wood truss ceiling. At this time, the church was celebrating its 70th anniversary in 1957, with Rev. Richard Aselford presiding. The parish register included the Gross, Findlay, Angle, Lewis, Hamor, Hodges, and Downs families. The church was unfortunately destroyed in the late 1970s to allow for the National Recreation Area. (Courtesy DF/DTHS.)

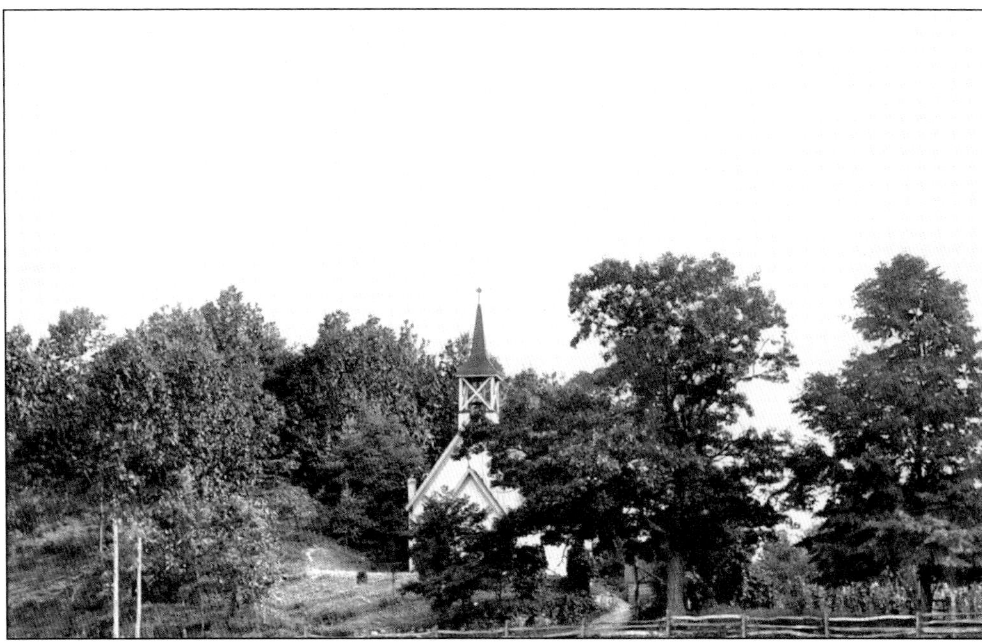

St. John's Episcopal Church appears in the distance of this view across Route 739. The church stood on Bethany Turnpike (Route 739) just below Tie Alley, which ran through to Main Street, just across from Johnny B. Road, later known as Dingmans Corner. (Courtesy DF/DTHS.)

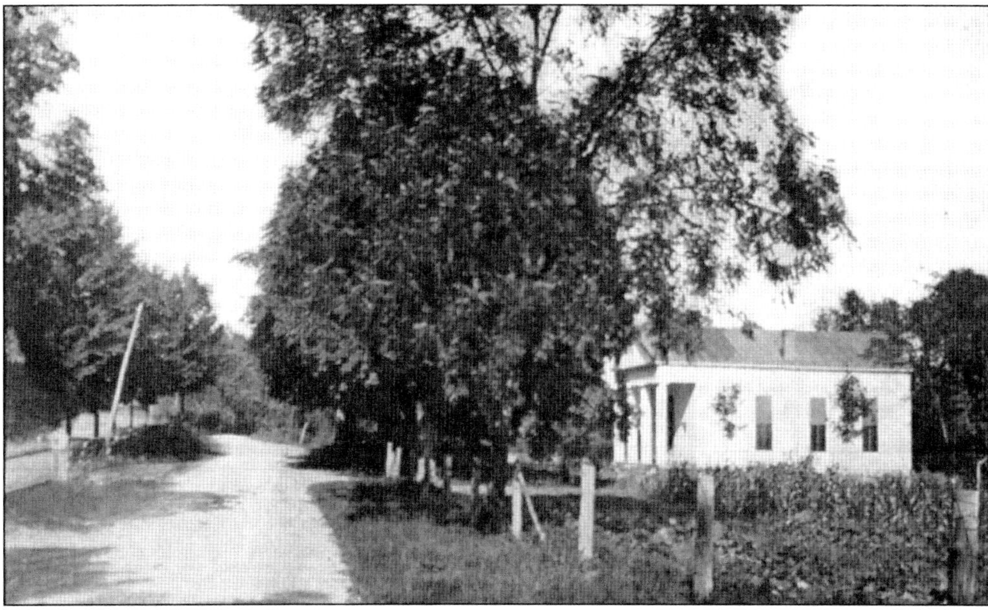

This early-20th-century view of the Dutch Reformed Church looks north on Main Street (Route 209). Organized as a congregation in 1737, in conjunction with Walpack, New Jersey, the first Dutch Reformed services in Pennsylvania were held in private homes. This building is now a private residence with a gift shop located in the outbuilding. (Courtesy Roberta and Leroy Cron.)

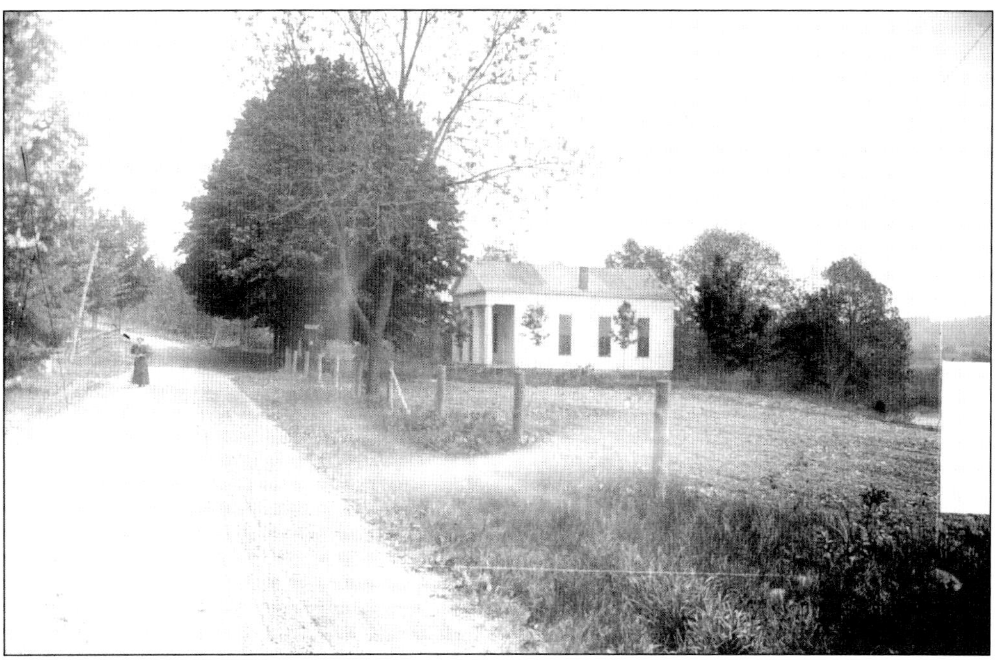

The Dutch Reformed Church is one of the remaining venerable structures of old Dingmans Ferry. Built in 1850 for $1,300, the graceful four-columned Greek-style church was originally known as the Upper Walpack Dutch Reformed Church. (Courtesy DF/DTHS.)

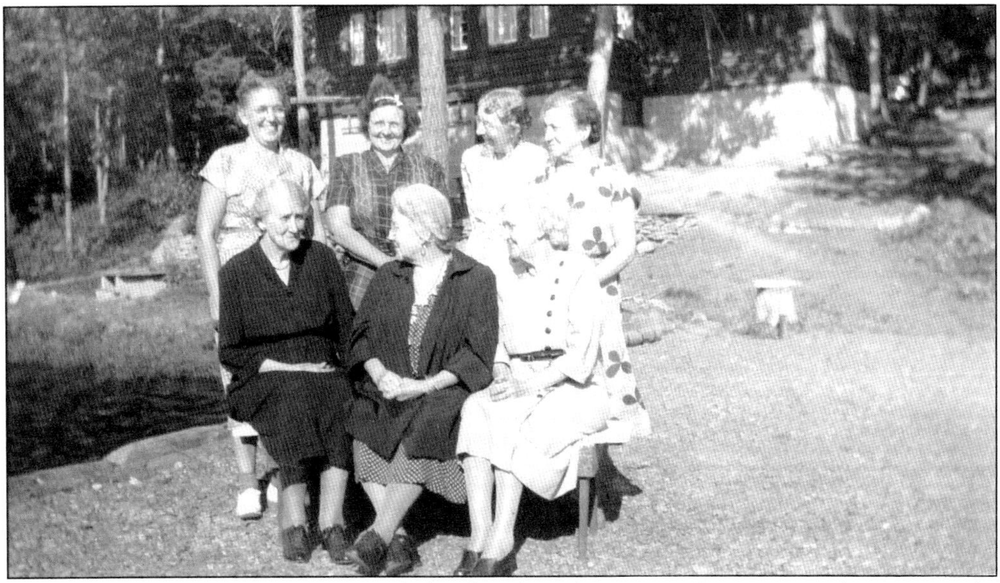

As in many small villages in this period, the churches of Dingmans Ferry were gathering spots for citizens. On Sunday, Delaware Township residents would come to town to worship and socialize. This group of women met at the Dutch Reformed church as part of the Daughters of Holland in August 1951. Pictured from left to right are (first row) Carrie Darragh Dingman Armstrong, Marion Darragh Faucett, and Kit Darragh; (second row) Mabel Bensley Dotey, Harriet Jagger Snyder, Caroline (Smith) Darragh, and Edna Darragh. (Courtesy Roberta and Leroy Cron.)

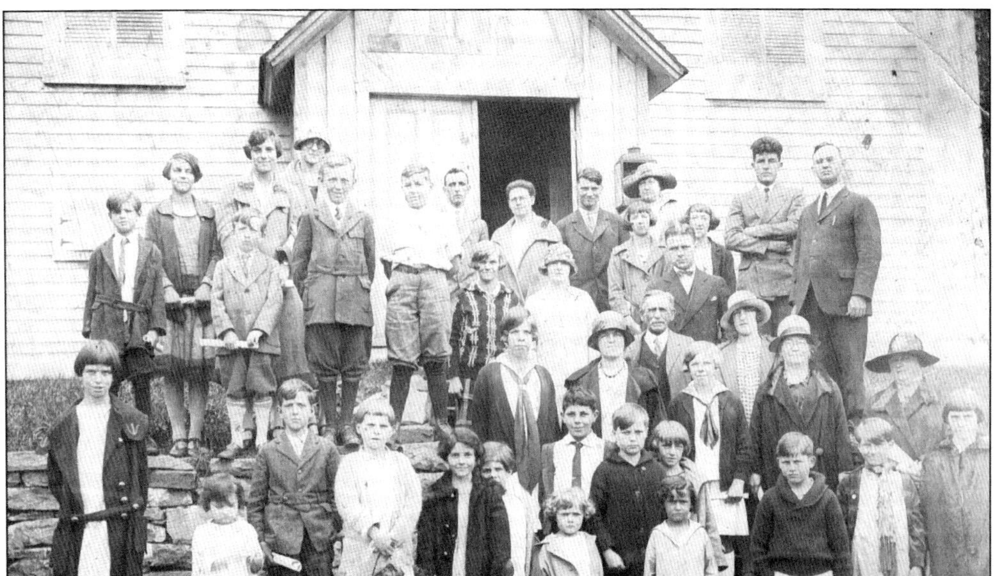

The United Methodist church Sunday school class of 1926 poses for a photograph. Identified here are Josephine Hotalen, Peggy Hesselman, Marge Shepherd, Anna Lagier, Dorothea Albright, Bill Hotalen, Floyd Hotalen, Claude Brown, teacher Ellen Smith, Lura Albright, Cora Albright, Irving Smith, and Edna Kupfer, the wife of Rev. Charles Kupfer. (Courtesy George and Carolyn Hotalen.)

The first Methodist Episcopal church in Dingmans Ferry welcomed parishioners in 1830. The lovely church graced Main Street just south of Wilson Hill Road. Dedicated in 1871, it was the second church to be an integral part of the village. (Courtesy DF/DTHS.)

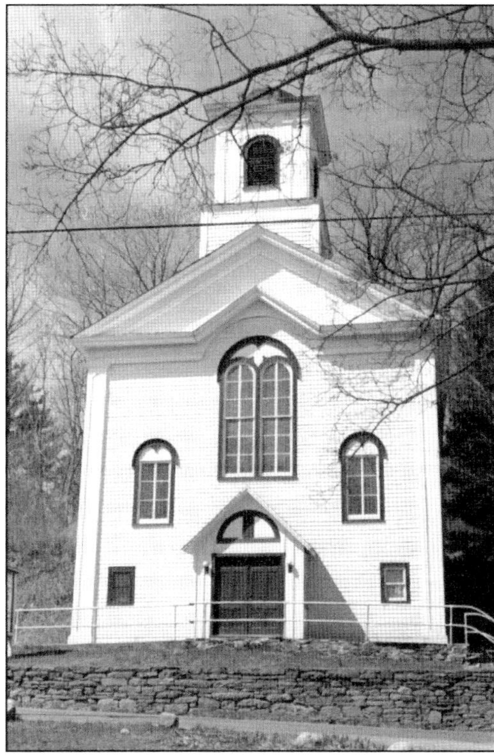

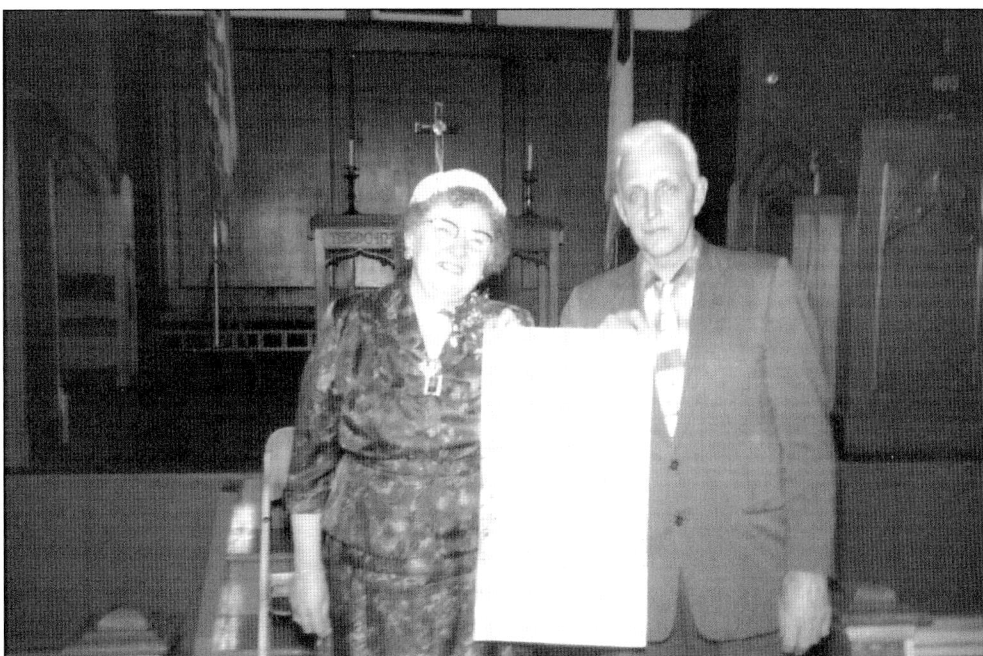

Even though many families belonged to the Methodist congregation, the Smith family received special recognition in March 1960 for 36 years of service in the Methodist Church School of Dingmans Ferry. Ellen Crone Smith and Irving Smith were given a scroll by the members of the church in a show of appreciation. (Courtesy Gen Stripple Collection.)

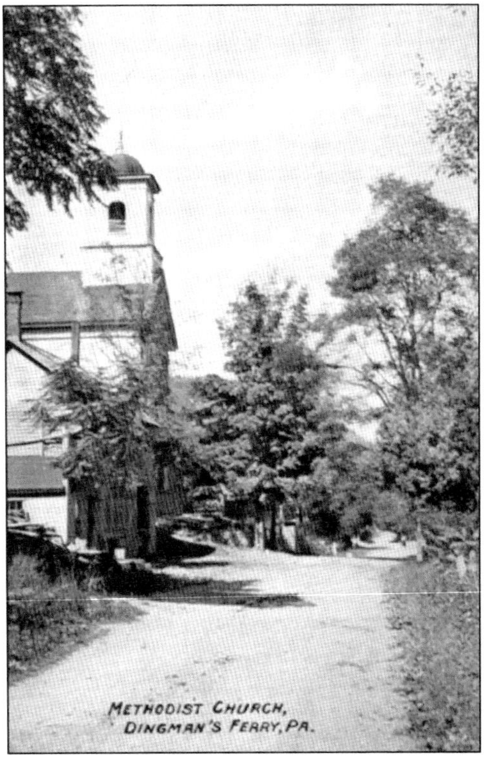

The bell of the Dingmans Methodist Church called its congregation for over 100 years. In the 1970s, the federal government purchased and demolished the structure, but not before parishioners had built a new church on Myck Road. (Courtesy DF/DTHS.)

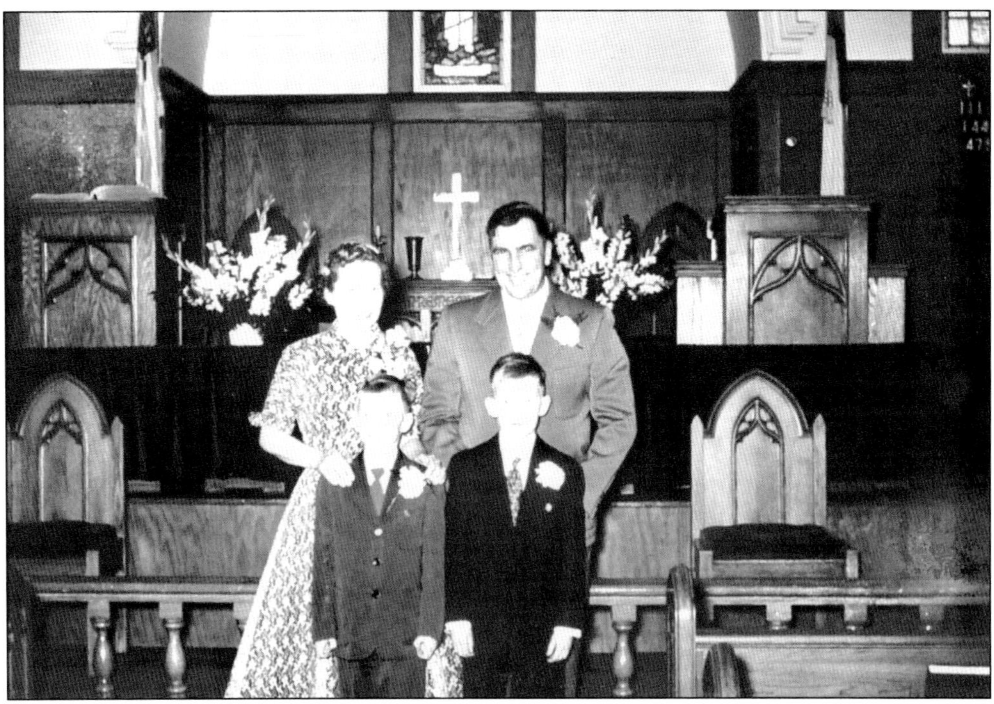

At the Dingmans Methodist Church, wedding bells rang on March 18, 1956. Elsie Kittel became the bride of Carl Bensley. Her children, Henry (left) and John Kraft, were at the ceremony to celebrate this happy occasion. (Courtesy Elsie Bensley.)

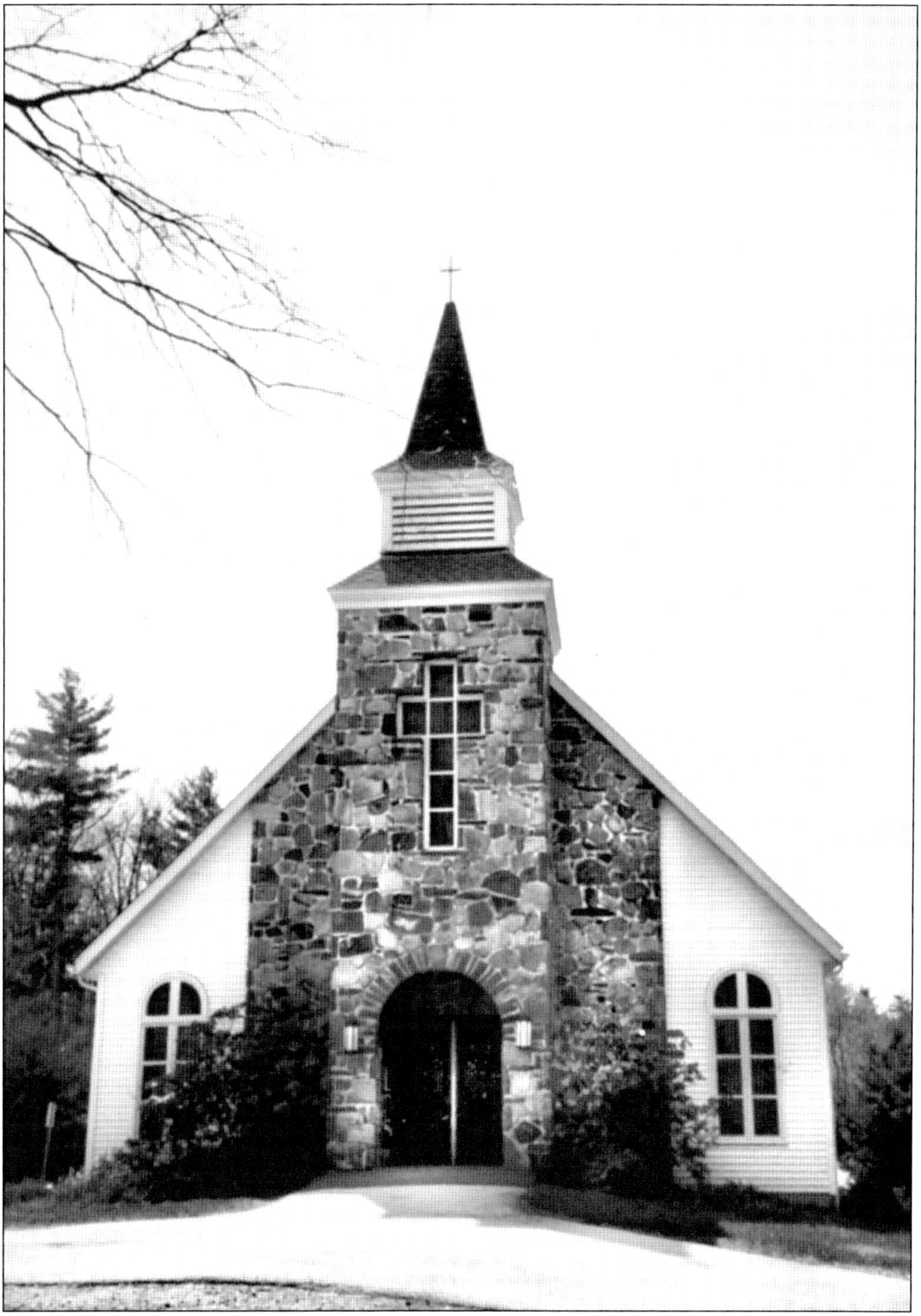

On June 29, 1978, the new Dingmans Ferry Methodist Church on Myck Road was dedicated. Known as the "Church in the Wildwood," it was constructed from salvaged materials of the original church. These items included the pews, stained-glass windows, and bell. (Courtesy Jo Ann and Ted Parsell.)

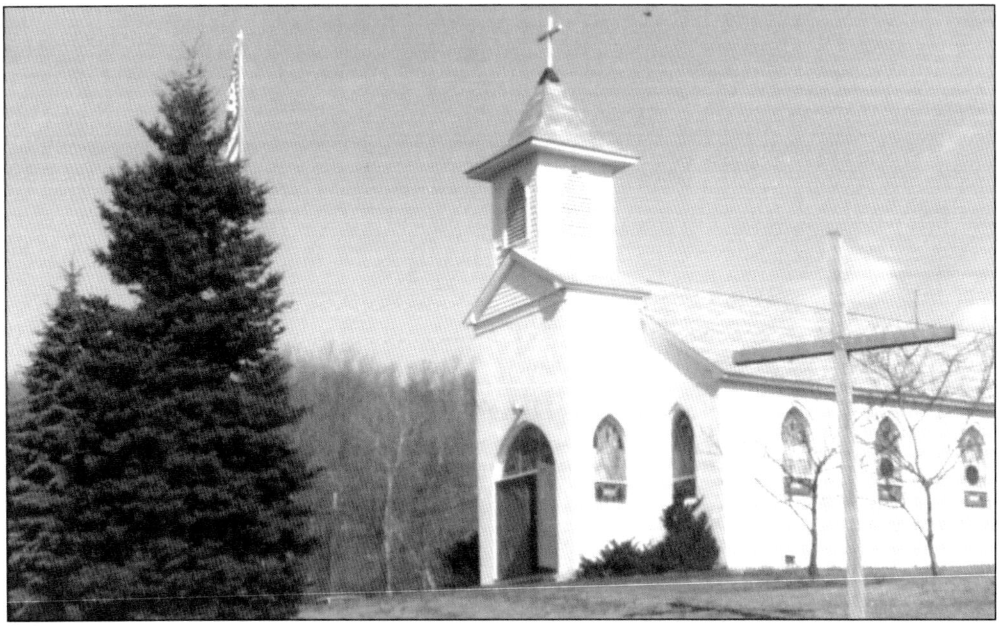

The first Holy Trinity Church was constructed in Dingmans Ferry in 1946 by Pastor Ernie Anderson and was expanded many times over the years. By 1992, a new sanctuary had been constructed. Pictured here in 1987 is the original Lutheran church. The building now houses the offices of the district magistrate serving the townships of Delaware, Porter, and Lehman. (Courtesy Virginia Oliver.)

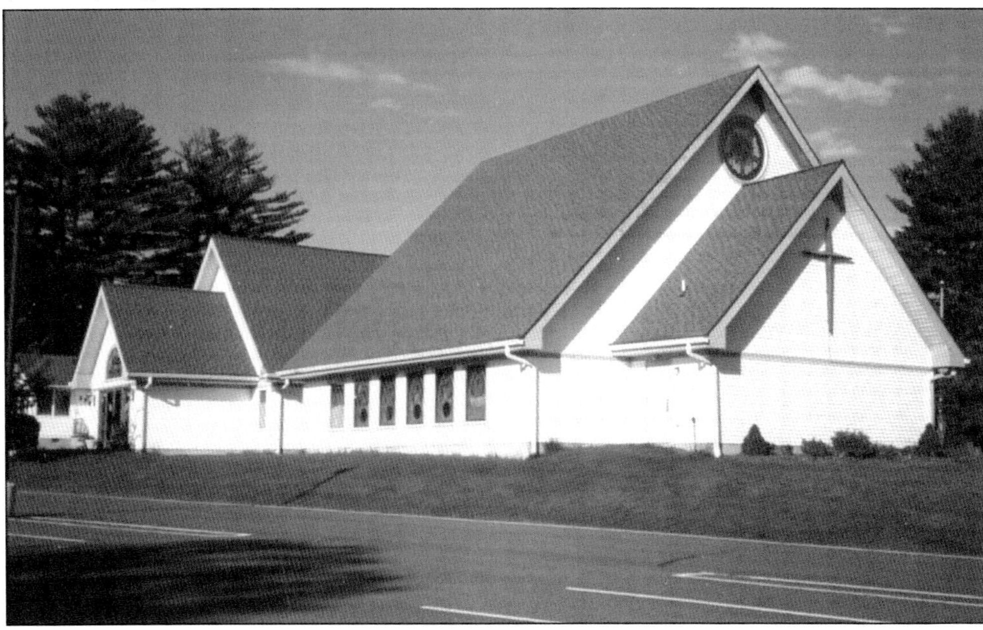

Located on Silver Lake Road, the new Holy Trinity Church was dedicated on December 6, 1992, to accommodate the growing Lutheran congregation. Leading the church for the past 23 years, Rev. Niels H. Nielsen was instrumental in the construction of the new sanctuary and the addition of a nursery school. The church continues to be a mainstay in the community. (Courtesy Jo Ann and Ted Parsell.)

Five

FARMING

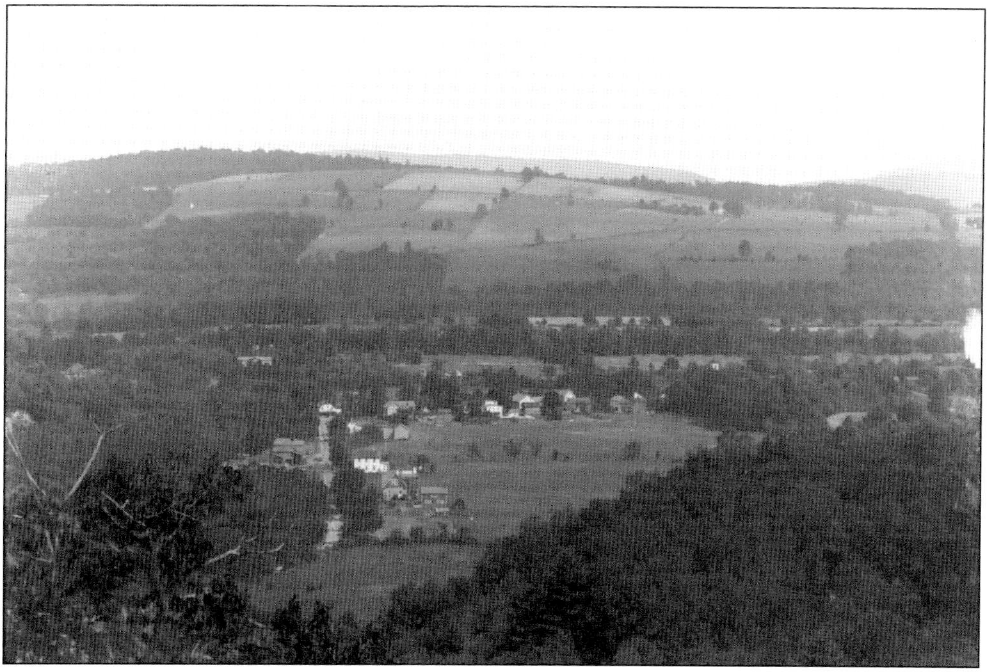

With the vast farm fields of New Jersey in the distance, this aerial view of Dingmans Ferry shows the tranquil setting of a quaint village. The main section of Dingmans is visible, with the Delaware River flowing in the middle of the photograph. Down Mill Street, the Darragh Mill is on the left, and the Thundercloud Homestead is on the right, with the Albright Store at the end of the road. The windmill of the Pine Hill House is to the left, while the bell tower of the Methodist church peeks from the trees on the far right. (Courtesy Sue and Carl Arnold.)

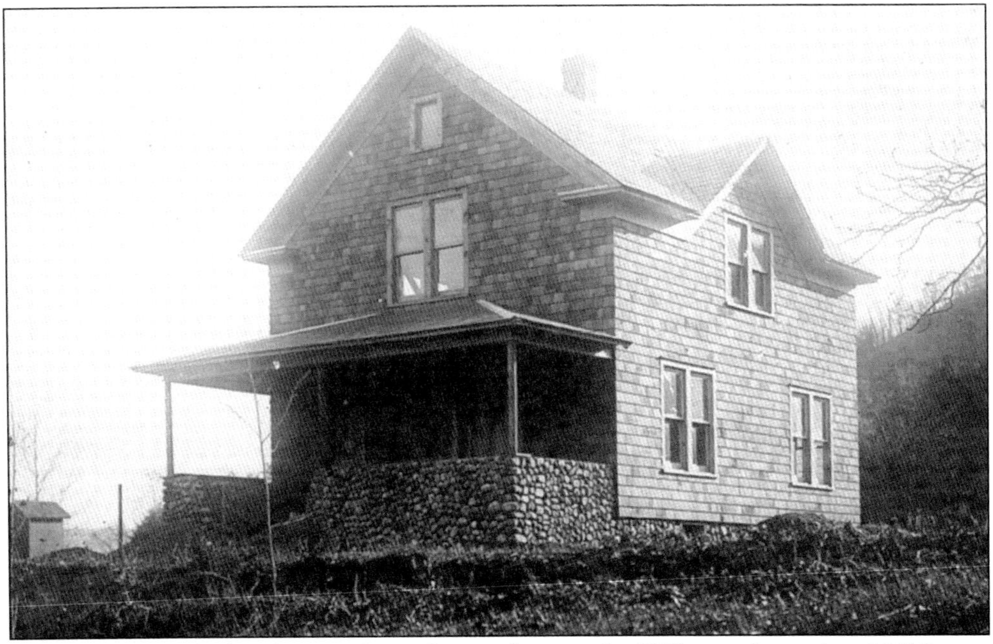

The farmhouse of Ed and Carrie Darragh, seen here in the 1920s, was located on Mill Street. (Courtesy Roberta and Leroy Cron.)

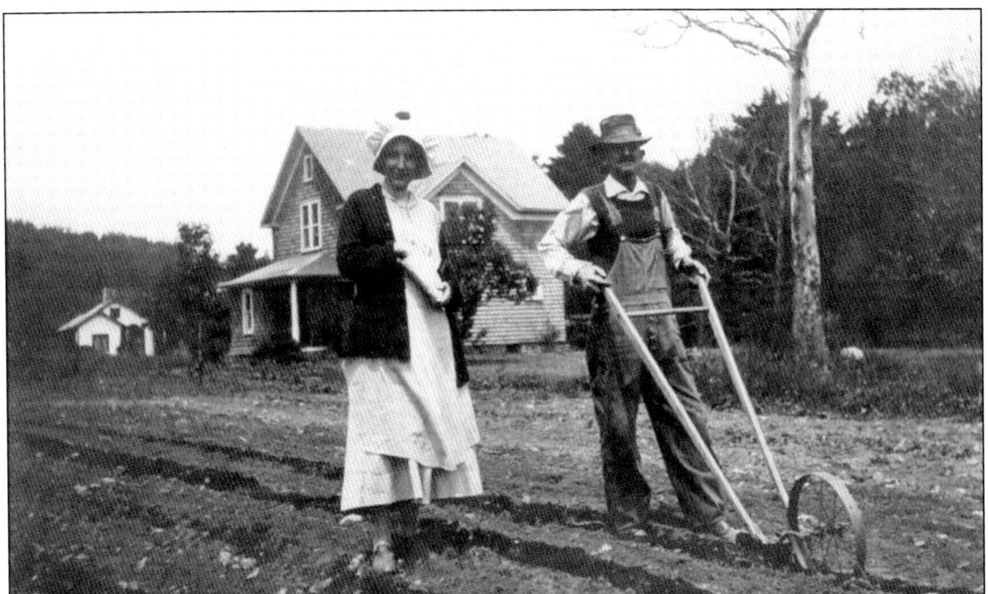

The Darraghs stop their farming chores for a moment to pose for this photograph. They operated a small farm in Dingmans Ferry for many years. (Courtesy Roberta and Leroy Cron.)

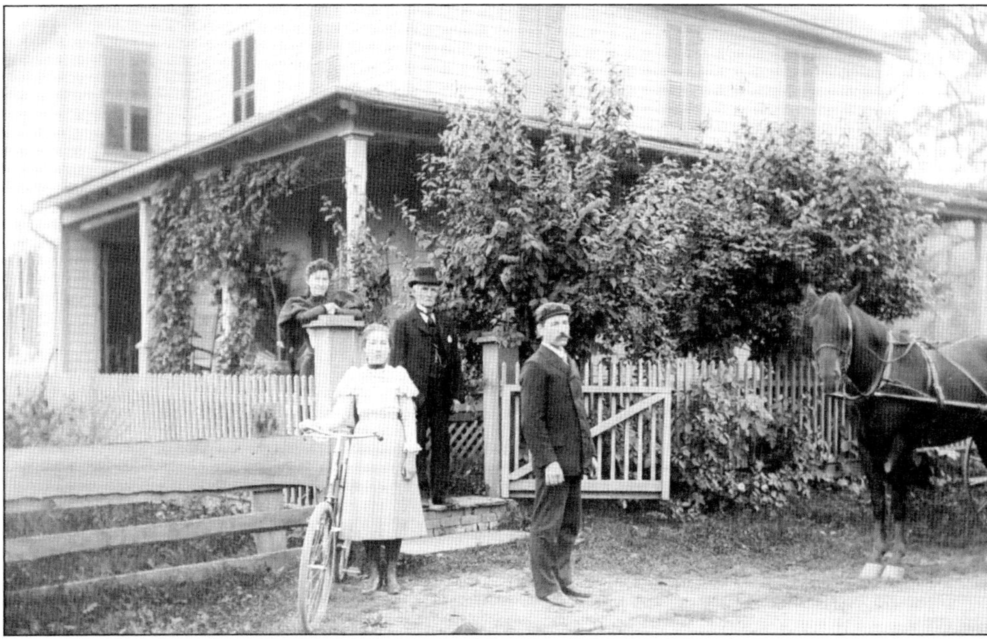

George VanAuken lived with his family on Mill Street. The lady standing on the left in this *c.* 1900 view is Emily VanAuken, and the gentleman in the top hat is her father, John Whittaker. In the foreground, George appears with his daughter Marilla (by the bicycle). George's father was John B., for whom Johnny B. Road is named. (Courtesy Inez E. Dickison.)

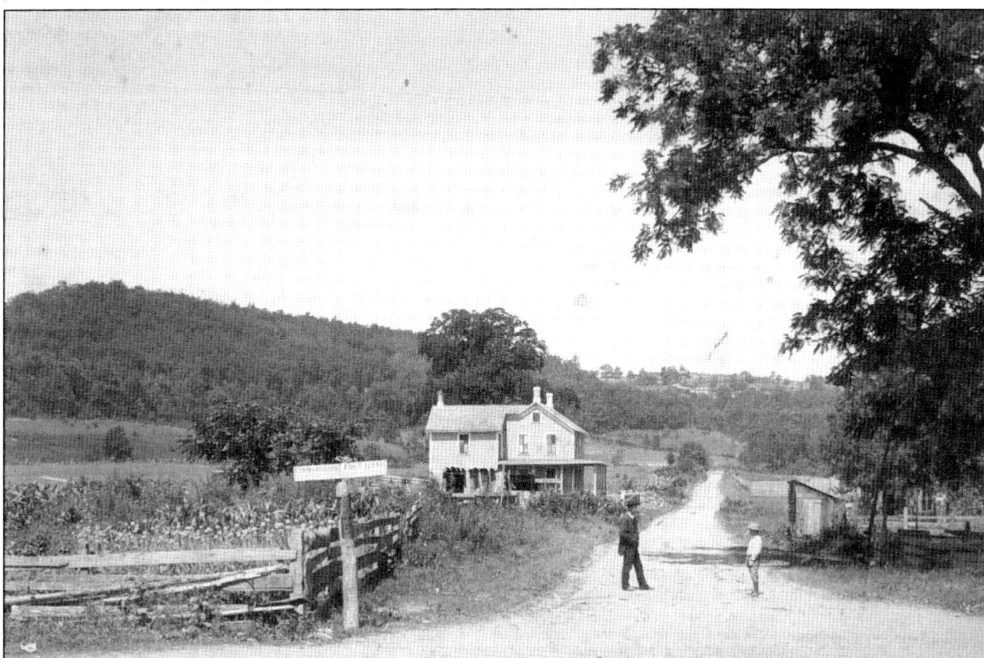

The Gen. George B. VanAuken house was built in 1850. This lovely Colonial-style residence also included an adjacent large farm, located on the corner of Mill and Main Streets. The house is shown here around 1890. (Courtesy Inez E. Dickison.)

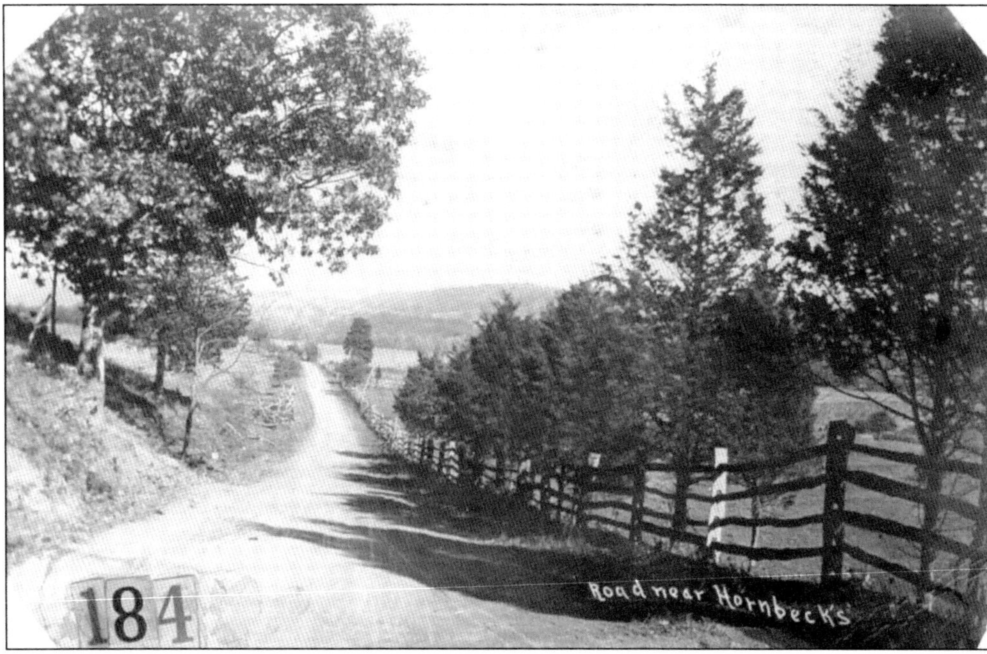

This early-1900s Allerton postcard view looks north on Main Street at Hornbeck's Creek. (Courtesy Laura and Jan de Graaf.)

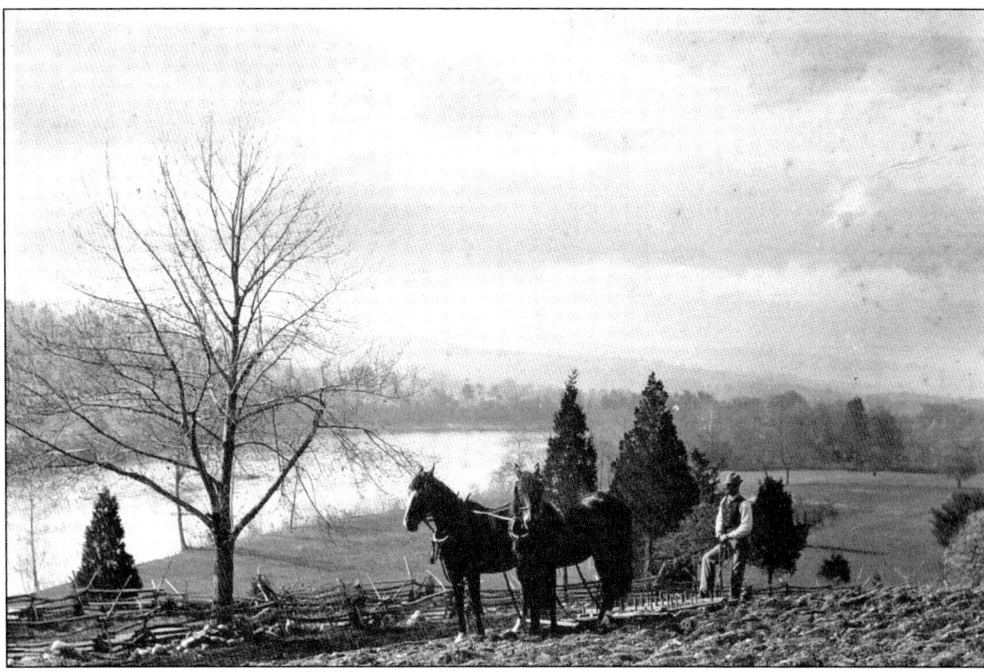

The area surrounding Dingmans Ferry flourished substantially as an agricultural community. These large farms provided the numerous hotels, inns, and boardinghouses with the fresh fruits and vegetables needed for guests' home-cooked meals. Here, Al Dingman plows the fields for his next planting of crops. (Courtesy Roberta and Leroy Cron.)

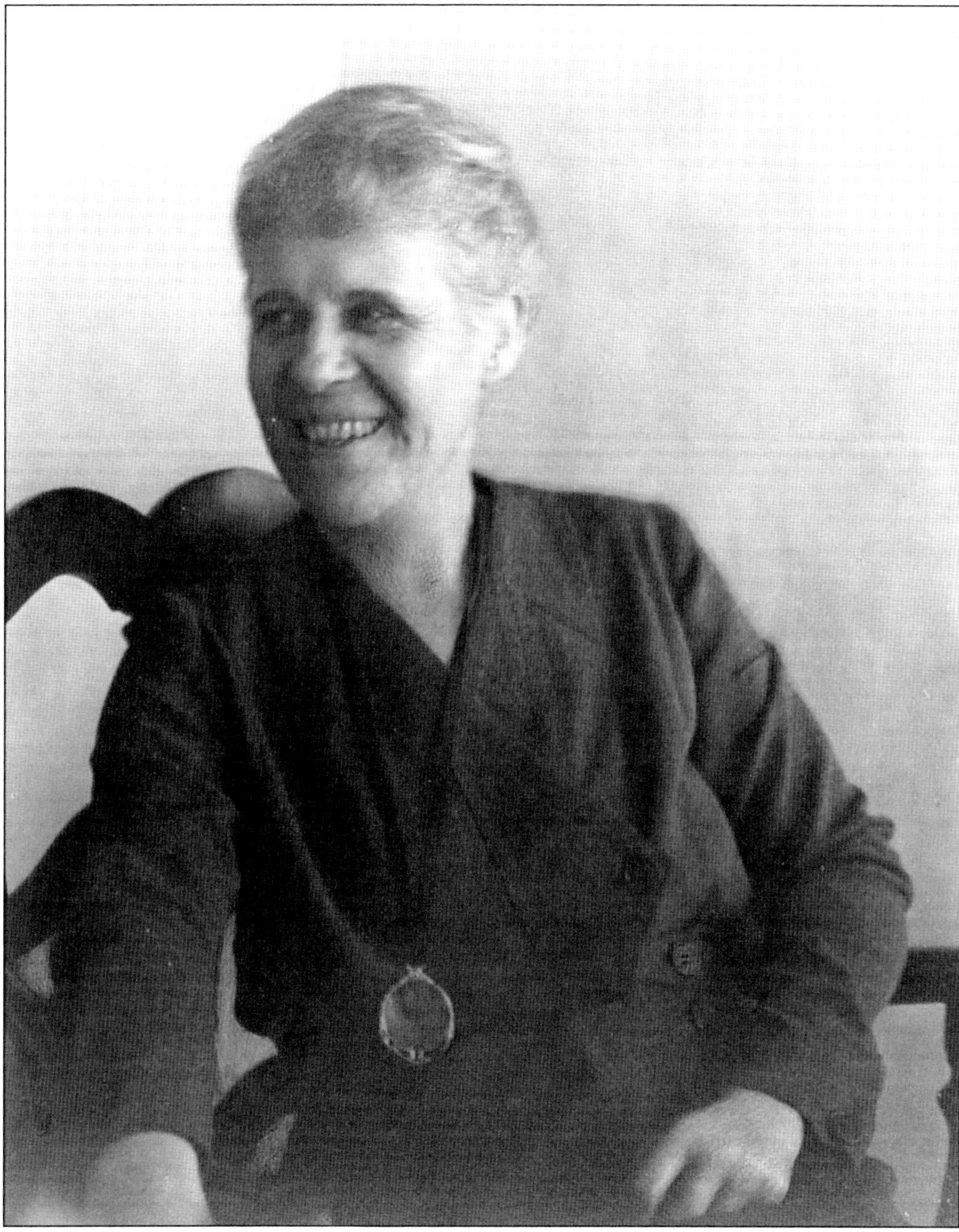

Marie Zimmermann (1879–1972) was a nationally acclaimed sculptress, painter, goldsmith, silversmith, cabinetmaker, wood carver, jeweler, and blacksmith. Her work has been displayed at many museums, including the Metropolitan Museum of Art in New York City. Born in Brooklyn, she also became an avid outdoorswoman at her family's farm on Route 209 in Dingmans Ferry. (Courtesy Jo Ann and Ted Parsell.)

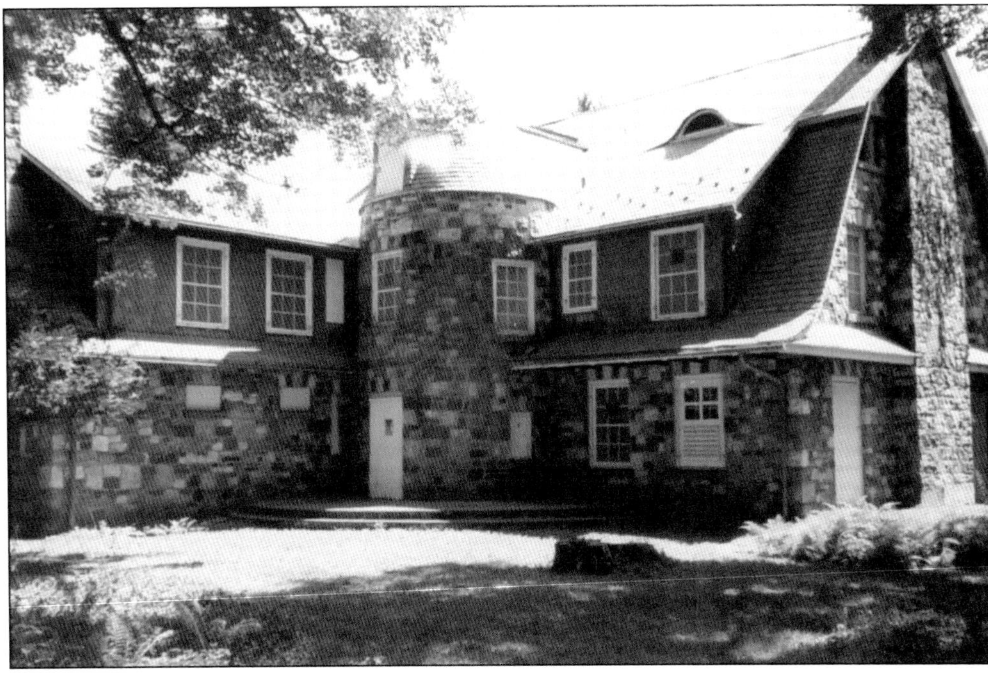

One of the few buildings still remaining in Dingmans Ferry is the Marie Zimmermann Home, built in 1912. This impressive residence was designed by Marie when she was 33 years old. Both the home and farm are now listed on the National Register of Historic Places. (Courtesy Jo Ann and Ted Parsell.)

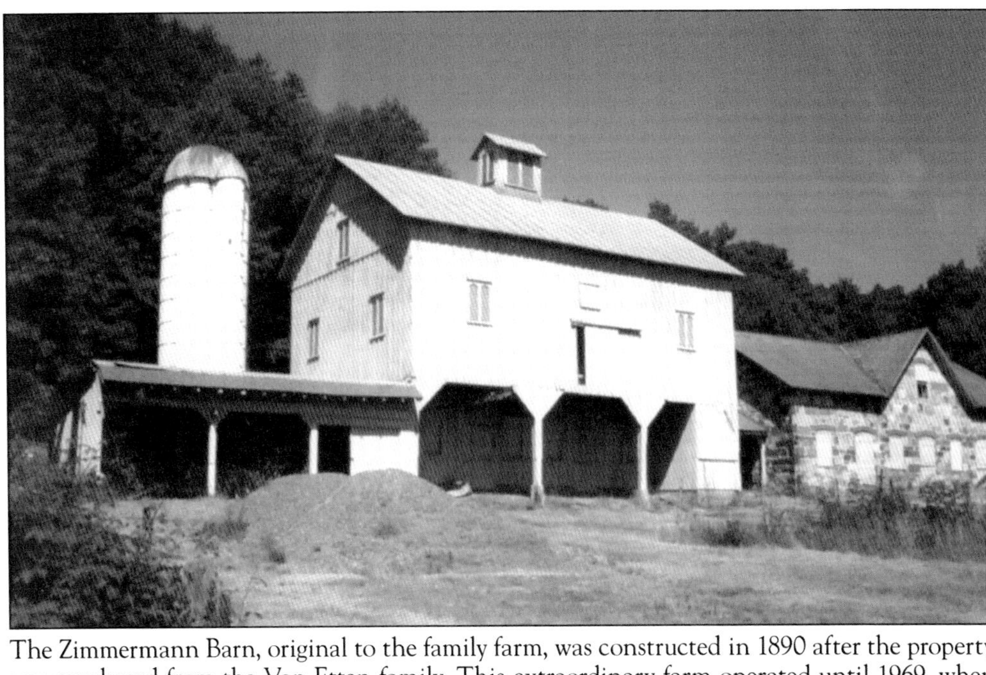

The Zimmermann Barn, original to the family farm, was constructed in 1890 after the property was purchased from the Van Etten family. This extraordinary farm operated until 1969, when Marie Zimmermann moved to Florida at the age of 90. (Courtesy Jo Ann and Ted Parsell.)

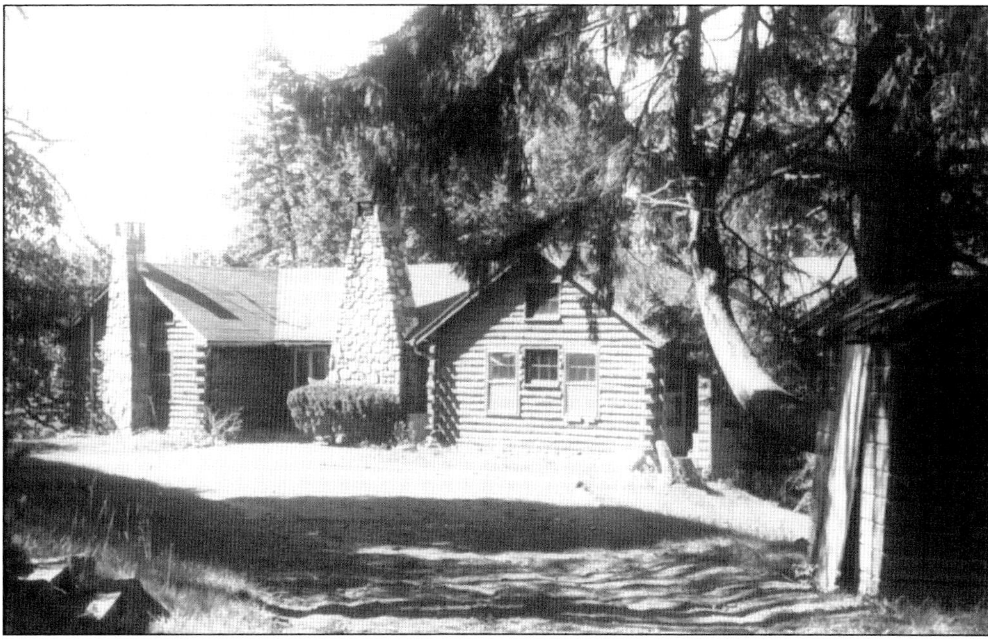

Originally called the Ardtarnish Farm, this farm was located on Wilson Hill Road and was owned by George Donaldson in 1833. It was later known as Loch Lomond. In the 1970s, the farm's new proprietor was Col. Dan Sullivan, who was active in county business and served as the head of Pike County Civil Defense. (Courtesy DF/DTHS.)

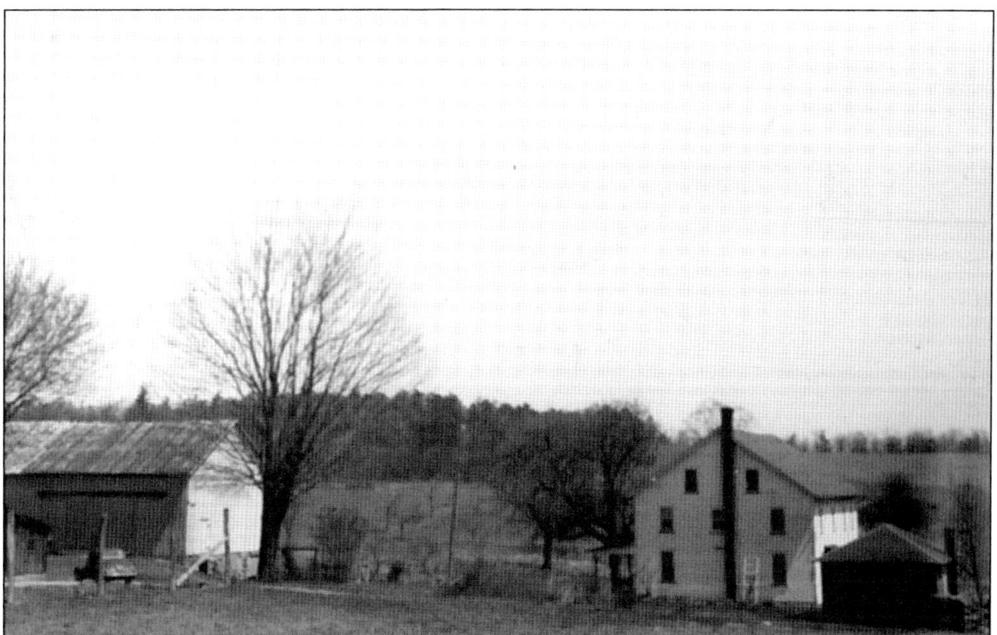

A ride to the end of Wilson Hill Road brought the traveler to the Smith Farm. Operated by Russell O. Smith and Clarence (Squire) Smith, it was one of the largest farms in the community. (Courtesy Roberta and Leroy Cron.)

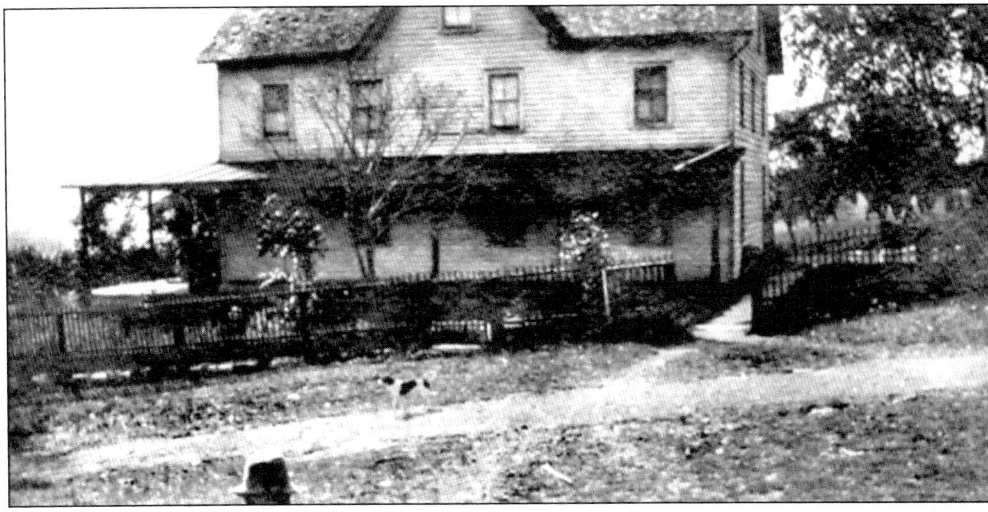

The Smith Homestead was a traditional farmhouse located opposite the present-day Delaware Township building on Wilson Hill Road. (Courtesy Leroy and Roberta Cron.)

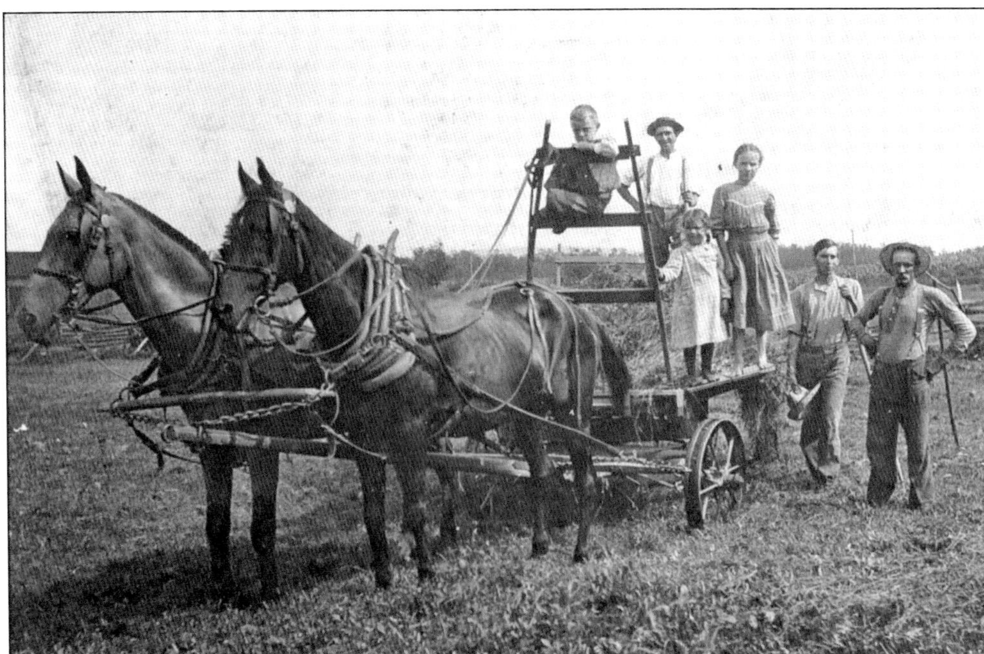

The fields of the Smith Farm would become the recreation area for the youth of Delaware Township and its surrounding communities. In this early-1900s image are, from left to right, Earl Jagger, George Smith, two unidentified people, Harold Smith, and Russell Smith. (Courtesy Roberta and Leroy Cron.)

Kitty Harker was born in 1868. Her grandparents William and Sarah Whittaker Harker arrived in Delaware Township in 1842. They cleared the land and built a homestead, which still stands on Kitty Harker Road. Kitty owned a pair of oxen used to haul and clear wood and to travel into Dingmans Ferry for supplies. She lived off the land and is considered by some to be the last pioneer of the village. The house remained without indoor plumbing and electricity until her health declined. It was sold in 1946. (Courtesy Mim Carpenter.)

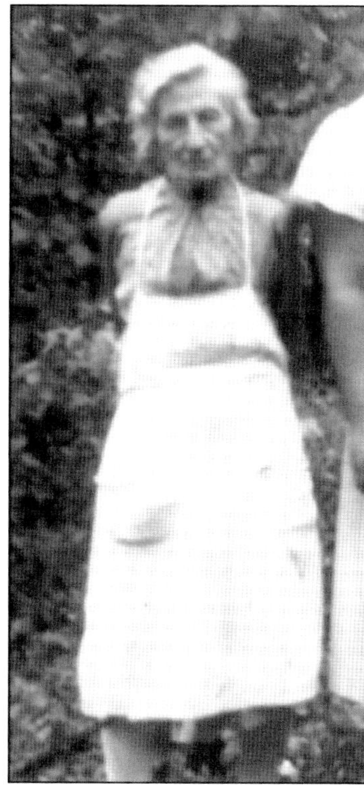

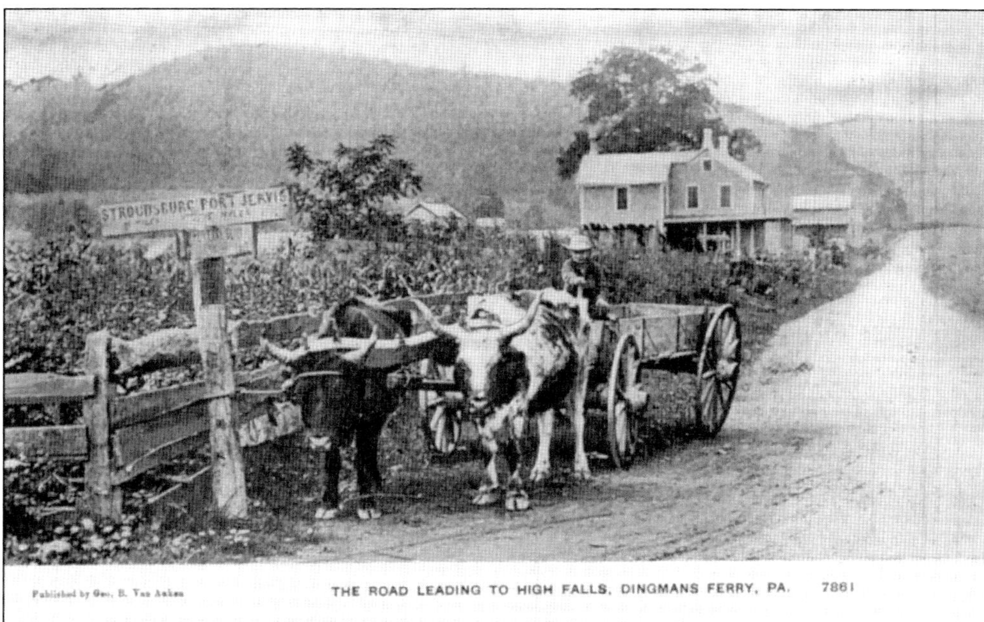

Though tourism was a major industry in old Dingmans Ferry, farming was how most of the residents earned a living. Shown here are Kitty Harker's oxen, a common sight in the village. (Courtesy DF/DTHS.)

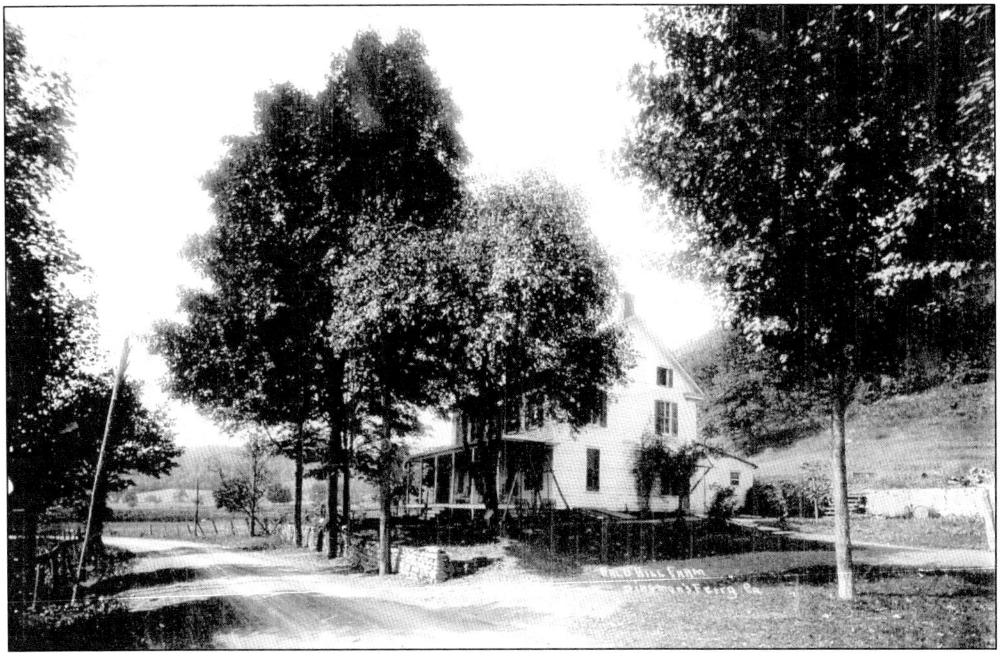

The Bald Hill Farmhouse stood on Route 209, south of the village of Dingmans Ferry. This farm was one of the earliest in the area, dating back before the Revolution. The original home was built in 1724, and this one replaced it in the 1870s. (Courtesy Flora Myers Collection.)

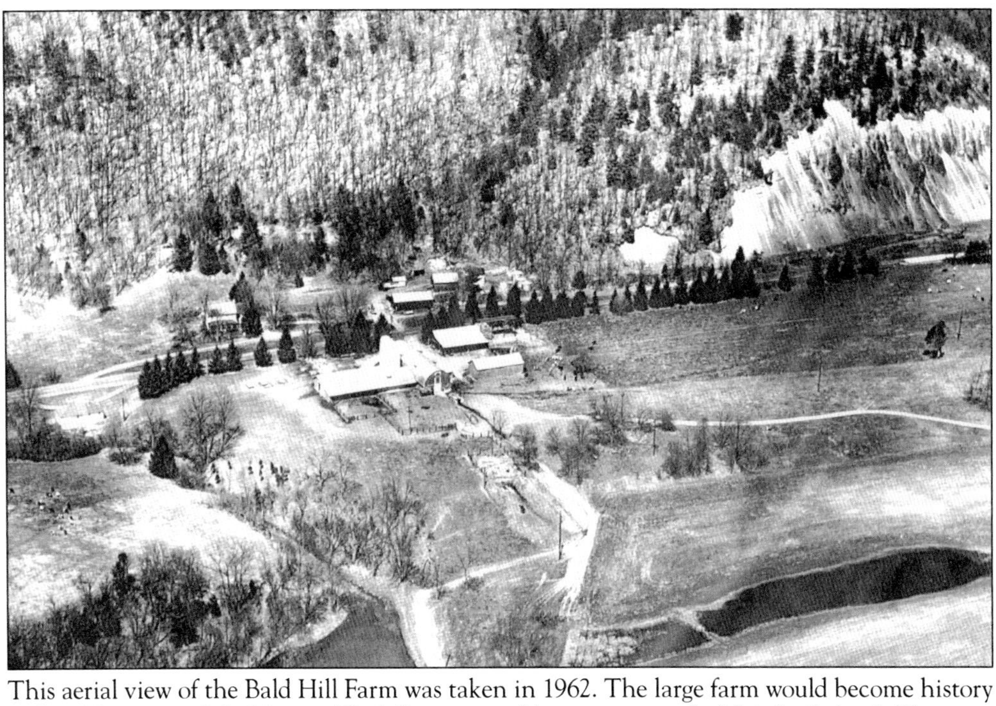

This aerial view of the Bald Hill Farm was taken in 1962. The large farm would become history within 20 years, and the National Park Service would assume control of this fertile land. (Courtesy Flora Myers Collection.)

Six

LIFE IN DINGMANS

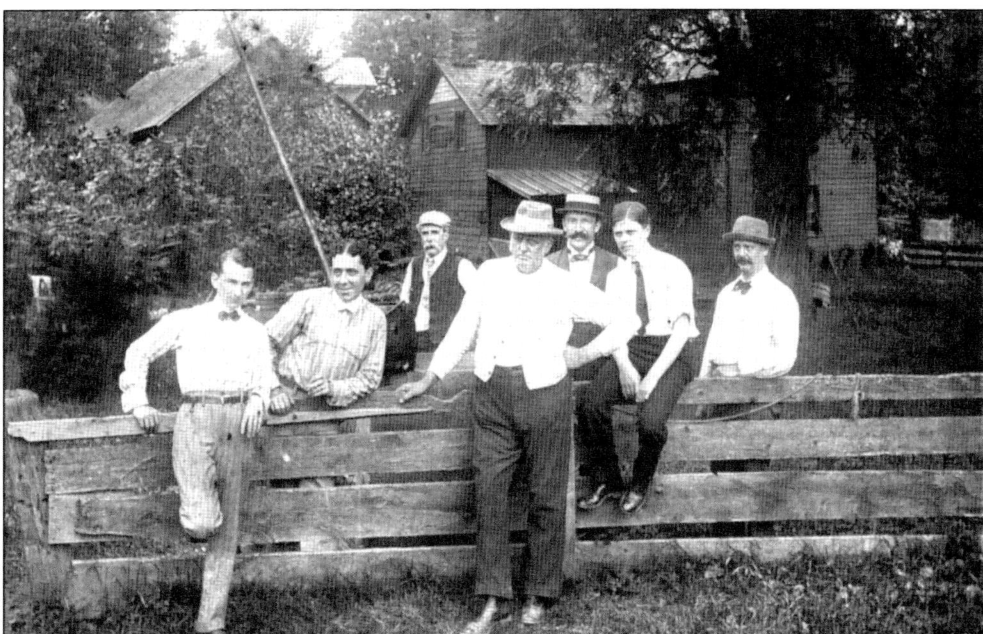

Delaware Township residents transformed the village of Dingmans Ferry into a center of commerce and the heart of the community. As early as 1735, enterprising settlers began to develop a small settlement into a bustling village. These men pose at the Old Oaken Bucket in the 1890s. Note the Darragh Mill in the background. (Courtesy Roberta and Leroy Cron.)

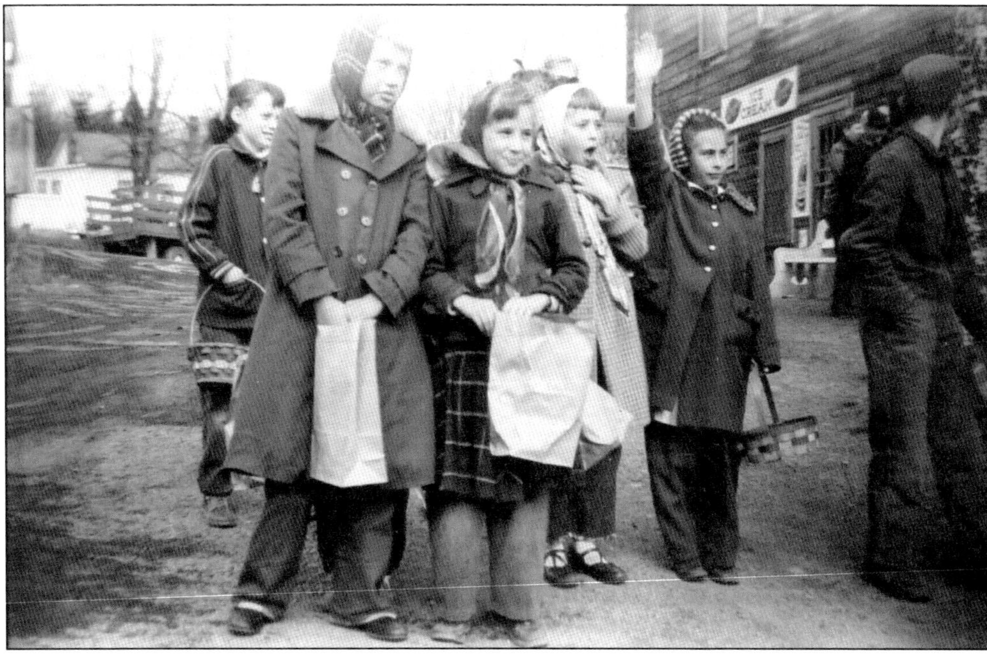

Excitement is in the air as these four local gals prepare for the 1955 Easter egg hunt at Sally and Lew's. Located at Shepherds Corner, Sally and Lew's is to the right, and the former Cole School is in the distance. Pictured here, from left to right, are Patricia Whittaker, Linda Lutz Davis, Jo Ann Whittaker Parsell, and Roberta Findlay Cron. (Courtesy DF/DTHS.)

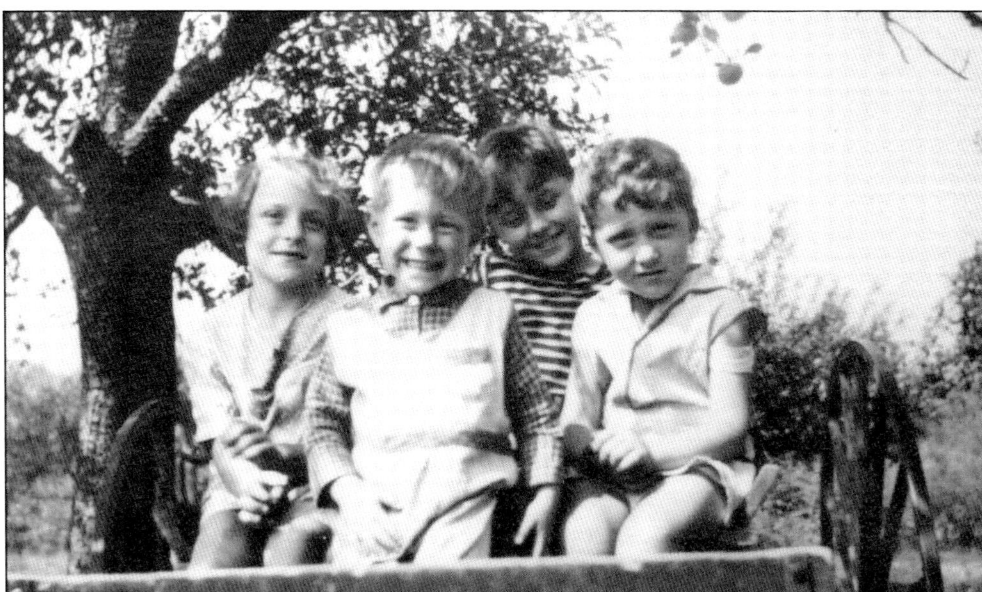

Dingmans Ferry children enjoy a wagon ride at the Ryder house on Johnny B. Road. This charming 1937 photograph shows, from left to right, Joan Ryder Mervine, Ollie Treible, Gerald Ryder, and Frank Ryder. (Courtesy Audrey Mervine.)

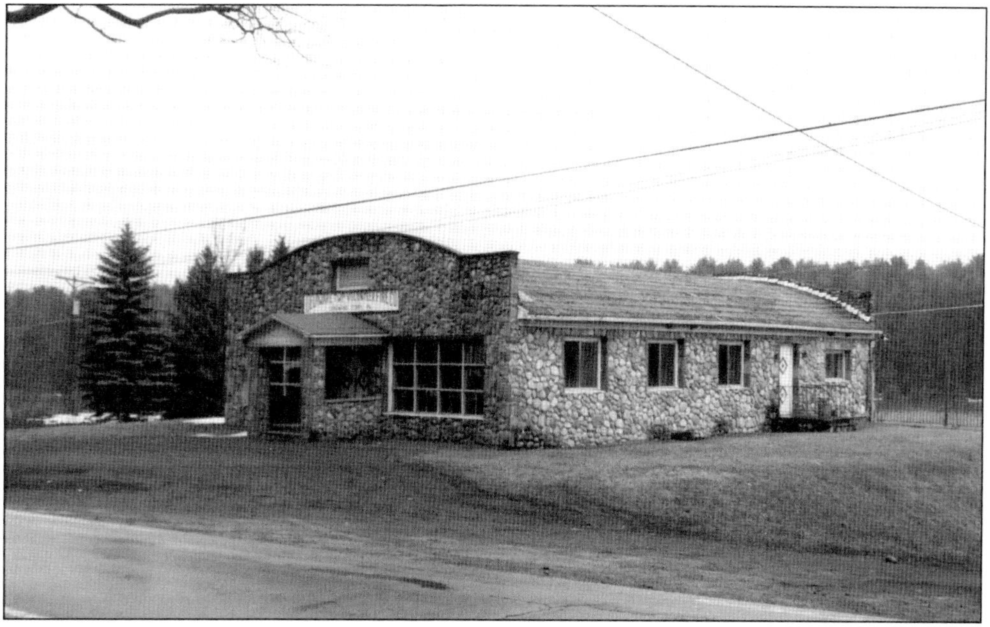

In response to the flood of 1955, village citizens formed a fire company. Previously, residents of Dingmans Ferry had to depend on Milford, Bushkill, and Layton, New Jersey, for fire protection, but with the aid of local craftsmen, this magnificent fire house was constructed on Route 209. The original fire house remains and is now used by the National Park Service. (Courtesy Delaware Water Gap National Recreation Area.)

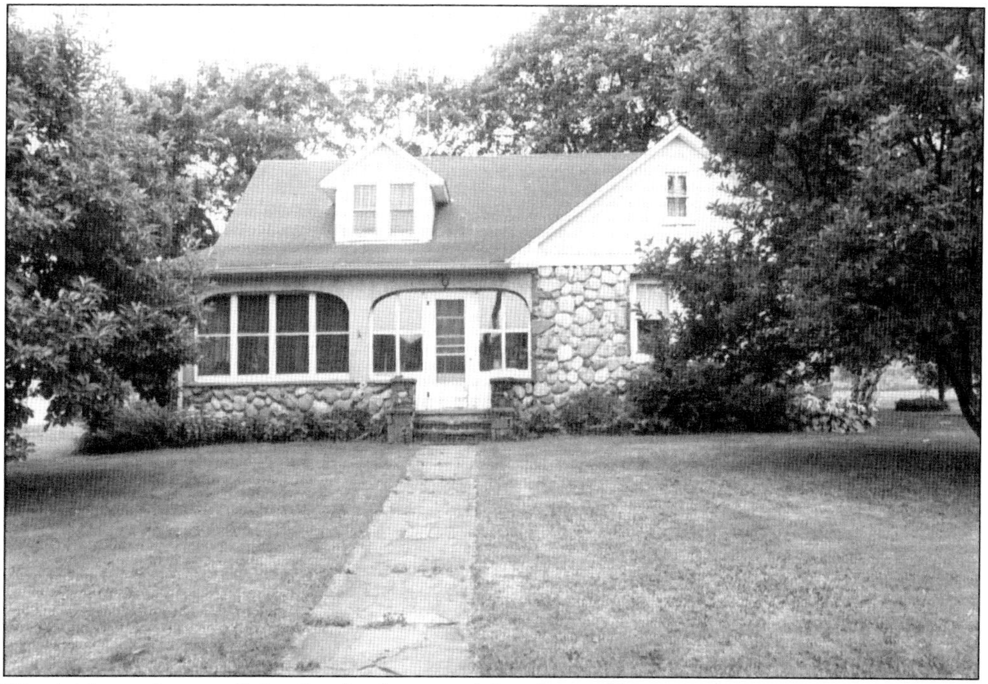

The fieldstone home of John Snyder decorates Main Street (Route 209) next to the fire house. A mason by trade, Snyder donated the property to the fire company and also aided in the construction of the beautiful stone fire house. (Courtesy Delaware Water Gap National Recreation Area.)

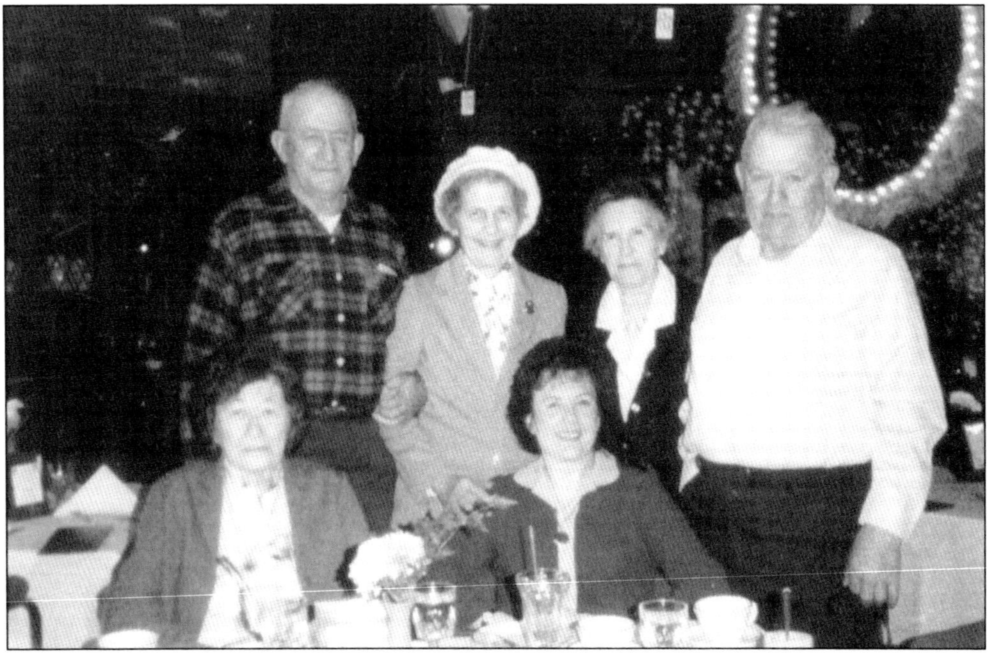

Family and friends gather to celebrate the 50th wedding anniversary of Bill and Ruth Reser in March 1988. Bill was a dedicated volunteer in Dingmans Ferry. Serving as a township supervisor for 25 years, he was also one of the founding members of the Delaware Township Fire Company. Pictured here, from left to right, are the following: (first row) Lillie Jagger and Joyce Reser Lewis, the daughter of Ruth and Bill Reser; (second row) Len and Margaret Herr, and Ruth and Bill Reser. (Courtesy Joyce Reser Lewis.)

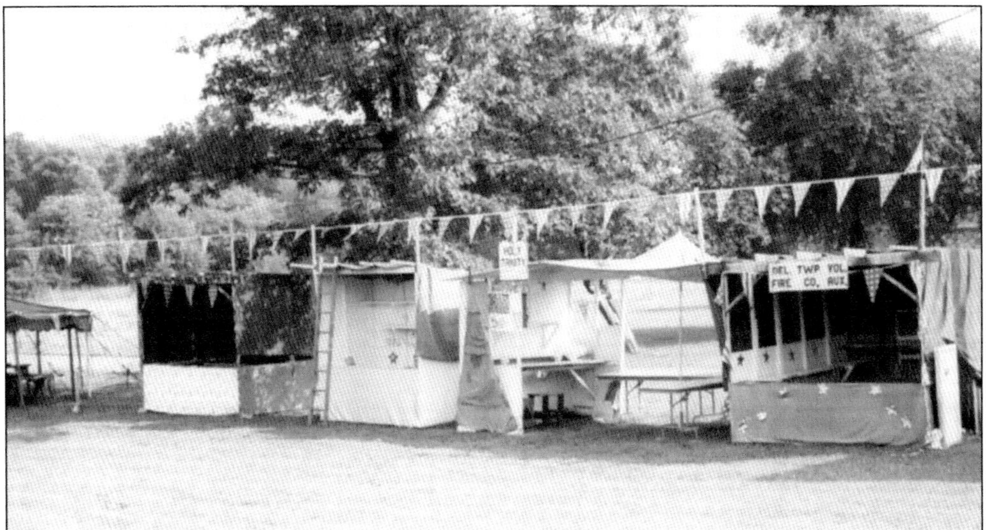

In 1976, the village of Dingmans Ferry held its last event. On the 200th anniversary of the country, a celebration occurred on the grounds of the fire house for local residents and tourists. (Courtesy DF/DTHS.)

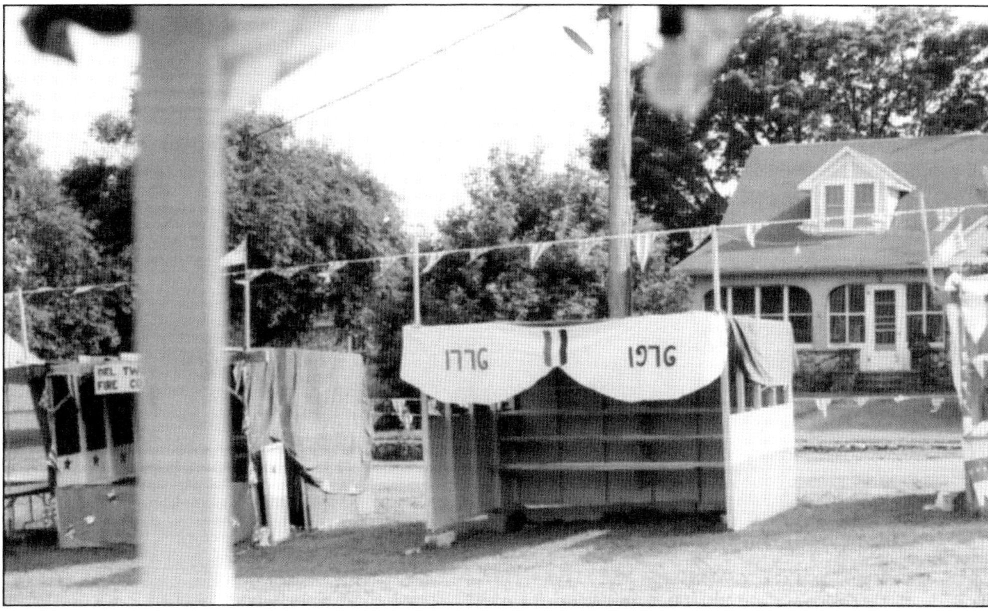

This carnival marked the end of this remarkable village that had prospered along the ancient banks of the Delaware River. As the country celebrated its 200th year, Dingmans Ferry proudly honored its 231st birthday. After more than two centuries of accomplishments, it took but a brief moment in time before the village landmarks became memories kept alive only through stories and photographs. (Courtesy DF/DTHS.)

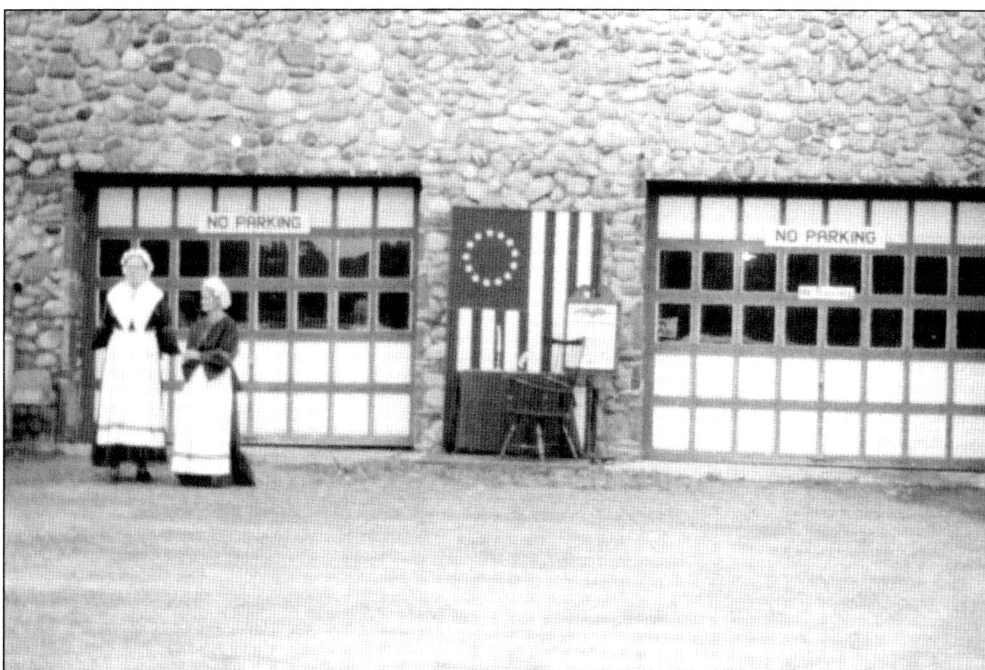

These costumed celebrants are Margaret Mary Jonas (left) and Minnie Lutz. At this time, Margaret Jonas was serving as Delaware Township supervisor, prior to being elected the first woman Pike County commissioner. (Courtesy DF/DTHS.)

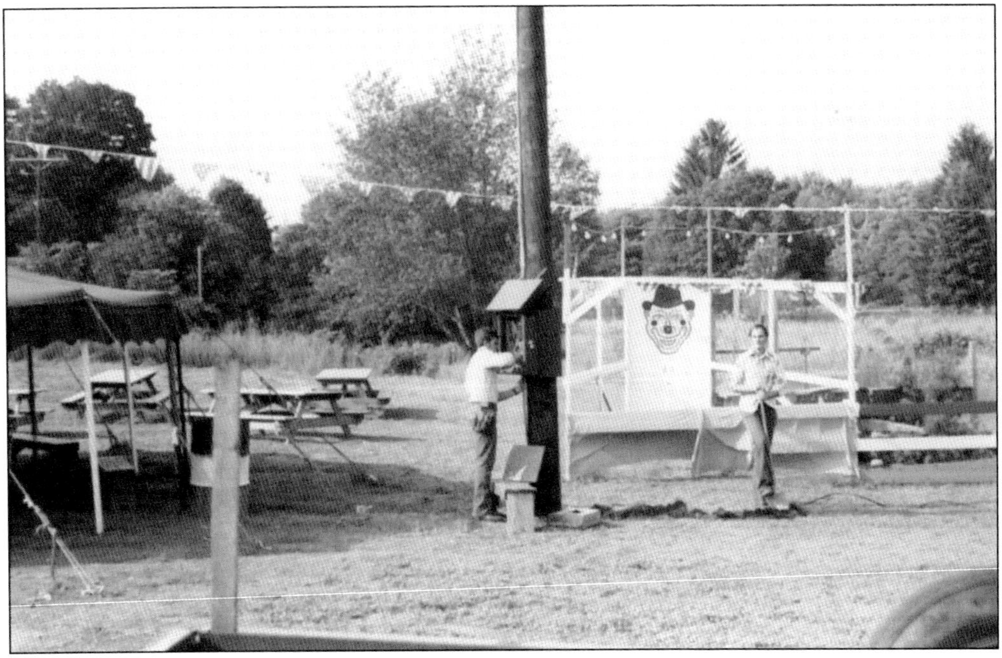

Fair workers Robert Schivert (left) and John Lyons complete the final preparations for the town carnival in Delaware Township. (Courtesy DF/DTHS.)

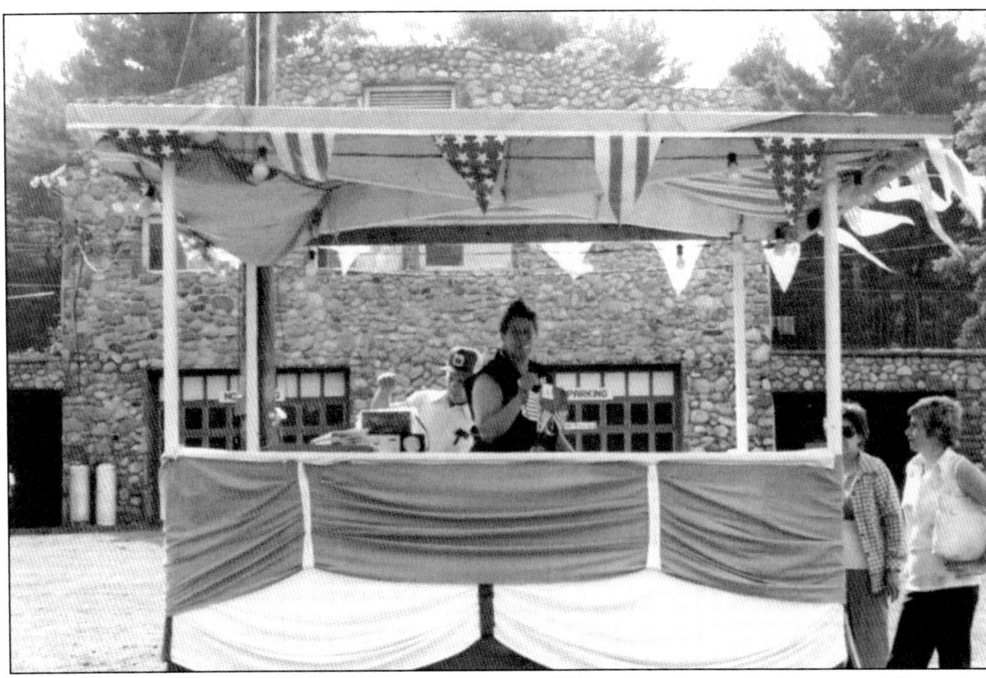

A fair fan arrives at the booth of Romain and Marjorie Whittaker during the bicentennial carnival held at the Delaware Township fire house. (Courtesy DF/DTHS.)

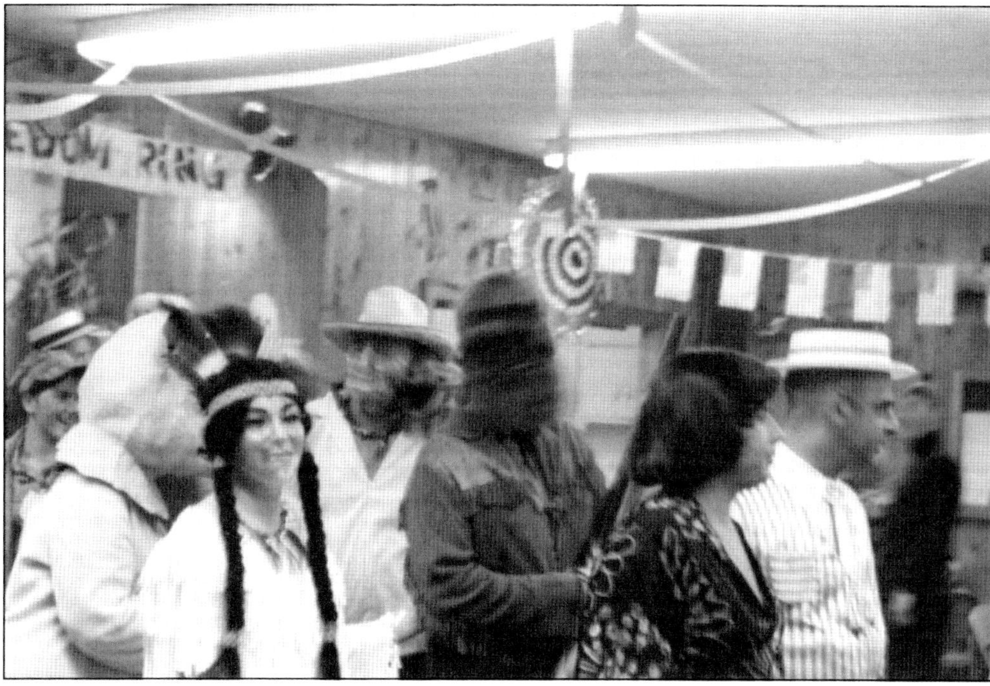

The fire house served as a community hall for parties and celebrations. This 1970s photograph depicts the annual Halloween party in Dingmans Ferry. Pictured here, from left to right, are Marjorie Whitthaker, Jo Ann Parsell, Romain Whitthaker, unidentified, Miriam Siegel, and Art Siegel. (Courtesy DF/DTHS.)

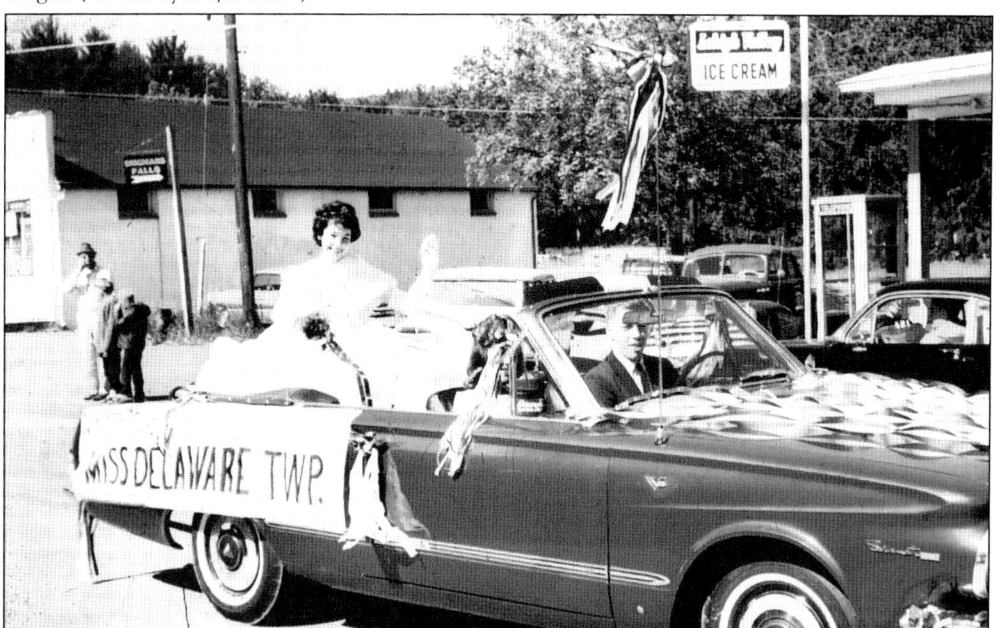

As in many small towns, parades were a special event for visitors and locals alike. A parade in Dingmans Ferry would not be the same without Miss Delaware Township, in this case Joanie Lentz, leading the marchers. This photograph was taken around 1968. (Courtesy Richard Heimbrook.)

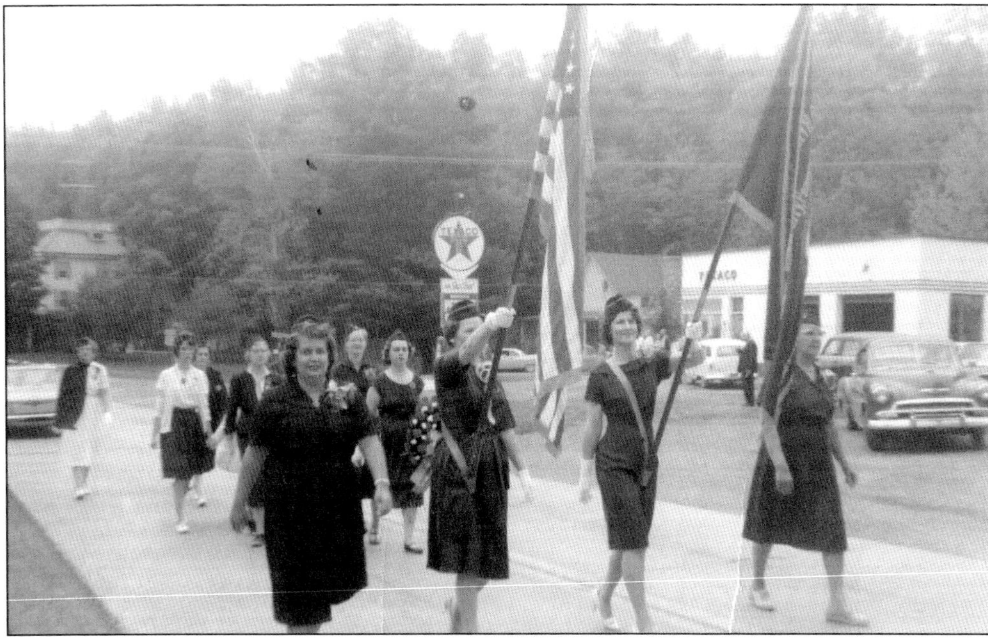

Local women celebrate Memorial Day in 1962. Pictured here are Mary Albright, Elsie Bensley, Margurite Gardner, Mabel Bensley, Pauline Lentz, Ida Brumbacher, and Betty Hotalen. The Dingman House is visible in the distance. (Courtesy Harry Arnold.)

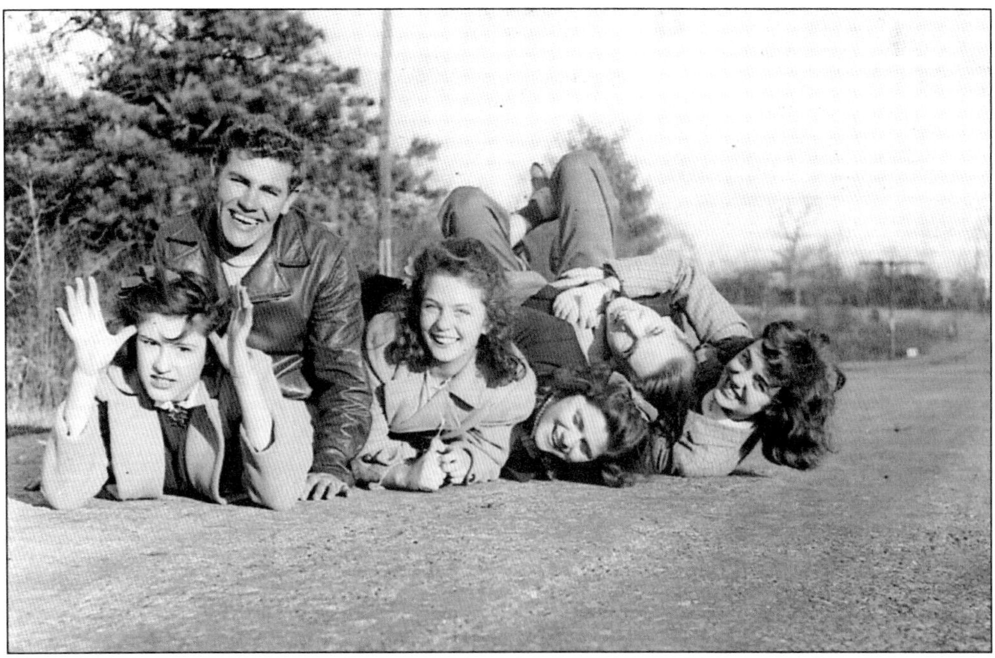

It was a slower time in Pike County when this photograph was taken on Halloween weekend of 1941. Pictured left to right are Evelyn (Metzger) Emr, Gerhardt Eckelmann, Verna (Rickard) Bumball, Doris (Metzger) Foos, Richard Arondt and Carmen "Pat" (Dillinger) Mescia. (Courtesy DF/DTHS.)

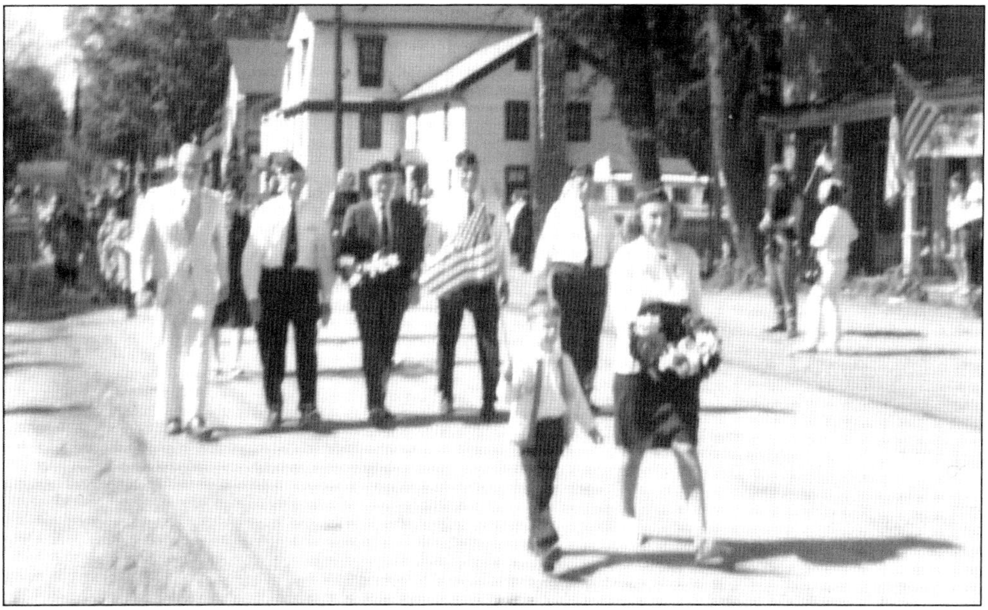

The Memorial Day parade in Dingmans Ferry marked the beginning of the summer season. As this parade proceeds down Main Street, members of the American Legion pass in front of the Delaware House. Pictured here about 1972 are the following, from left to right: (first row) Pauline Lentz and her son Charles; (second row) Jim Duffy, Tom Hotalen, unidentified, Carl Bensley, and unidentified. (Courtesy Inez Dickison.)

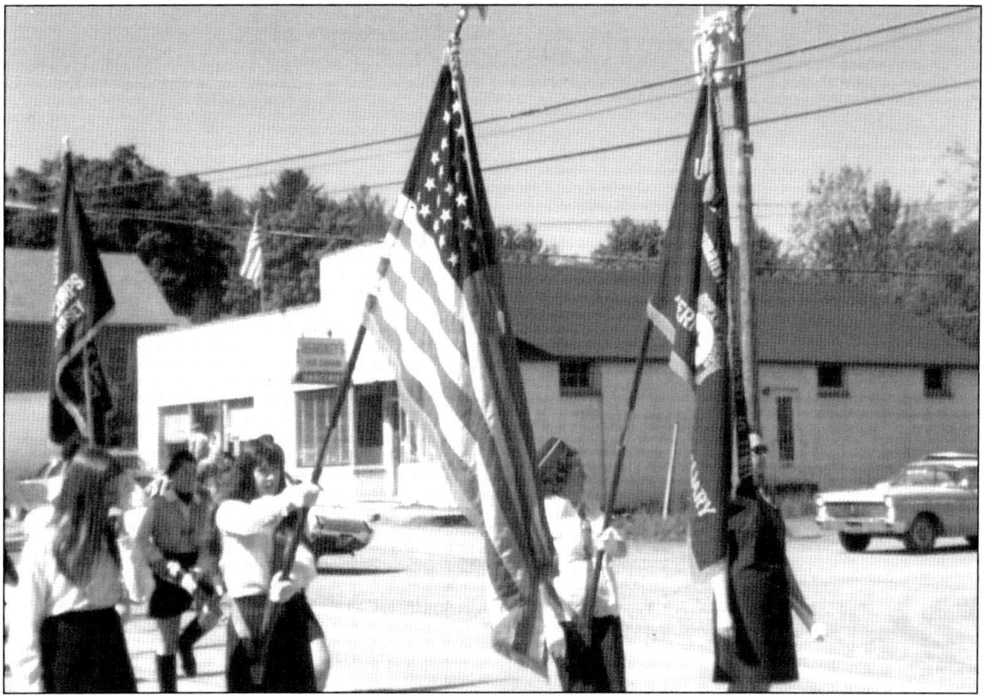

The color guard pauses in the 1972 Memorial Day parade, with Grace Drake's store and the Dingmans Ferry Post Office in the background. Seen here, from left to right, are Kathy, Sheri, Doris, and Betty Hotalen. (Courtesy Inez Dickison.)

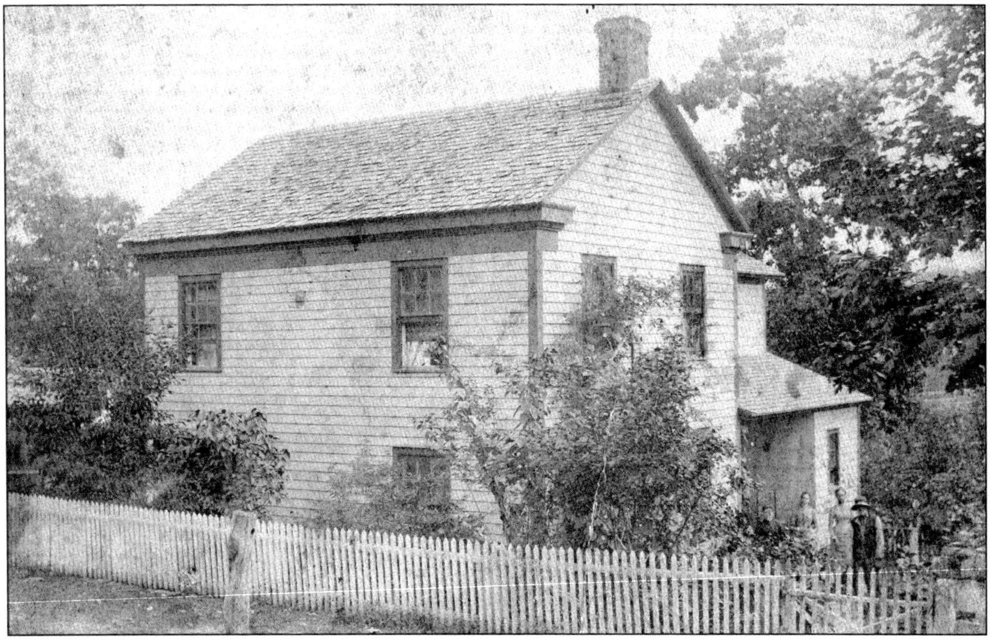

This home, shown in the early 1900s, was built in the 1850s for William Angle and his new bride, Margaret Middaugh Angle. In recent years, it served as the residence of Herbert and Laura DePue. When Herbert was a teenager, he worked for local photographer William Allerton. (Courtesy Laura and Jan de Graaf.)

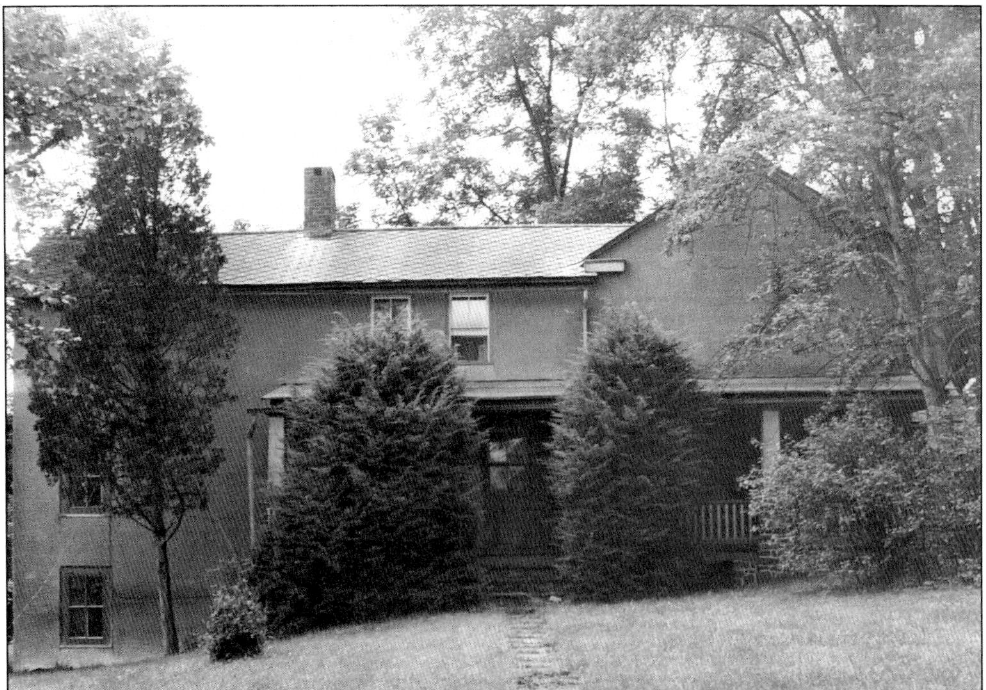

The lovely DePue home still stands on the corner of Wilson Hill and Chestnut Ridge Roads. (Courtesy Laura and Jan de Graaf.)

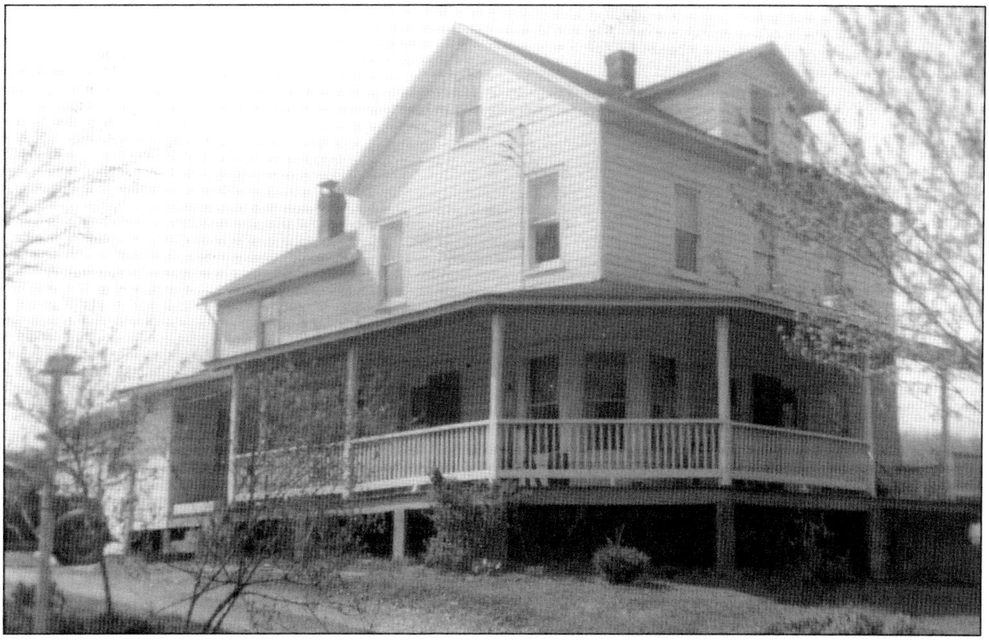

Constructed in the late 1800s by Thomas Shepherd, this graceful country home is located on the corner of Milford and Spencer Roads. Owned over the years by the Tuthill, Lutz, and Whittaker families, it is now the residence of Jo Ann (Whittaker) and Ted Parsell. (Courtesy Jo Ann and Ted Parsell.)

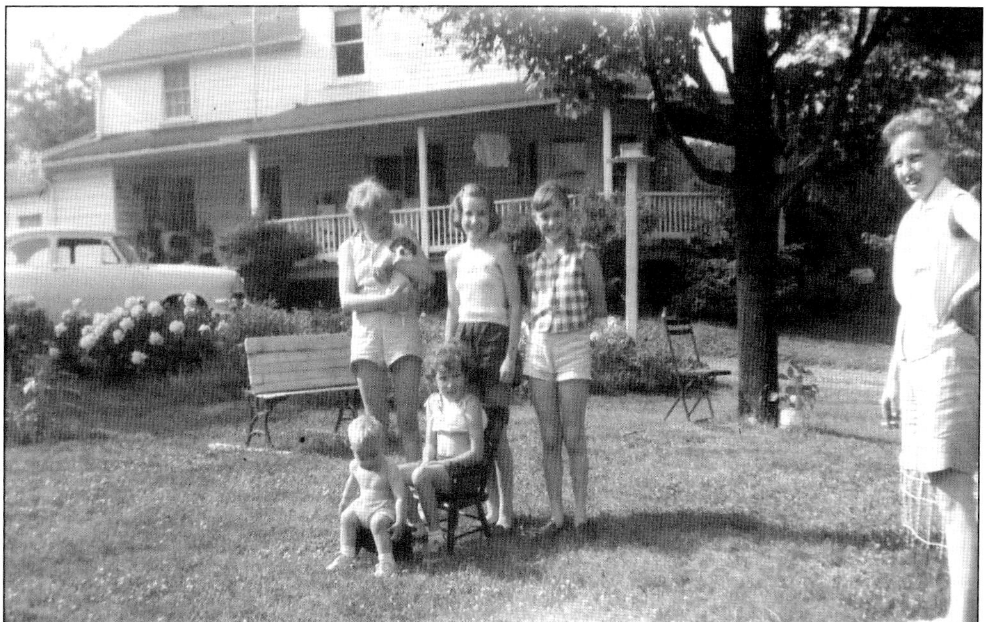

The Lutz and Whittaker children pose in their grandmother's front yard in 1957. Pictured here, from left to right, are the following: (sitting) Douglas and Dawn Lutz; (standing) Patricia "Patsy" Whittaker, Linda Lutz Davis, and Jo Ann Whittaker Parsell. Edna Lutz looks on. (Courtesy Jo Ann and Ted Parsell.)

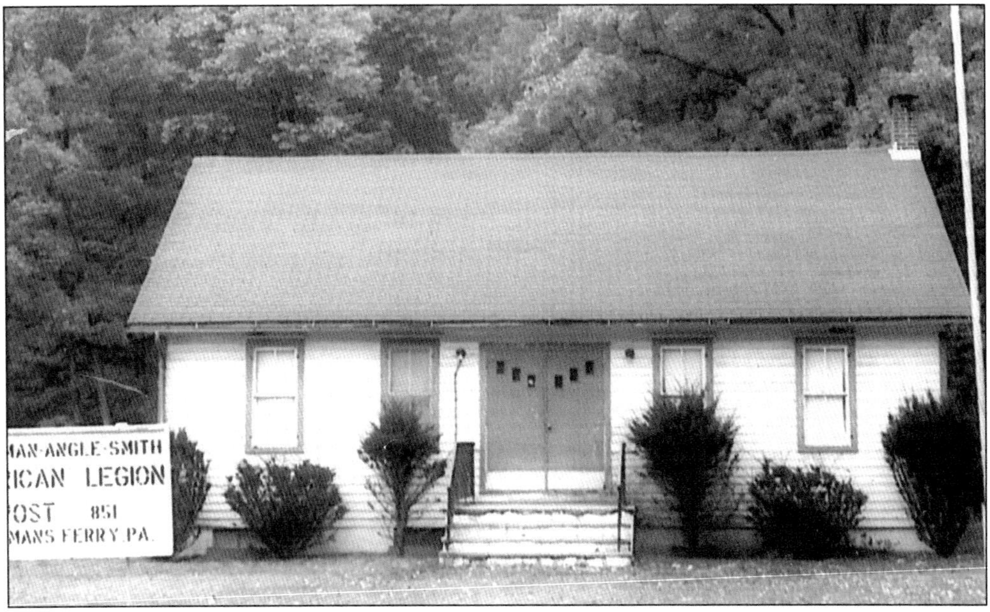

Tilghman Angle Smith American Legion Post No. 851, located on Route 209, is seen here in the 1980s. This single-story structure, originally the second floor of the Academy School, was purchased by the legion in 1953. The top half of the school was preserved and lowered onto a foundation, where it served as the post's home until 1985. (Courtesy Jo Ann and Ted Parsell.)

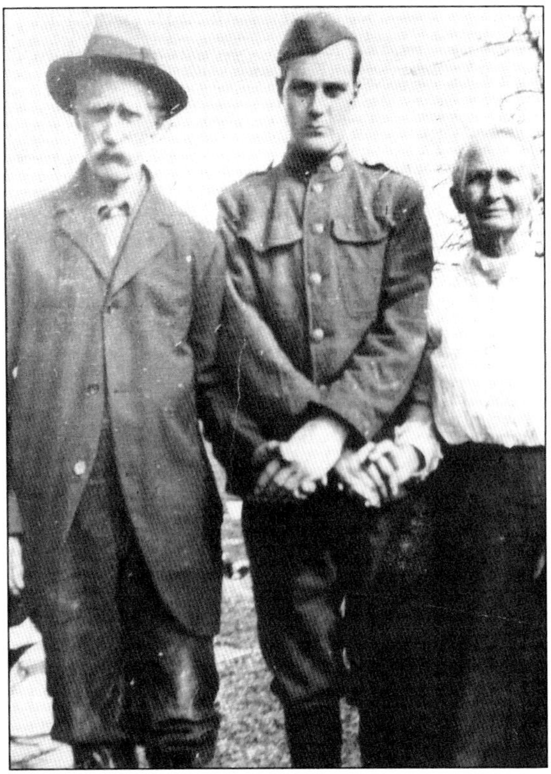

From the Revolution to Vietnam, Dingmans Ferry was honorably represented by its brave young men. Theodore (left) and Charlotte Simpson Howey stand with their son Henry, who is dressed in his World War I uniform. (Courtesy Raitt family.)

Dingmans Ferry native Lester Jagger served his country in the Navy. Pictured here on June 23, 1947, Jagger stands proud for his commitment to his country. (Courtesy Roberts and Leroy Cron.)

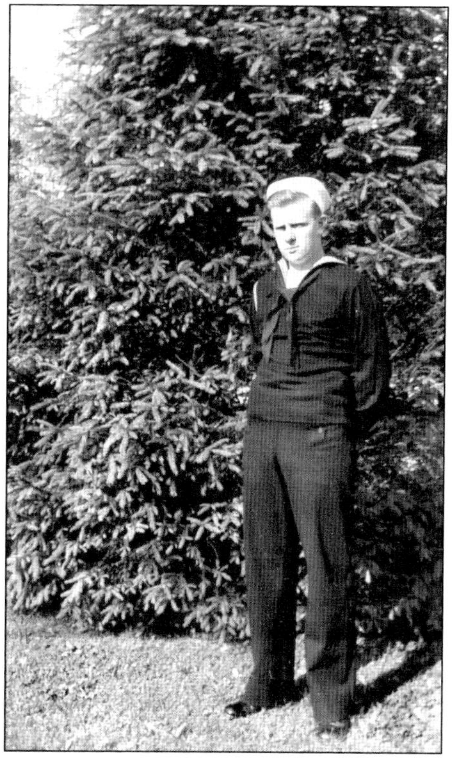

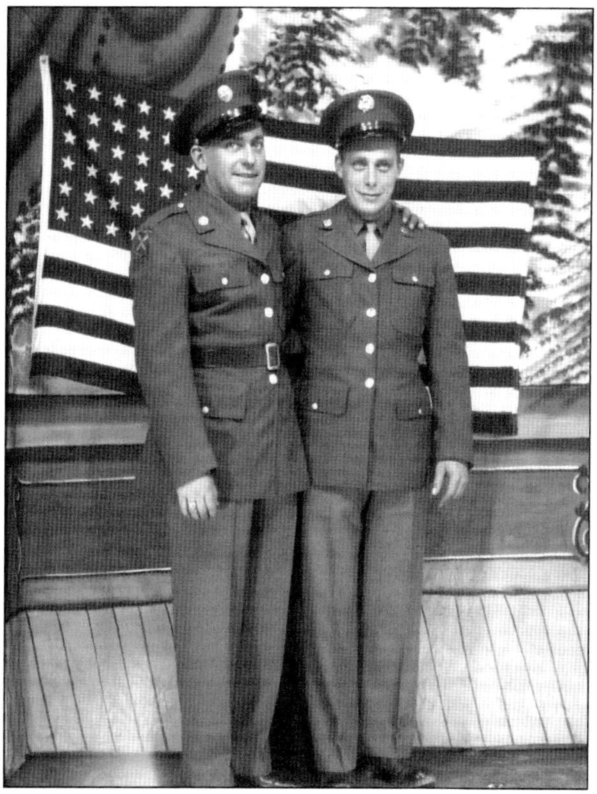

Carl Snyder (left) and Charles Howey stand proudly in front of the American flag in February 1943. (Courtesy Raitt family.)

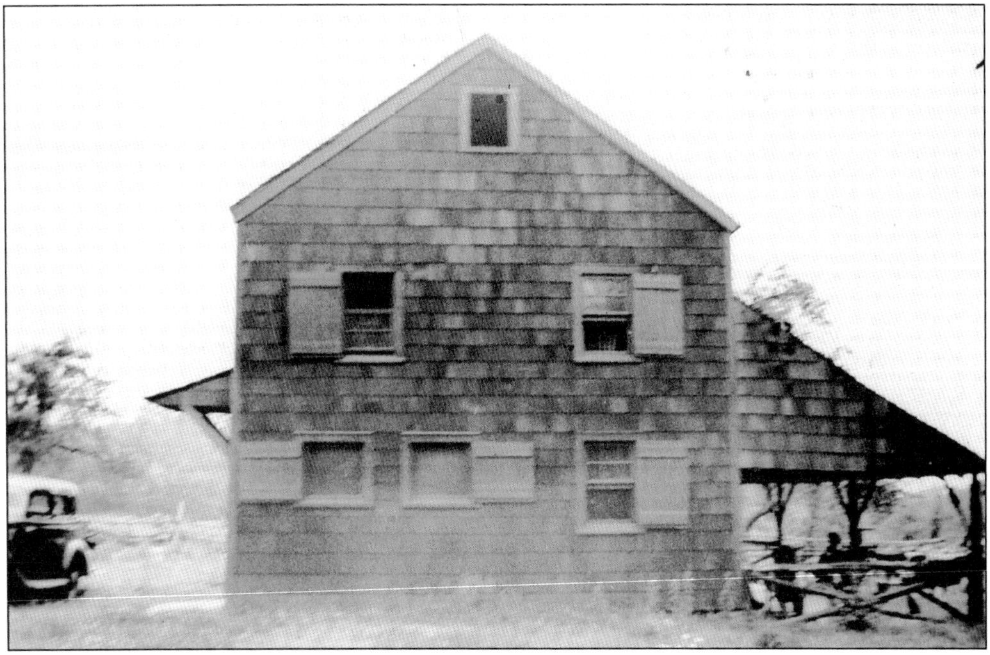

The Howey Homestead, located in Deep Hollow, was constructed of solid logs with shake siding. (Courtesy Dorthann and Joe White.)

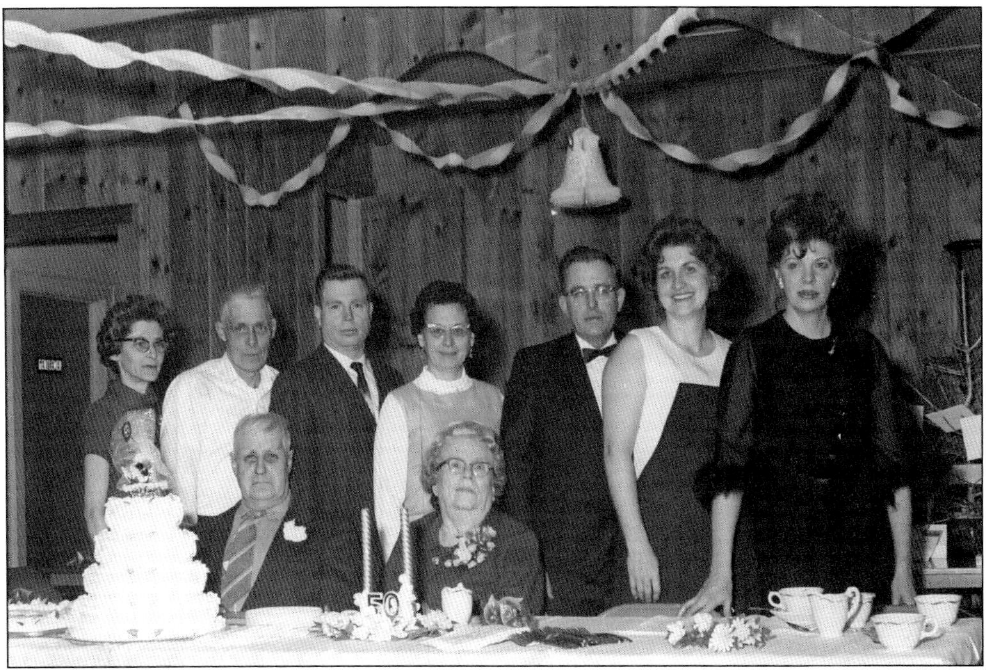

Henry and Mabel Walters Howey (seated) celebrated their golden wedding anniversary on February 18, 1978. They lived their entire married life in Dingmans Ferry. Seen in the back, from left to right, are the following: Jennie Ada Howey Place Grygo, Charles Howey, Walter L. Howey, Dorothy Howey Raitt, Kenneth Howey, Irene Howey Travis Kinney, and Amy Howey Widdos Safin Kulp. (Courtesy Raitt family.)

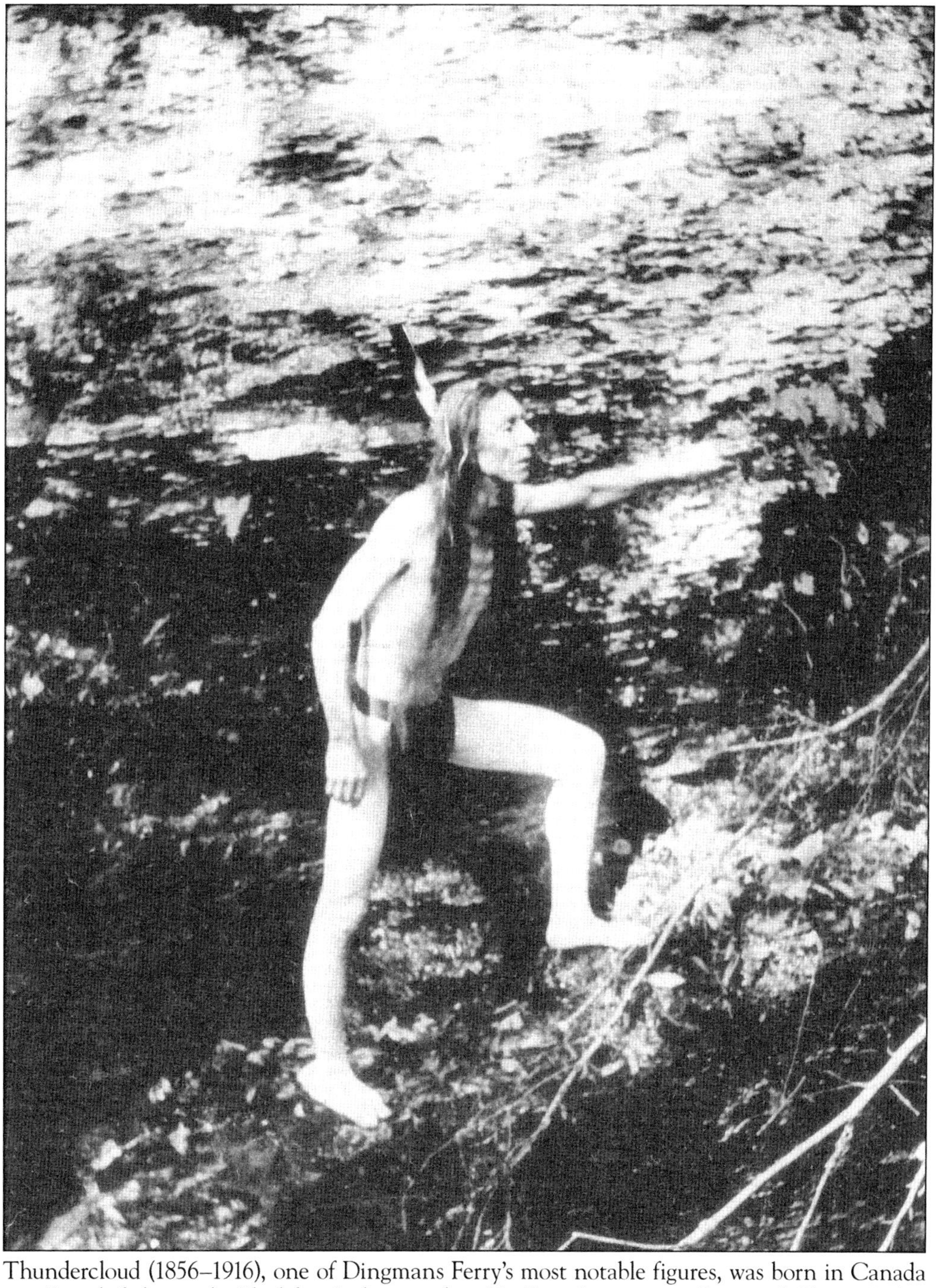

Thundercloud (1856–1916), one of Dingmans Ferry's most notable figures, was born in Canada to a French father and a Blackfoot Indian mother. His French name was Dominick Plante. In his early life, he served in the army as a scout during the Indian Wars. Later, he toured with the famous Buffalo Bill Wild West Show. During this time, he was hired as a model and posed for many famous artists of the day, including Frederic Remington and John Singer. His likeness adorns the last $5 gold piece produced by the U.S. government. (Courtesy Pike County Historical Society.)

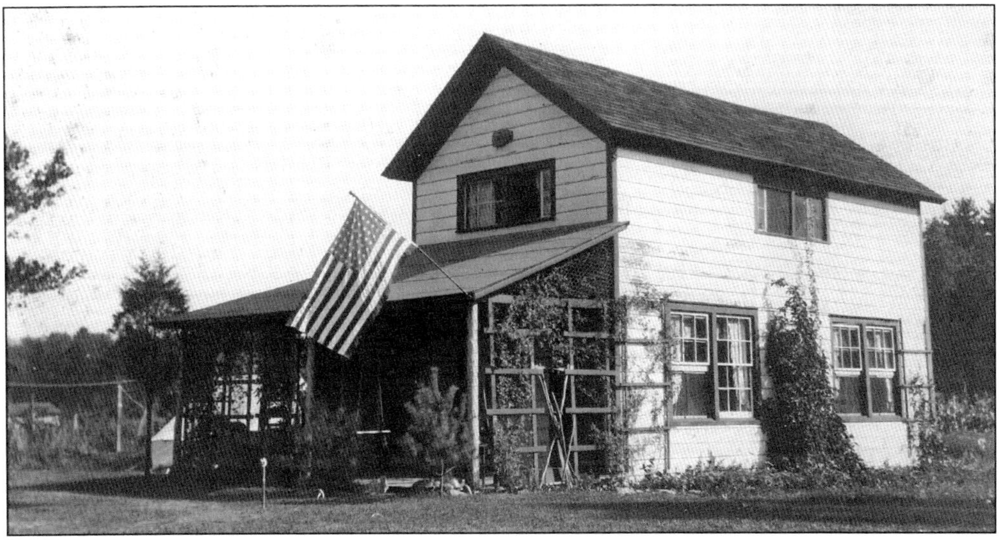

Chief Thundercloud found Dingmans Ferry so pretty and peaceful that after he married in 1887, he settled in there. Pictured is his first home, on Mill Street (Johnny B. Road). Thundercloud would later build a new house nearby, which the family used until 1968. (Courtesy Roberta and Leroy Cron.)

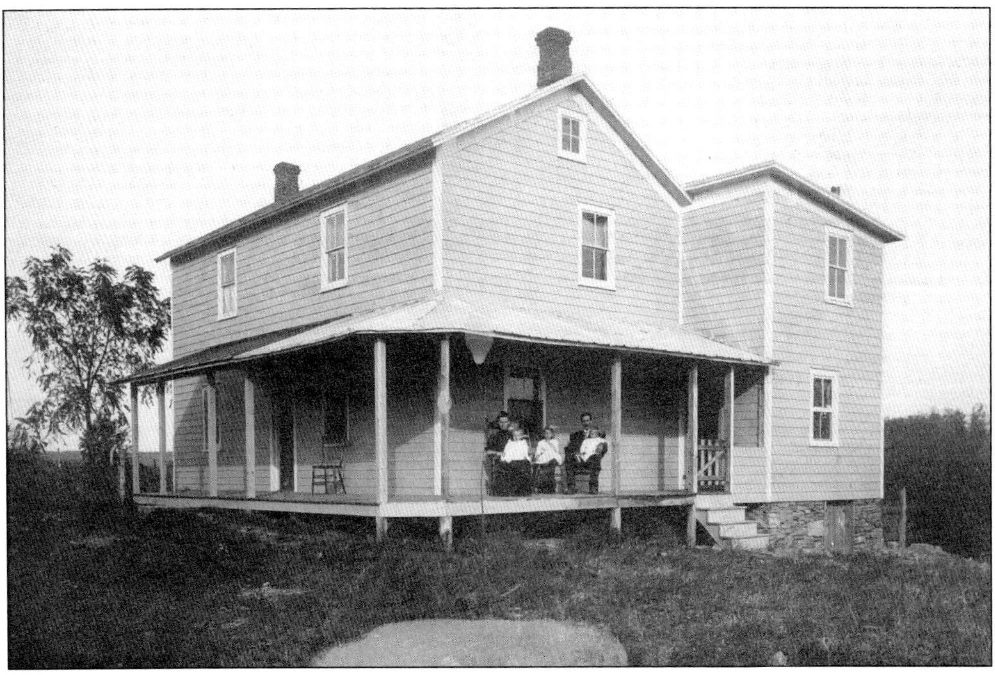

This simple but quaint farmhouse belonged to John and Edith Albright. Built in 1903 on the corner of Route 739 and Milford Road, it is now the home of Pike County Motors. Shown in the photograph are Edith and John and their children: Mary (left), Arthur (center), and Lura. At one time, the Albrights owned all four corners of the intersection, and today it is known to locals as Albright's Corners. (Courtesy Mary and James Albright Sr.)

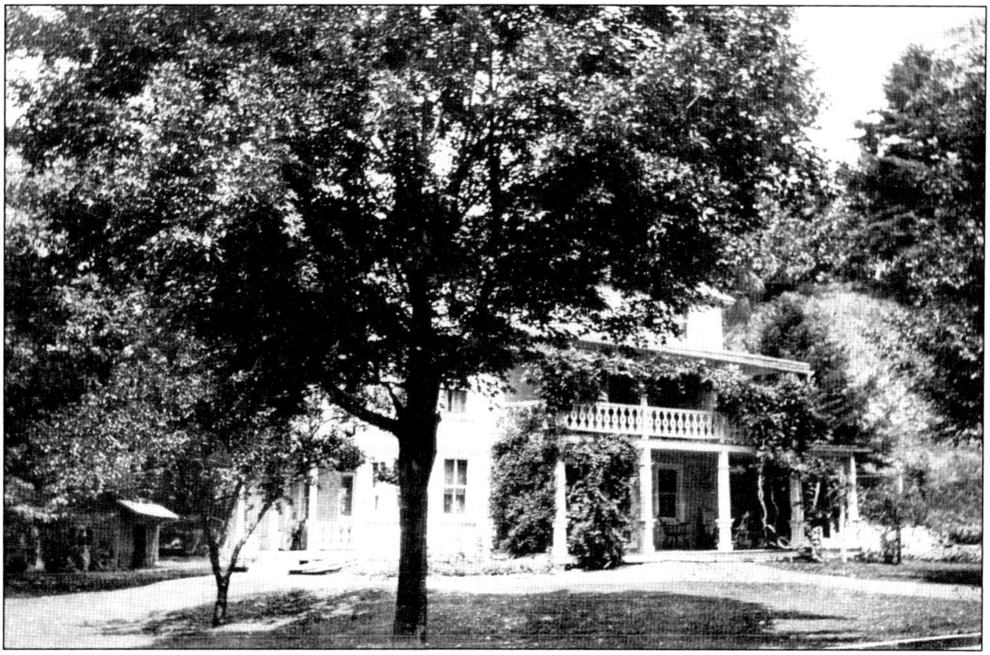

The Darragh Homestead was first sited next to the original mill on Main Street (Route 209) and was later moved closer to the creek. A modest home, it was enlarged and renovated to this stature after the dismantling of the Darragh Mill in 1903. (Courtesy Roberta and Leroy Cron.)

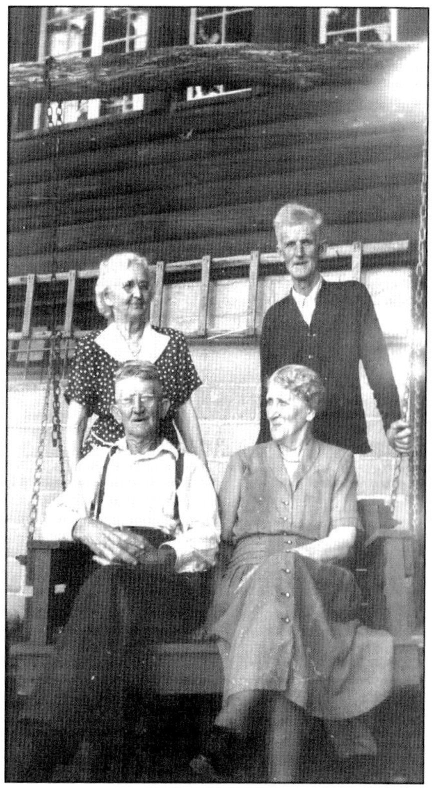

The Darragh family came from strong stock. Like many Dingmans Ferry families, its members lived long and fulfilling lives. The children of Thomas and Margaret Cole Darragh are seen here. Sitting are Edgar Darragh (1871–1956), left, and Carrie Darragh Dingman Armstrong (1875–1973). Standing are Kittie Darragh Buckley (1873–1969), left, and George Elston Darragh (1879–1969). (Courtesy Sylvia Miller.)

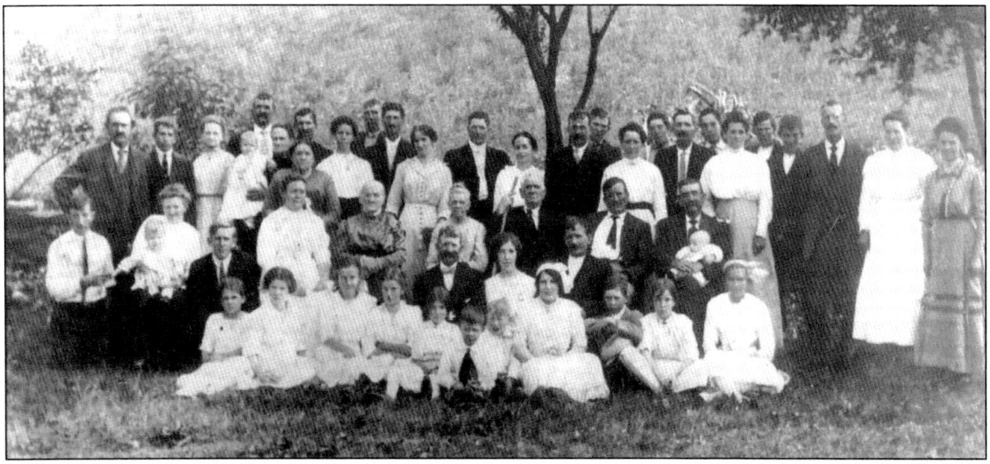

Pictured here is the 1915 Bensley family reunion photograph. Identified here are Girl Huff, Lena Bensley, Orilla Layton, Rena Bensley, Nina Bensley, Harry Bensley, Lena Cron, Alpheus Bensley, Harold Treible, Percy Bensley, Ada Martin, Harold Bensley, Virgie Bensley, Mabel Bensley, Mercer Bensley, Jennie Bensley and baby Raymond Bensley, Levi Jagger, Ida Bensley, ? Huff, ? Huff, Almeda Bensley, Oliver Bensley, James Bensley, Romaine Bensley, baby Evan Treible, Mr. Huff, Chester Bensley, Cora Bensley, Saul Bensley and baby, Mrs. Huff, Isiah Bensley, Margaret Bensley, Wallace Bensley, Ed VanAuken, Ada VanAuken, Mark Bensley, Elmira Bensley, Frank Layton, Eva Layton, Chauncey Bensley, Emmett Bensley, Charlie Bensley, Art Cron, Josephine Bensley, Roy Bensley, Arthur Bensley, Calvin Cron, Ida Cron, and Minerva Treible. (Courtesy Elsie Bensley.)

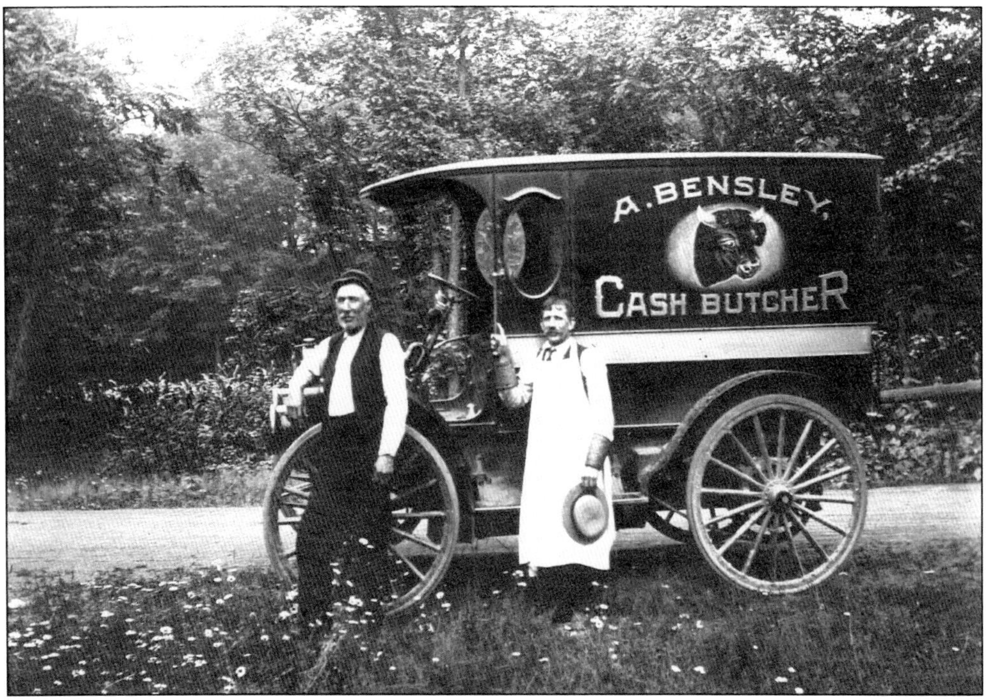

For many years, Alpheus Bensley operated a butchering delivery service by horse and wagon. As evidenced here, by 1910 he had upgraded his operation to include a horseless carriage. With Bensley is Dan Smith. (Courtesy Roberta and Leroy Cron.)

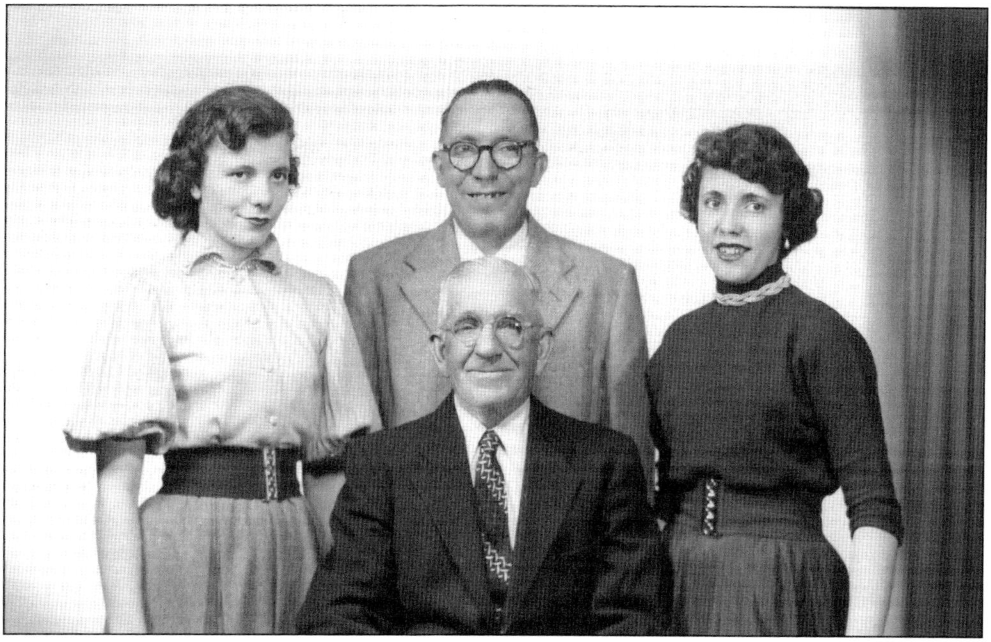

Local butcher Alpheus Bensley appears front and center in this photograph of three generations. Standing in the back is his son Herbert Bensley (center) and his granddaughters Barbara Bensley Cole (left) and Joan Bensley Stasa. The girls are the daughters of Herbert and Elaine Eshback Bensley. (Courtesy Barbara Bensley Cole.)

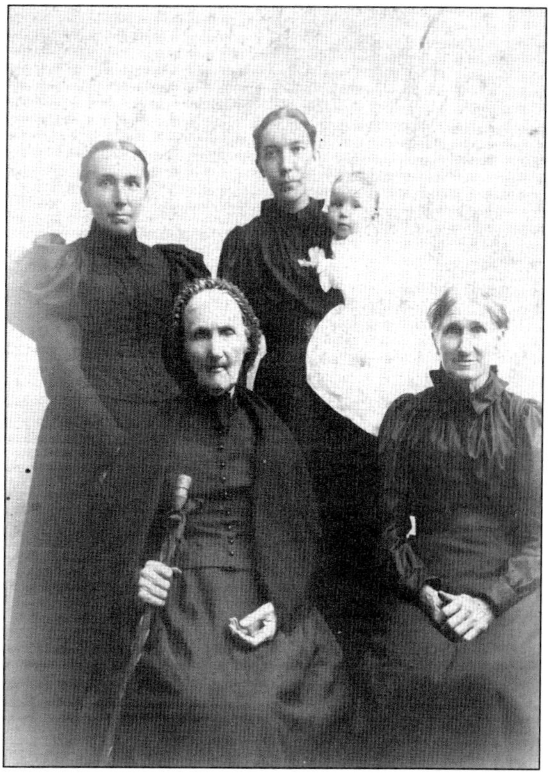

This five-generation photograph was taken in the late 1890s. Sitting are Jane Hornbeck Everett (left) and her daughter Hannah A. Everett Middaugh. Standing are Mary Frances Middaugh Smith (left) and her daughter Hannah Smith Bensley, holding her daughter Vienna S. Bensley. (Courtesy Barbara Bensley Cole.)

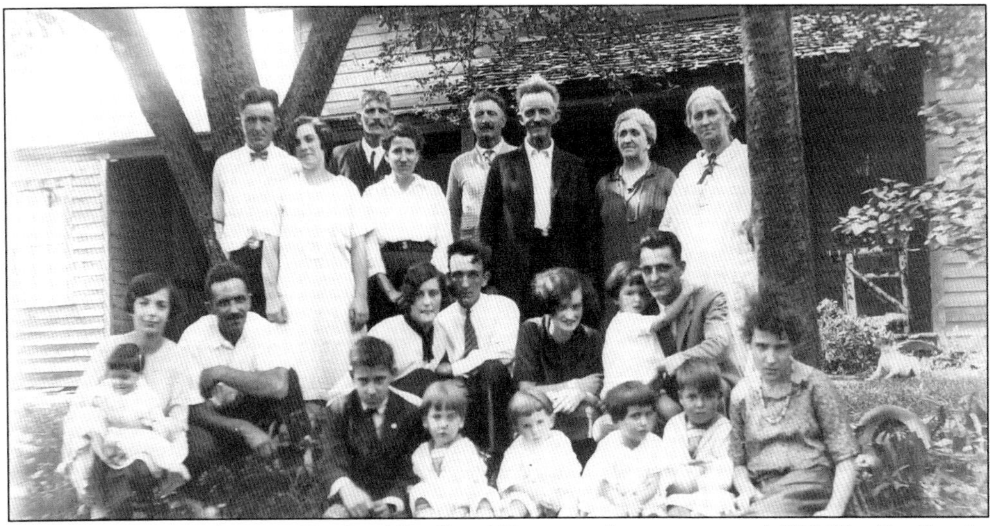

The Hugh Owen and Emma Shepherd Brodhead Homestead appears around 1927. The Brodheads, like the Dingmans, have a long history in the village and surrounding area. In the mid-1700s, they were members of the pioneers that settled the Delaware River Valley. Pictured here, from left to right, are the following: (first row) Margaret Retallick Brodhead and John Shepherd Brodhead; Edna Brodhead and Welcome Haines Brodhead; and Audrey Rathburn Brodhead and William A. Brodhead; (second row) David Owen and his wife, Hazel; three unidentified people; Hugh and Emma Brodhead; and her mother, Mrs. Shepherd. In the foreground are the grandchildren. (Courtesy Edwin Brodhead.)

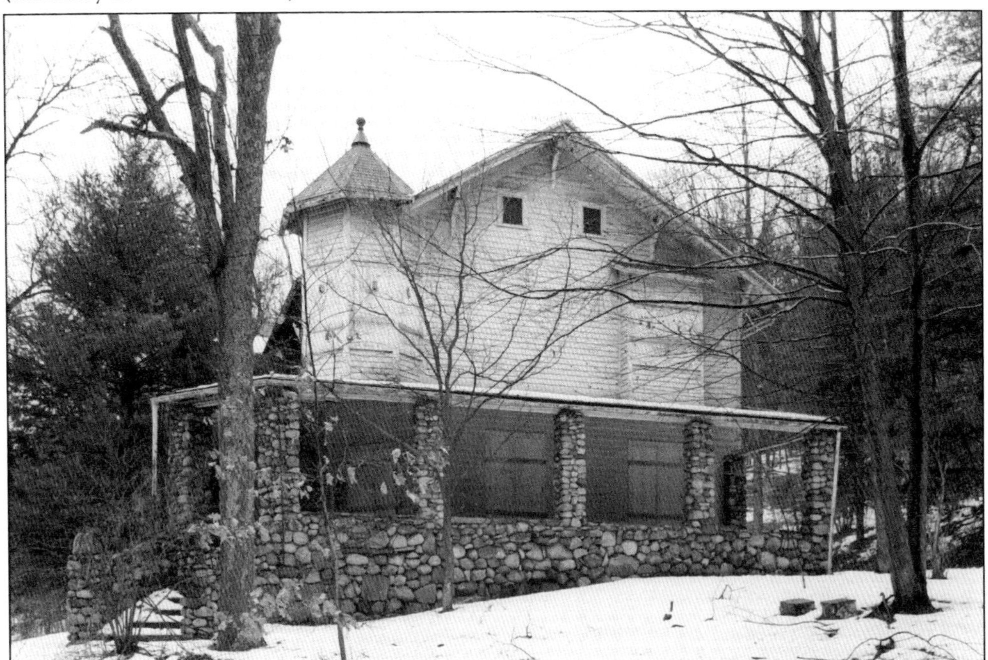

The Crane/Goldhardt home remains on Route 739, just north of Route 209. Now owned by the National Park Service, this property was once a retreat for vaudeville actors in the mid-1900s. In the 1930s, it was owned by theatrical celebrity Edward Darling. Margaret Crane built the home, and its final owner was William Goldhardt. (Courtesy Jo Ann and Ted Parsell.)

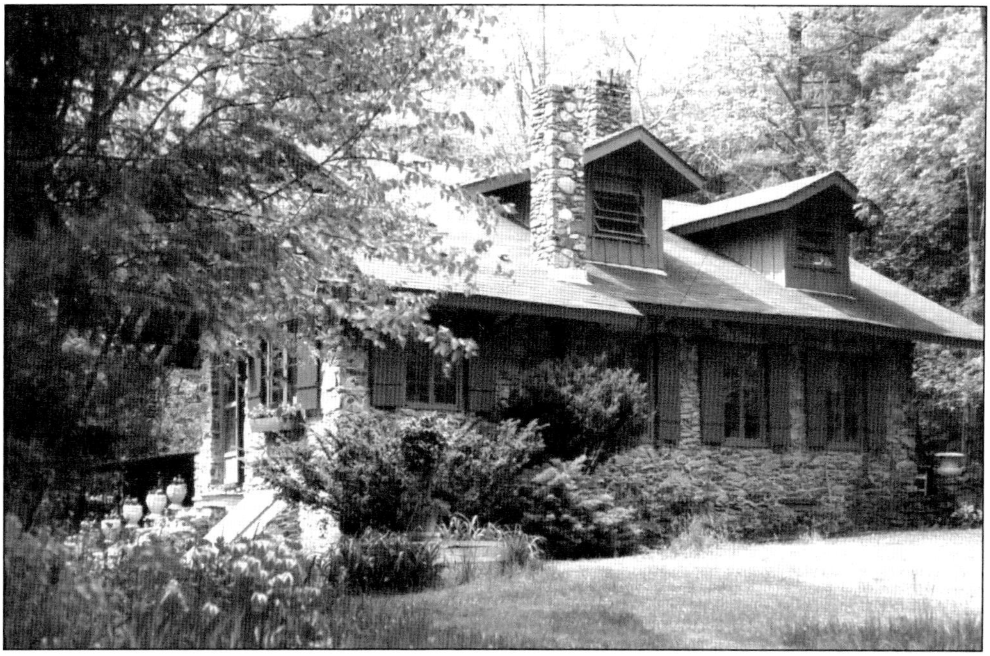

This arts-and-crafts-style retreat is located on the Dingmans Creek. Constructed in 1906 by future Pennsylvania governor William C. Sproul (1919–1923), this home has been completely restored by its current owners, Sonda and Lee Miller. (Courtesy Sonda and Lee Miller.)

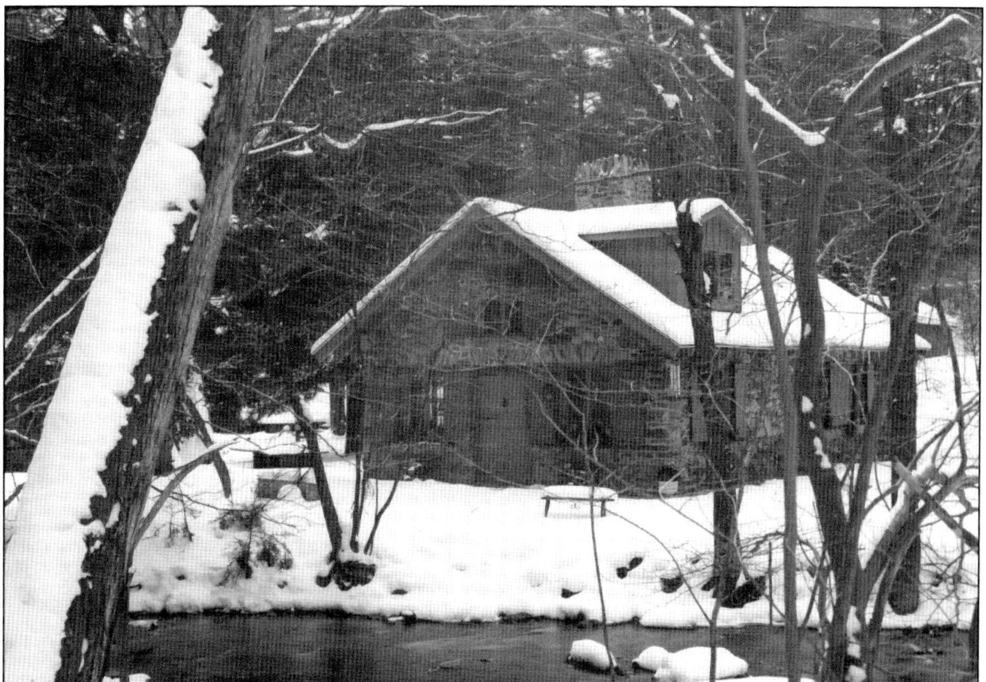

Originally the horse barn on Governor Sproul's private retreat, this native stone cottage is an example of the keystone design, in which triangular stones are used for support. Transformed from its 1906 use, it is now a weekend retreat showplace. (Courtesy Sonda and Lee Miller.)

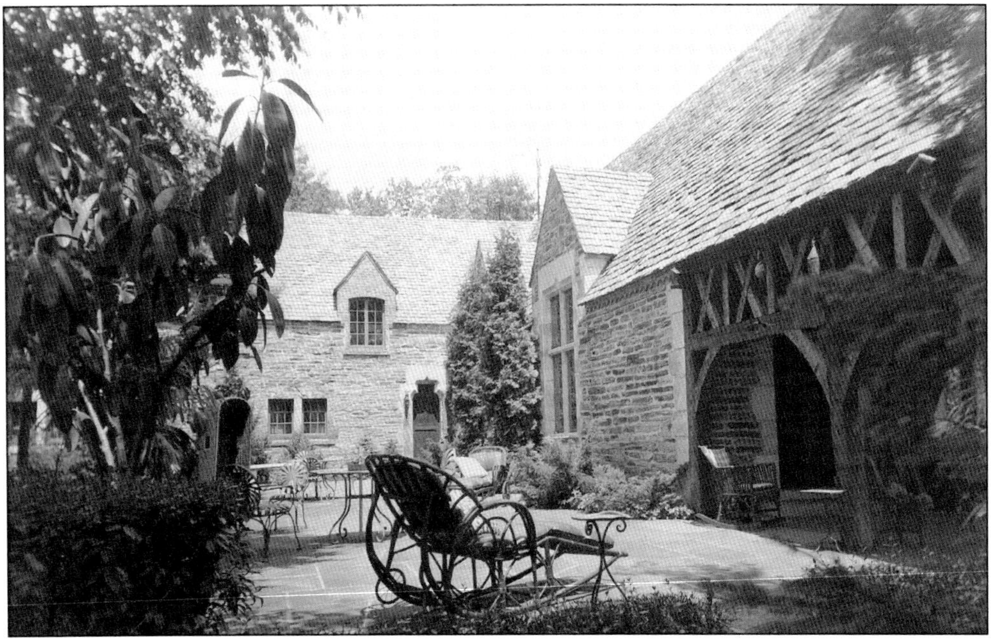

This spacious home was built in the 1920s by August Kiel, known nationally as the "Marble King." Constructed by local craftsmen on the property that is now Wild Aces, the retreat was the setting for hunting and fishing getaways and lavish parties. Included in its construction were large, lavish marble bathrooms and spacious bedrooms. (Courtesy Bill and Patsy Kiger.)

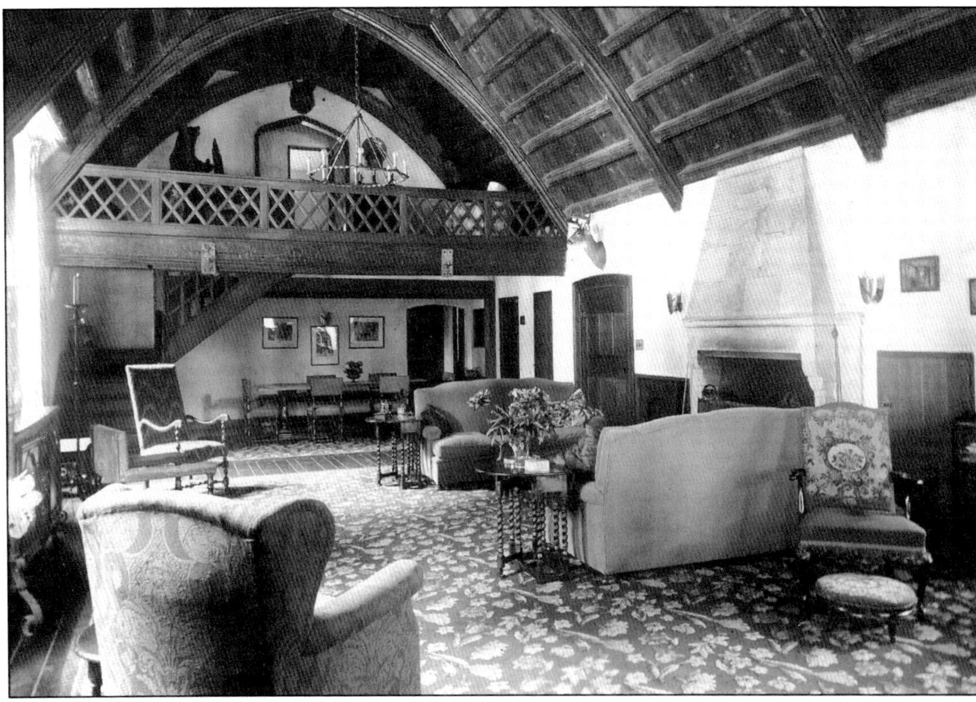

The main living room, with its wood truss ceiling, is a fine example of the work done by local craftsmen. This magnificent home is owned today by the Alan and Julianne Leverten family. (Courtesy Bill and Patsy Kiger.)

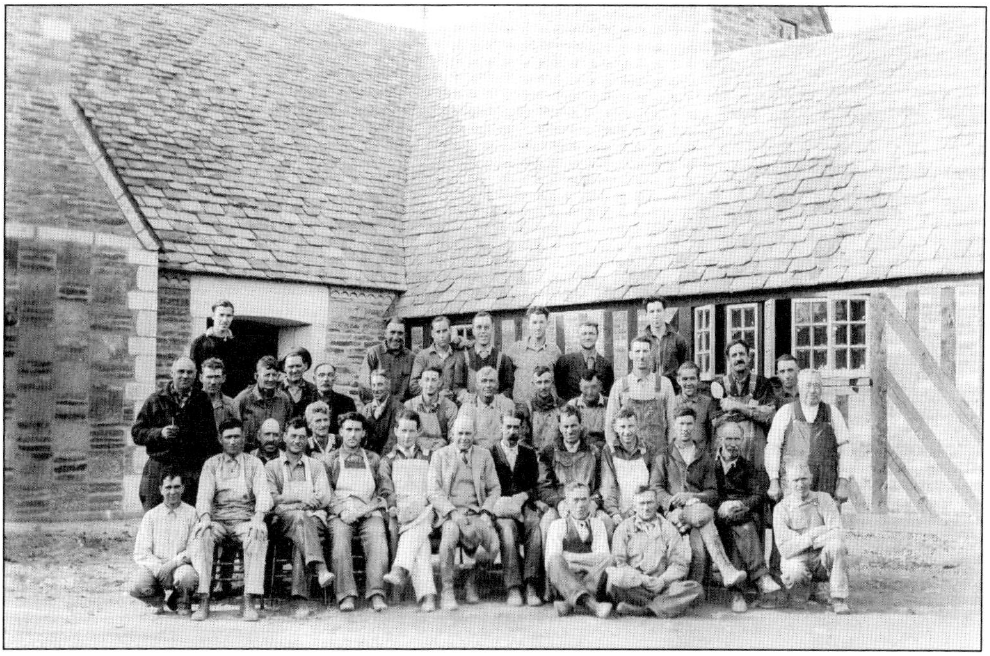

Around 1925, August Kiel sits among the local craftsmen and artists who created his illustrious estate in Delaware Township. (Courtesy Dorthann and Joe White.)

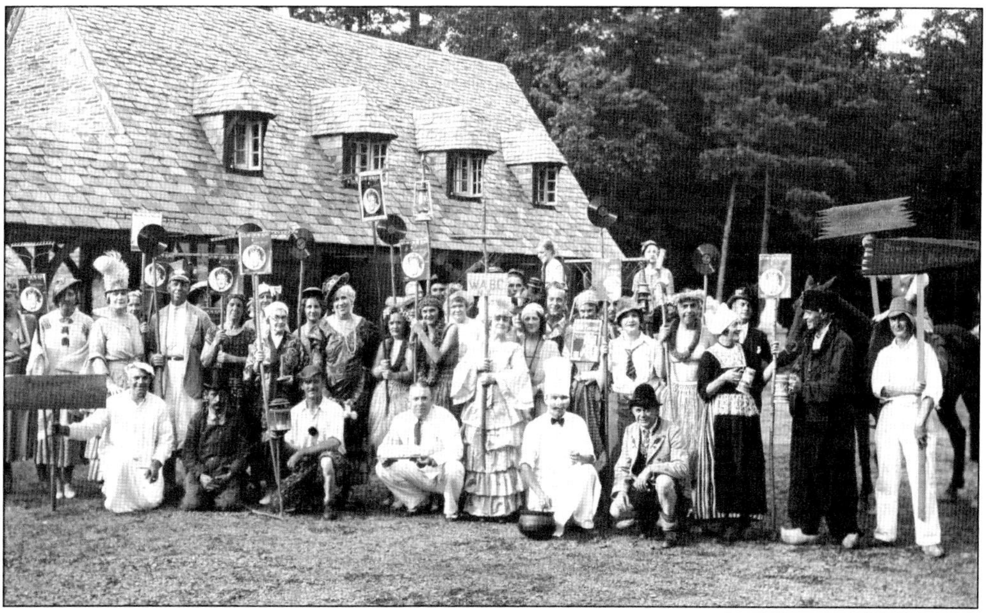

At the Kiel Estate in 1932, people celebrate the release of "Let's Put Out the Lights." This hit song was written that year by Herbert "DoDo" Hupfeld and performed by Rudy Vallee. Hupfeld, the man in the hula skirt to the right, was also noted for his huge hit "As Time Goes By." August Kiel appears in front, dressed in lederhosen. In the center, just right of the WABC sign, is possibly Rudy Vallee. This celebration turned into a march from Milford to Dingmans Ferry called DoDo's Parade. (Courtesy Bill and Patsy Kiger.)

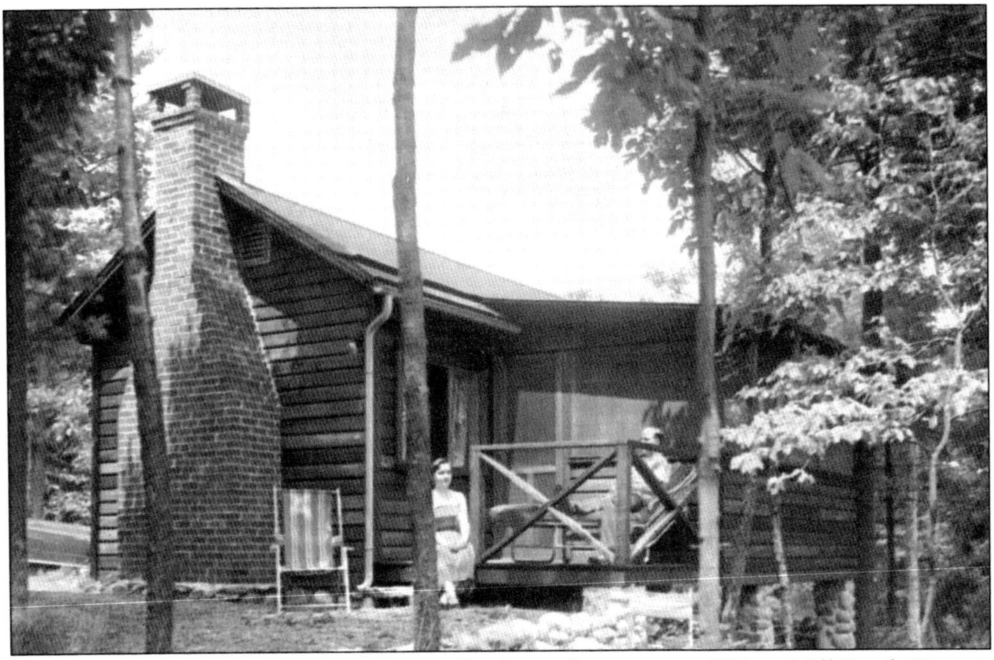

Luke Locke and his family operated a small colony of cottages on Wilson Hill Road. Since it stood atop the ridge, it was called Lockes Barrel Ridge. (Courtesy DF/DTHS.)

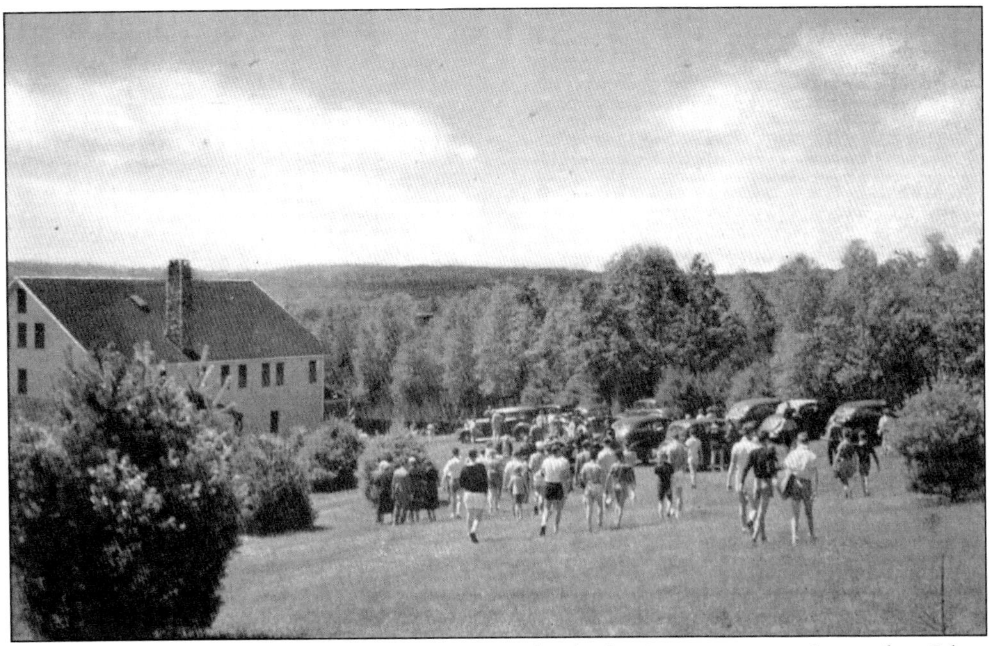

"Munsee Makes Men" reads the 1927 advertisement for this boy's summer camp. Located on Silver Lake Road, it is the present site of Camp Massad. (Courtesy Kathleen and Stephen Bumball.)

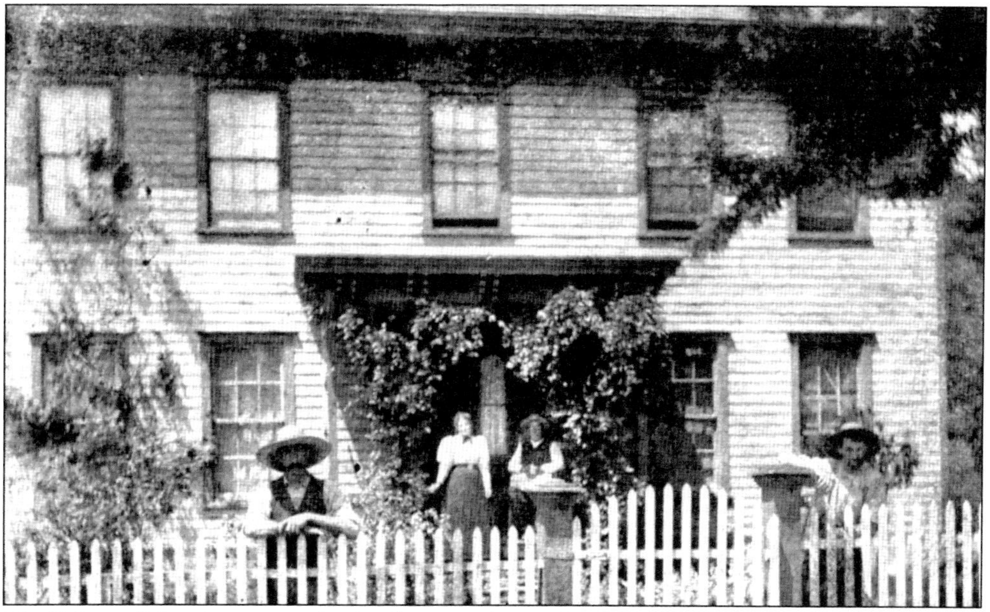

The Whitesell family poses at the farmhouse on Route 209 South. The Whitesells were residents of Dingmans Ferry earlier than the 1870s. In later years, the farm belonged to Alpheus Bensley, the noted door-to-door butcher salesman. Standing by the fence are Harry (left) and Charles Whitesell, the sons of Jane Angle Whitesell and Benjamin Whitesell, pictured on the porch of this lovely home. (Courtesy Eugene Whitesell.)

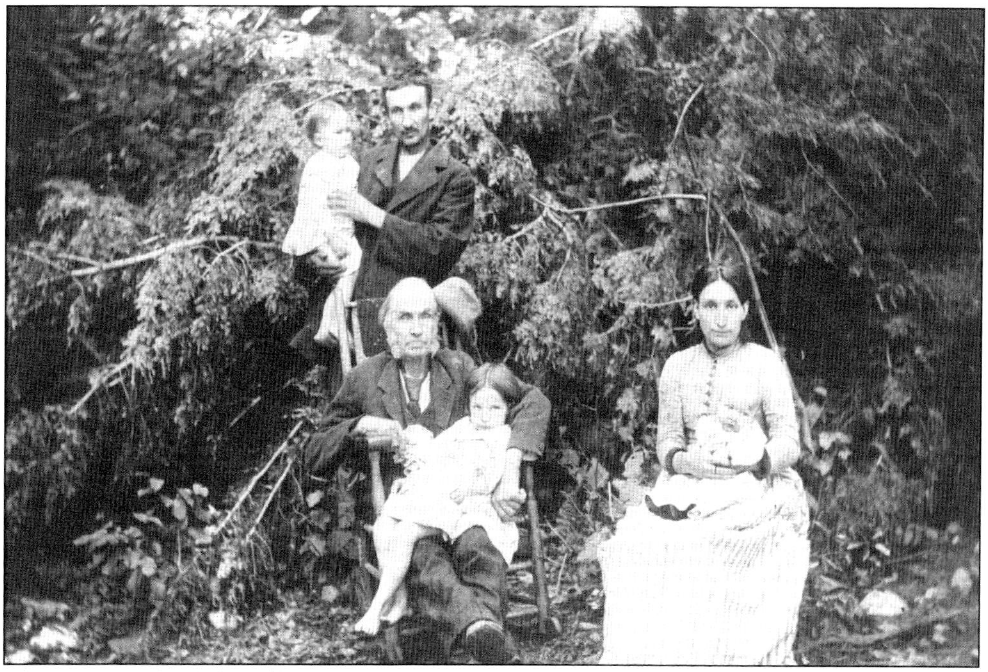

The First Family of the village will always be the Dingman family. Shown here *c.* 1888 are the following, from left to right: (sitting) Andrew Dingman, holding Melissa; and Charlotte Conklin Dingman, wife of Isaac, holding an unidentified girl; (standing) Isaac Dingman, son of Andrew, holding his daughter Caroline Dingman Zimmermann. (Courtesy Jacqueline Dougherty.)

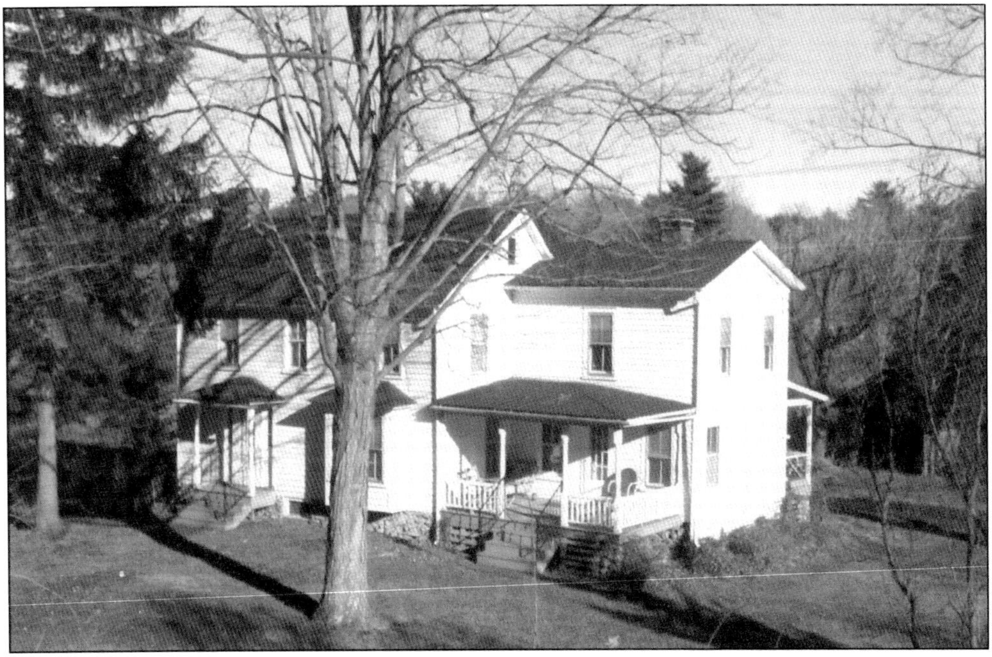

The Nina Layton Ford home, seen in 1973, was located on School House Road. Nina's husband operated Ralph Ford's service station on Main Street for many years. (Courtesy George and Carolyn Hotalen.)

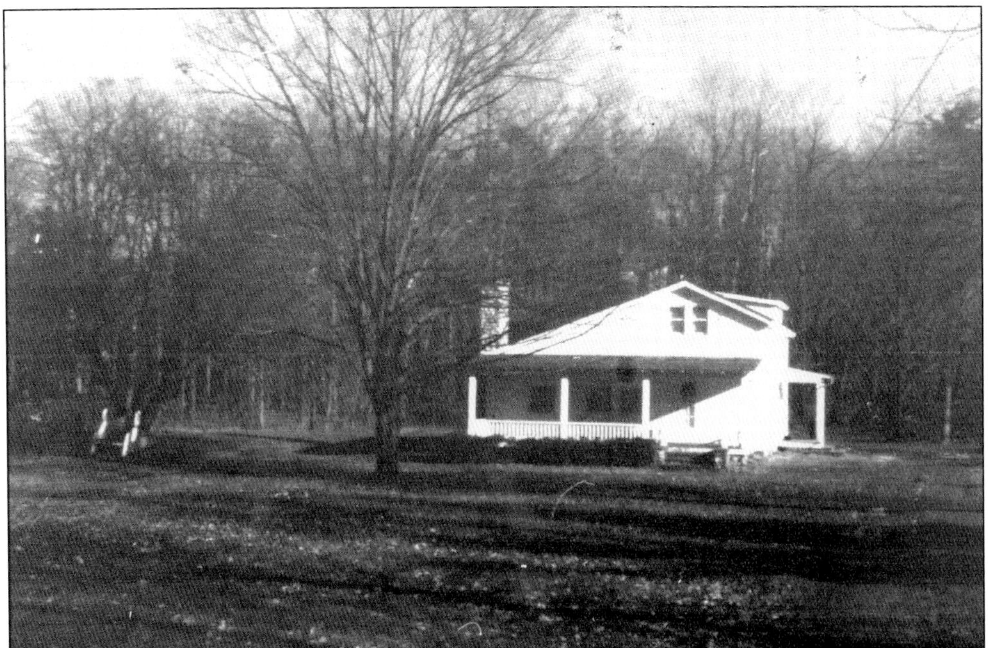

The family home of Tom Parkinson, this quaint farmhouse was located just off of Main Street (Route 209). (Courtesy George and Carolyn Hotalen.)

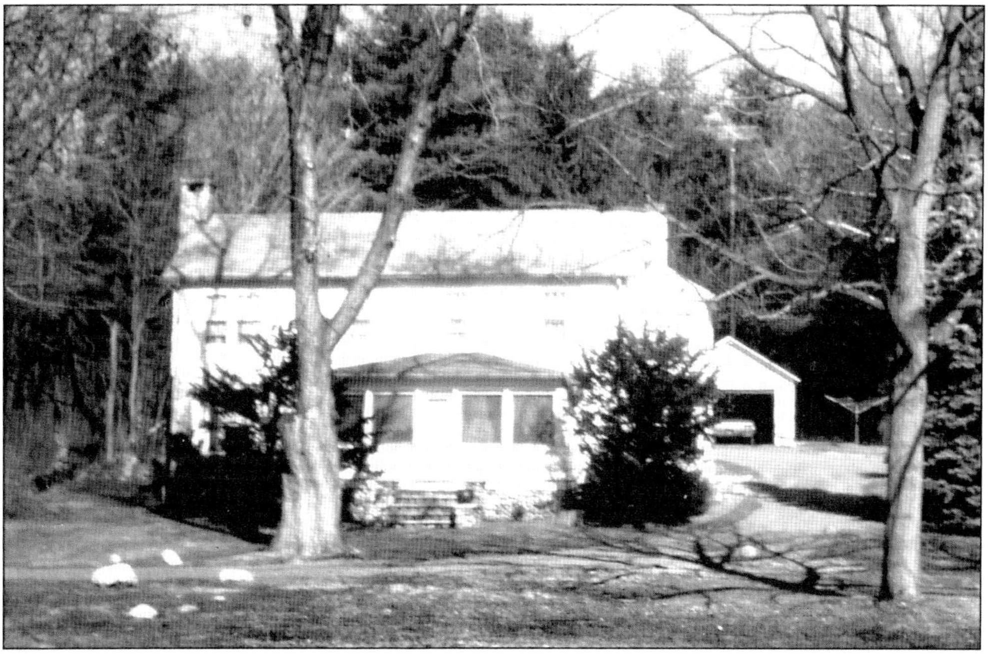

The Paul Smith house on Tie Alley was a lovely home standing adjacent to the Hotalen Homestead. (Courtesy George and Carolyn Hotalen.)

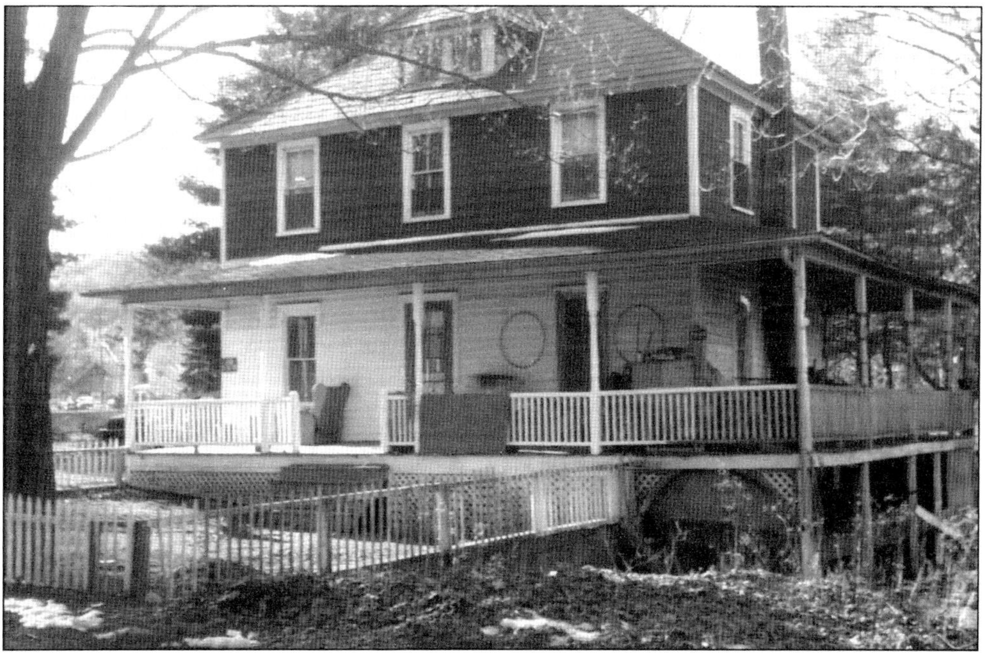

The four-square-style home of Lou Myer was located on Tie Alley. This street began on Route 739 and exited on Route 209 opposite Johnny B. Road. (Courtesy George and Carolyn Hotalen.)

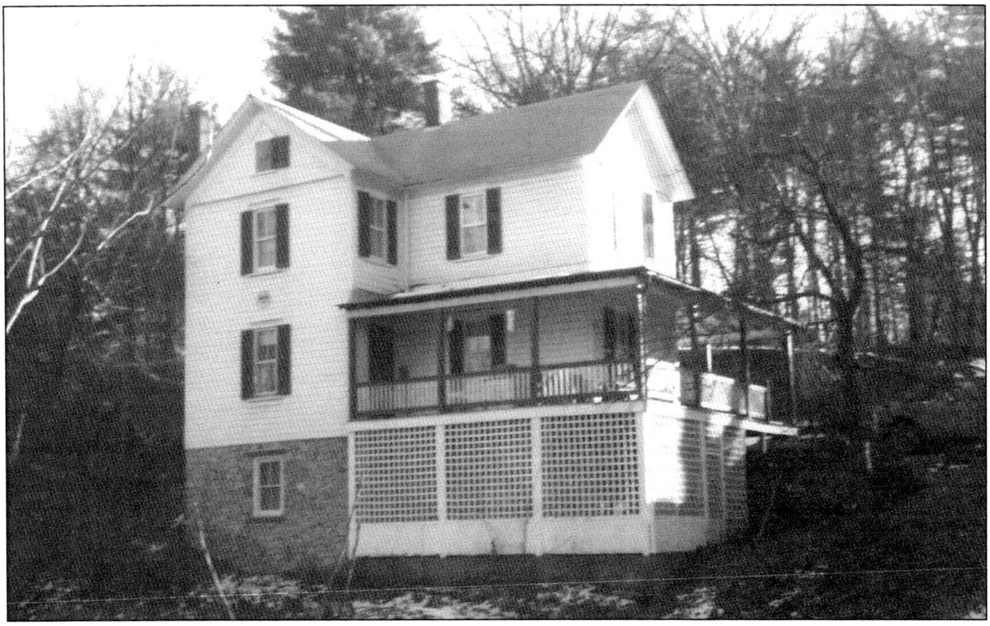

The residence of Fred and Edna Gunn Hotalen also stood on Tie Alley. Here, the Hotalens raised their children, many of whom still call Delaware Township home. This typical American home, shown in 1973, was destroyed to make way for the Tocks Island Dam Project. (Courtesy George and Carolyn Hotalen.)

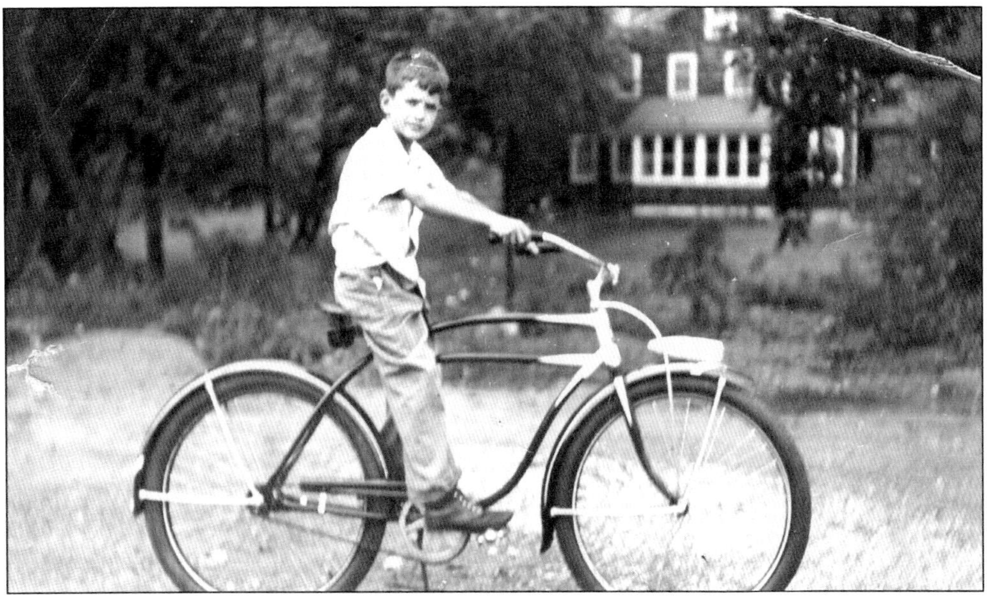

The children of Dingmans Ferry had many activities to keep them busy, some coming just from the natural wonders of the area, like hunting, fishing, and exploring the surrounding woods. But just like most small American towns, kids were kids. George Hotalen proudly shows off his new bicycle in this image. The building in the background is the home of Richard Boby. (Courtesy George and Carolyn Hotalen.)

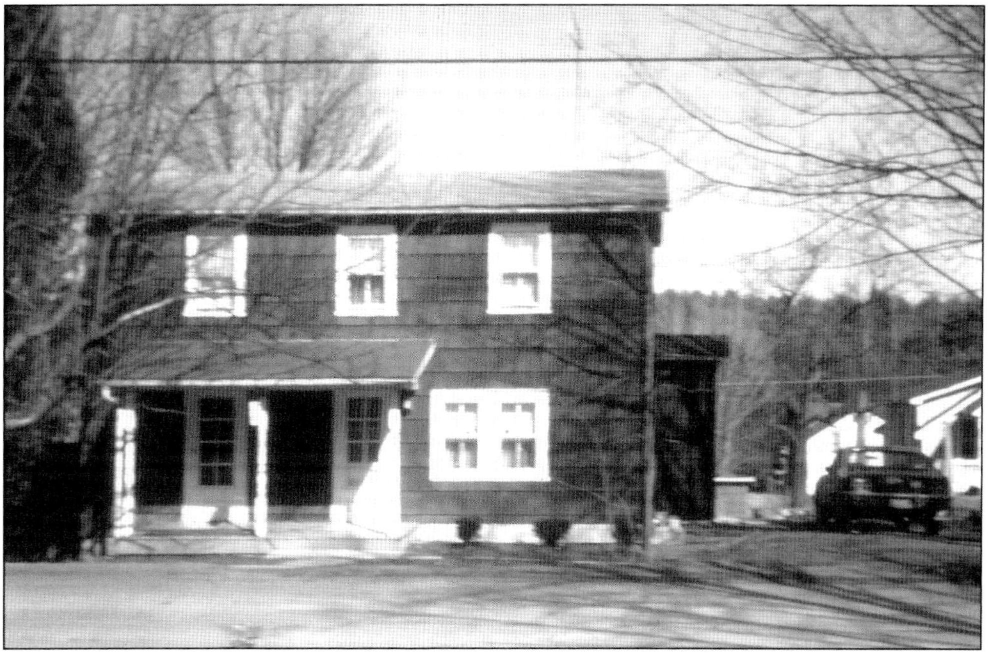

This quaint home, standing on Main Street (Route 209) across from the Bellevue Hotel, was the residence of Blace and Betty Hotalen. (Courtesy George and Carolyn Hotalen.)

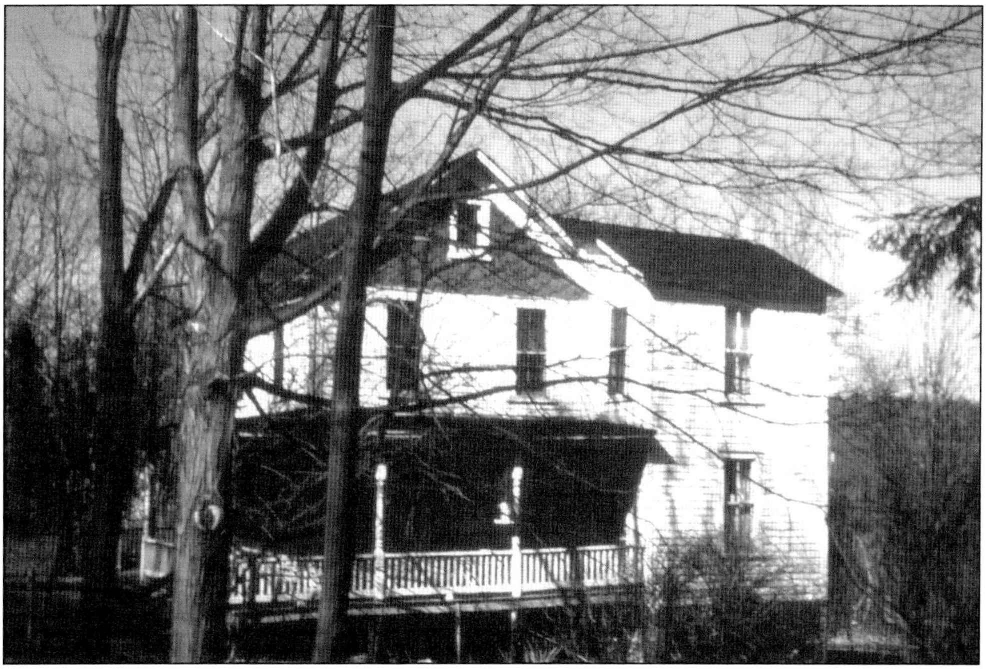

This beautiful wraparound porch graces a lovely home belonging to Tom and Doris Hotalen. The Hotalen family all lived nearby in the village of Dingmans Ferry. (Courtesy George and Carolyn Hotalen.)

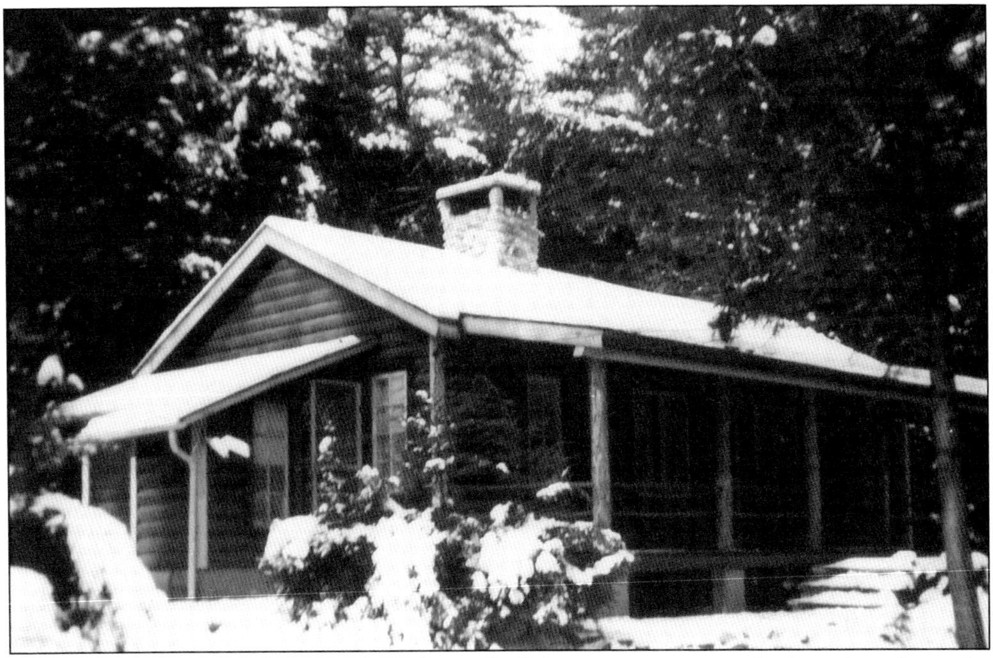

Many homes in the old Dingmans Ferry located off the main streets were built in the cabin style, like the O'Neill House on Mill Street. (Courtesy Roberta and Leroy Cron.)

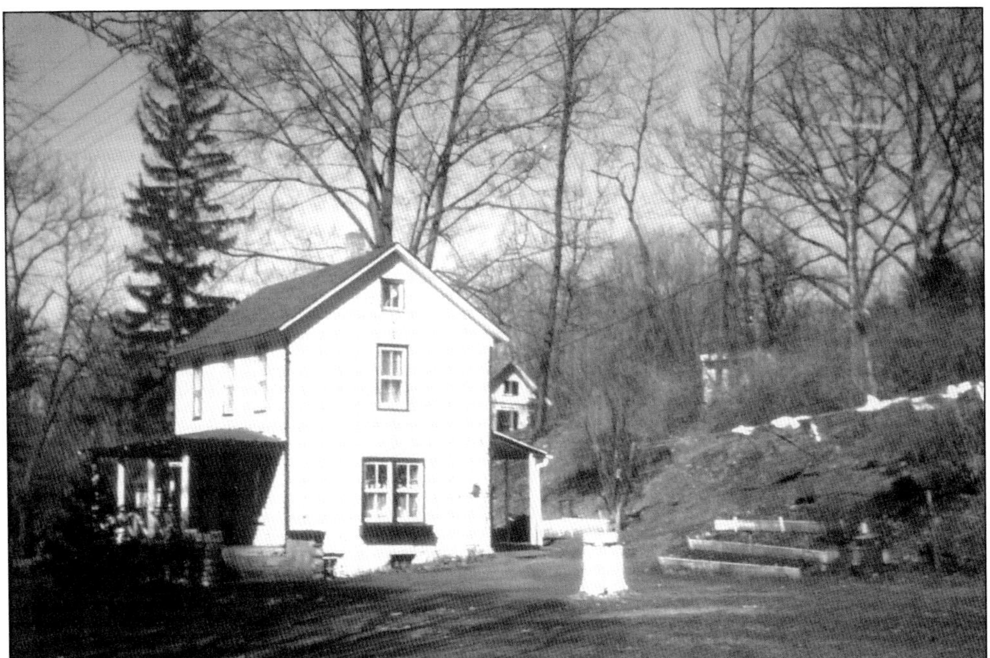

The farm-style Howard Smith home was situated on Tie Alley adjacent to the Hotalen Homestead. (Courtesy George and Carolyn Hotalen.)

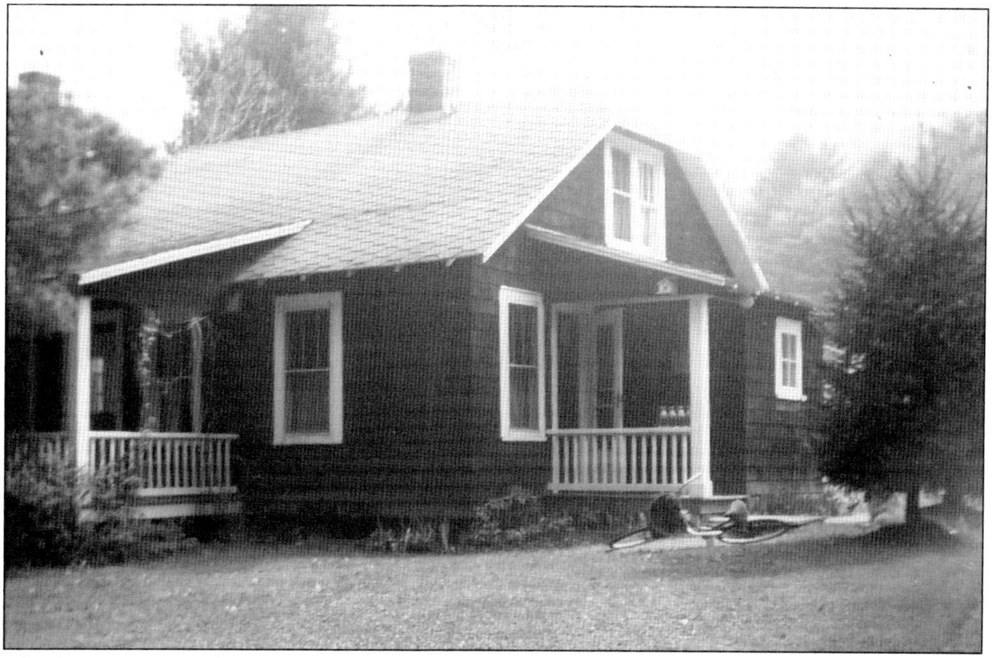

Charles Cron owned this home on Mill Street. Like many other buildings pictured on these pages, it was lost to the Delaware Water Gap National Recreation Area. It was in these homes that children grew and families thrived. (Courtesy George and Carolyn Hotalen.)

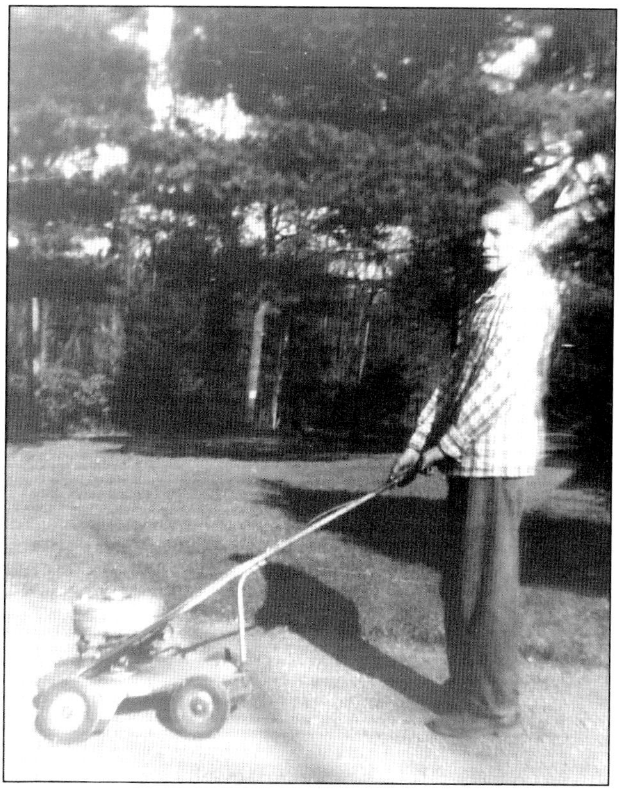

Leroy Cron takes a break to show off his new power mower around 1940. (Courtesy Roberta and Leroy Cron.)

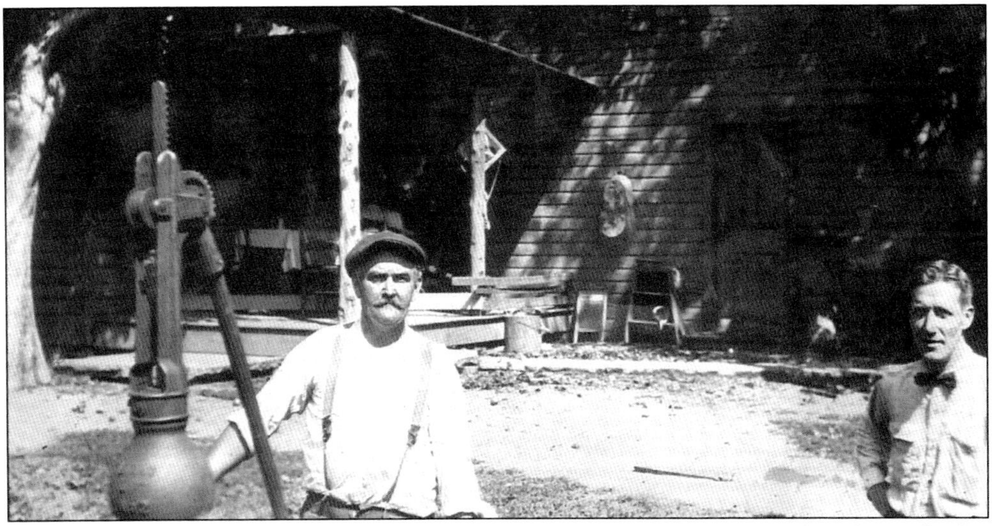

Mr. Willis, pictured on the right with Mercer Jagger, owned a farm on Conashaugh Road. This c. 1927 image shows a rare pressure water pump, used to water the crops of the large family farms. (Courtesy Jagger family.)

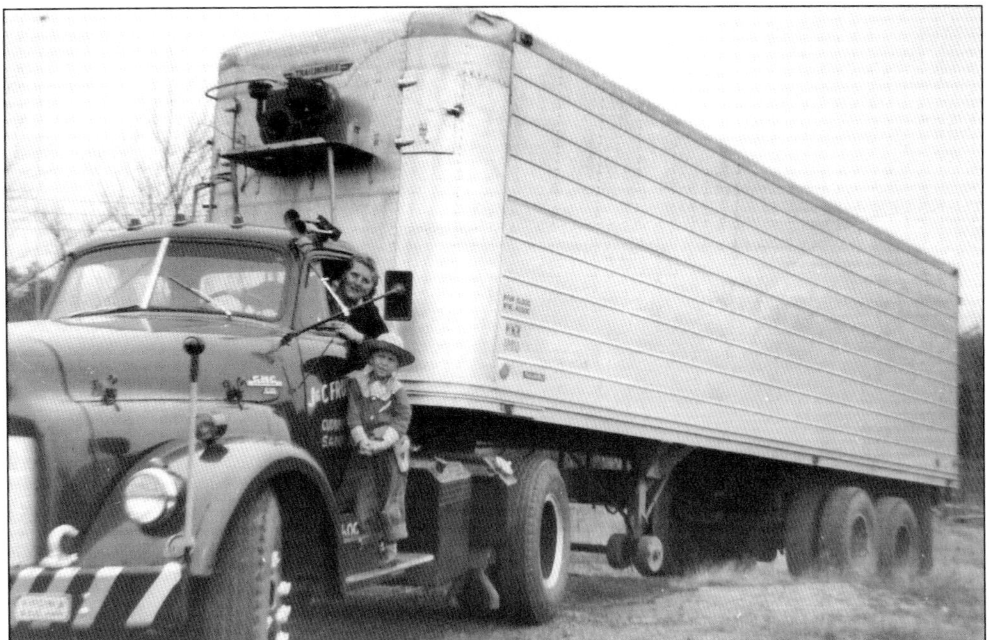

In her rig, in the 1950s, is Daisy Jagger. One of only a few women hired as truck drivers in an era when it was a man's job, Daisy was a pioneer for women's equality. Many articles were written about her in various local publications. Raised on a farm in Dingmans Ferry, she worked many years for Cicerone Trucking of Milford. (Courtesy Linda Davis.)

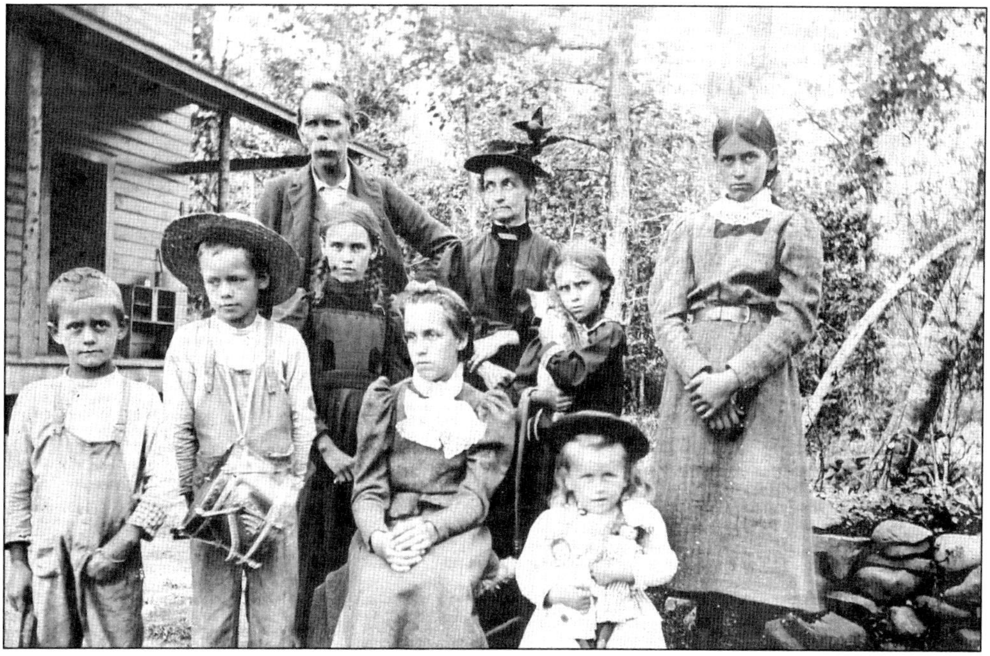

The Eugene and Bertha Emery Raitt family members pictured here, from left to right, are as follows: (first row) Clyde, Earl, Jess, and Beryl; (second row) Bess and Inez; (third row) Eugene, Bertha, and Emma. (Courtesy Raitt family.)

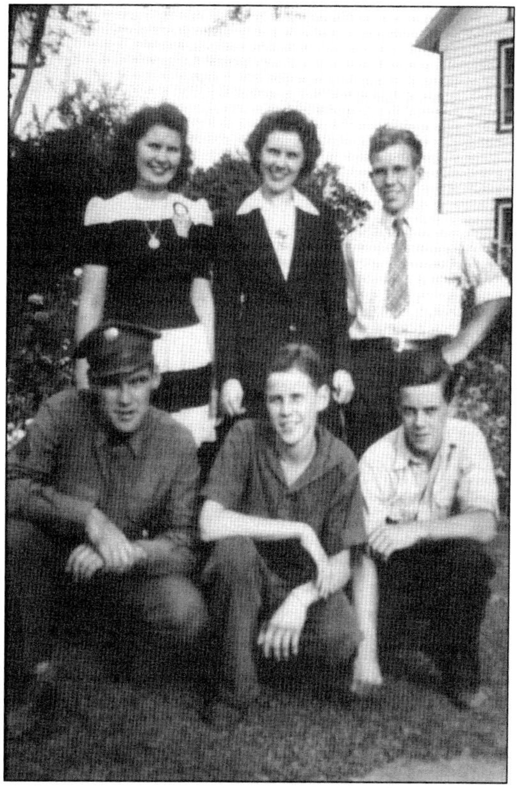

On September 7, 1942, the six children of Mercer and Bess Raitt Jagger posed for a portrait. Shown here, from left to right, are the following: (first row) Mercer, Walter, and Richard; (second row) Ella May, Bertha, and Willis Berne. (Courtesy Jagger family.)

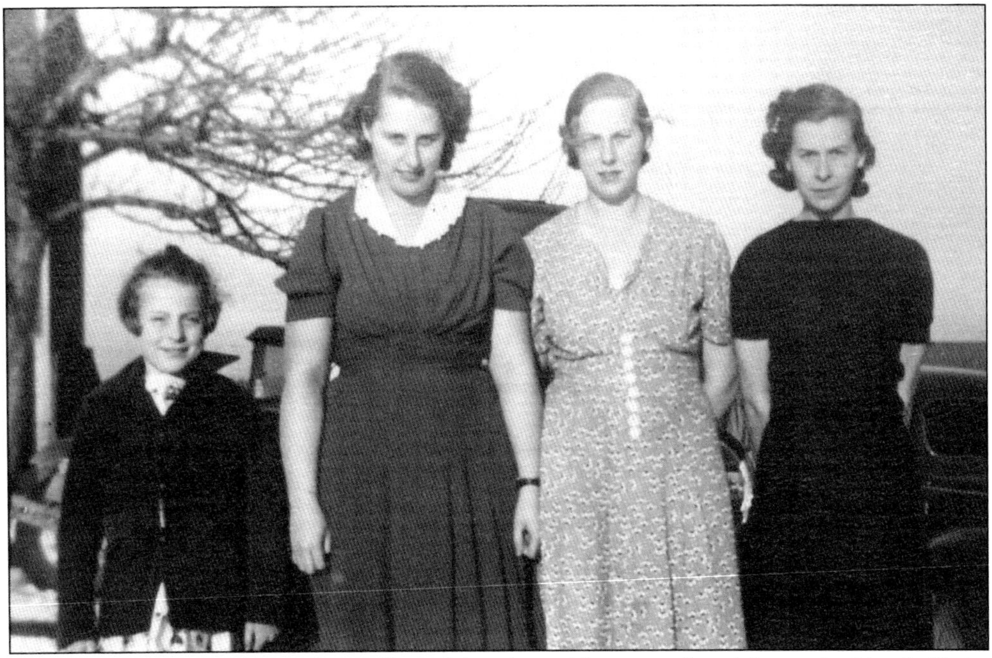

Joan Ryder Mervine (left) stands proudly with her three older sisters, from left to right: Natalie Ryder Snyder, Lillian Ryder Treible, and Mildred Ryder Jagger. Mildred is one of the oldest Dingmans Ferry natives, and she remembers this community in its glory days. (Courtesy Audrey Mervine.)

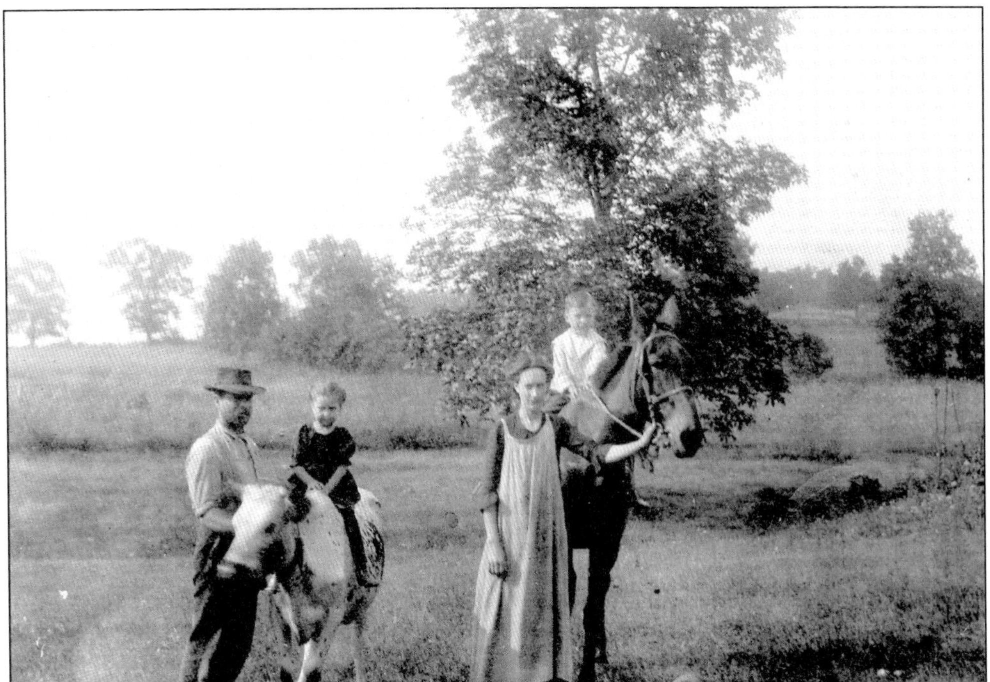

Mr. and Mrs. Henry Cron take their children for a summer stroll in the pastures of their Dingmans Ferry farm about 1906. August Cron rides the horse, and Anna Cron Gavoille the Guernsey. (Courtesy Dorthann and Joe White.)

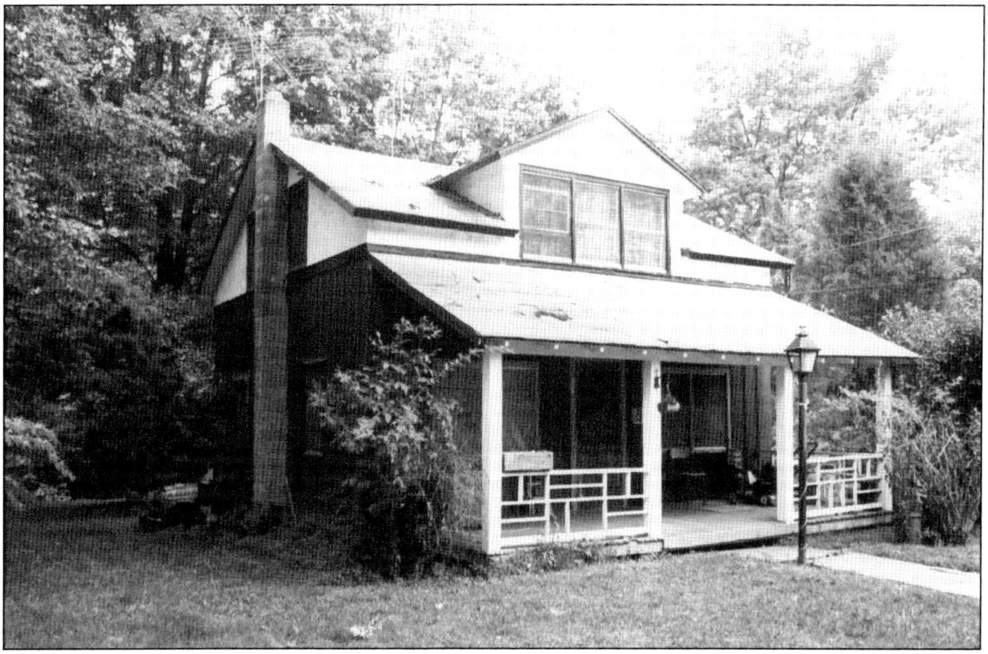

This home originally belonged to the Allerton family. Located on Mill Street (Johnny B. Road), in more recent years it was the home of Pat Herberz, the Dingman Township historian who wrote extensively, keeping the stories of Dingmans Ferry alive. (Courtesy Delaware Water Gap National Recreation Area.)

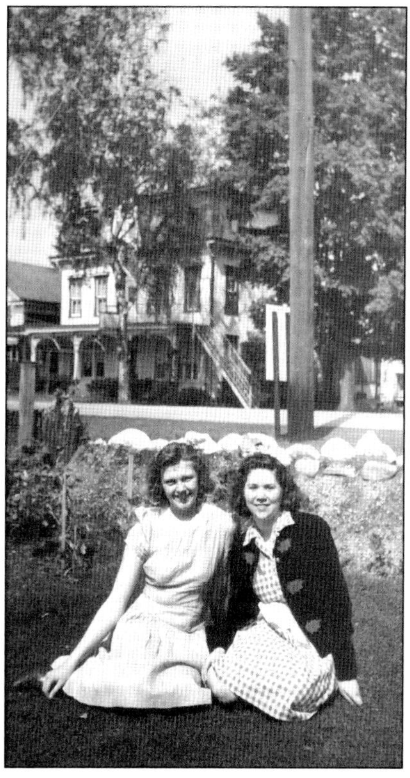

In 1943, Mary Hoffman Froese (left) and Geraldine Goodman Pugh relax on the lawn across the street from the elegant Mansion House. (Courtesy Marie Hoffman.)

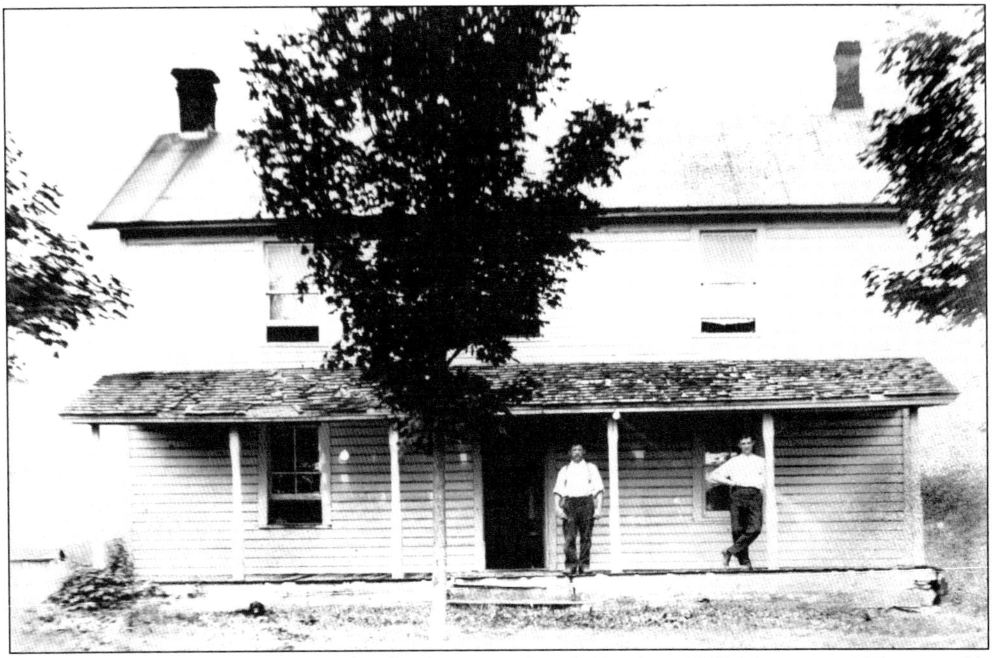

Robert and Frances Findlay bought this house on Myck Road in 1947. Now over 130 years old, the building was home to the Findlays for 52 years. In 1999, it was sold to Matthew and Jennifer Foley. (Courtesy Roberta and Leroy Cron.)

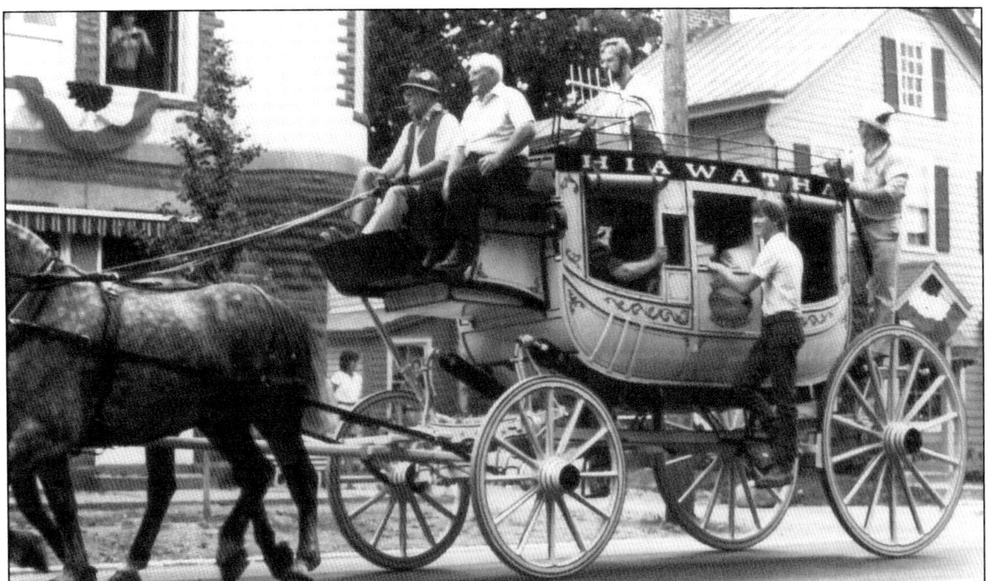

The Findlays have been a part of Pike County for more than 100 years. The family owned the stagecoach that operated from Milford to the Delaware Water Gap from 1860 to 1900. Here, in a 1982 Milford parade, Robert Findlay (left) rides aboard the Hiawatha Stagecoach. He is the grandson of the original owner, Robert Watson Findlay. The stagecoach has been magnificently restored by the Pike County Historical Society and is on display at the museum in Milford. (Courtesy Roberta and Leroy Cron.)

Members of the Judd family have lived in Dingmans Ferry for over 100 years. This photograph depicts Philip Truswell Judd (1846–1890), who served in the Civil War as a "drummer boy." (Courtesy Mim Carpenter.)

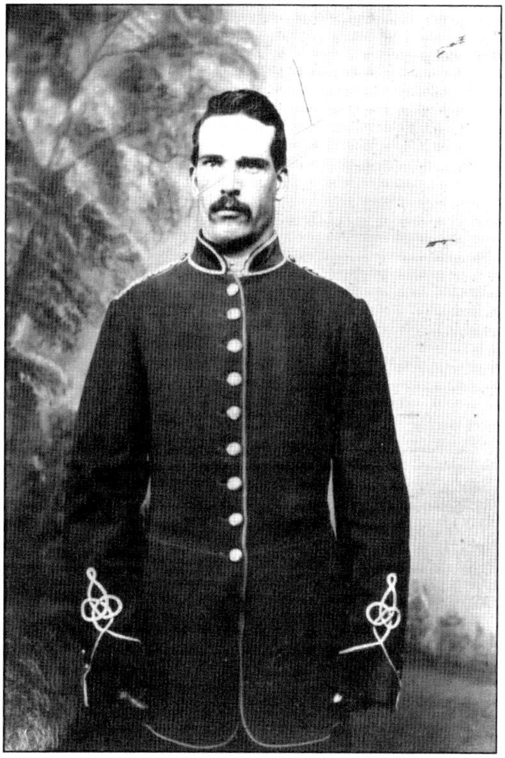

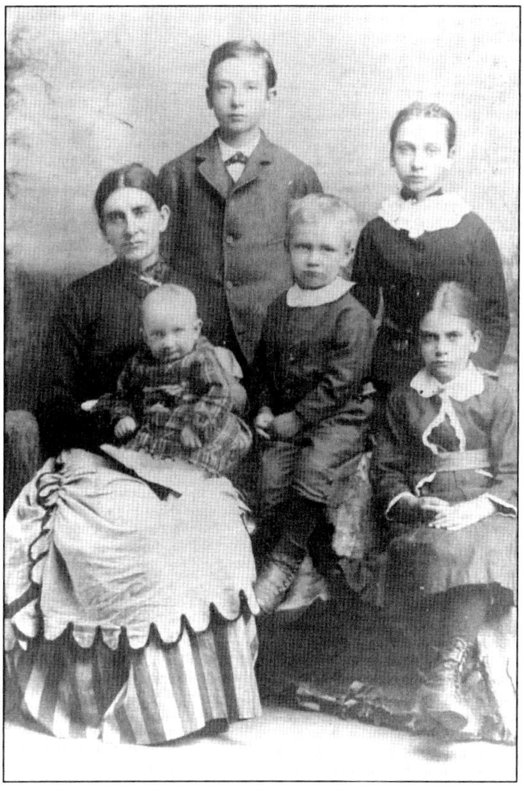

The Philip Judd family poses for local photographer W. H. Allerton around 1889. Judd married Susan Catherine Meakin of Delaware Township on January 6, 1873. Susan is pictured here with her family: Philip Charles, Catherine Estella, Mehetabel, Joseph Lewis, and Elizabeth Mary. (Courtesy Mim Carpenter.)

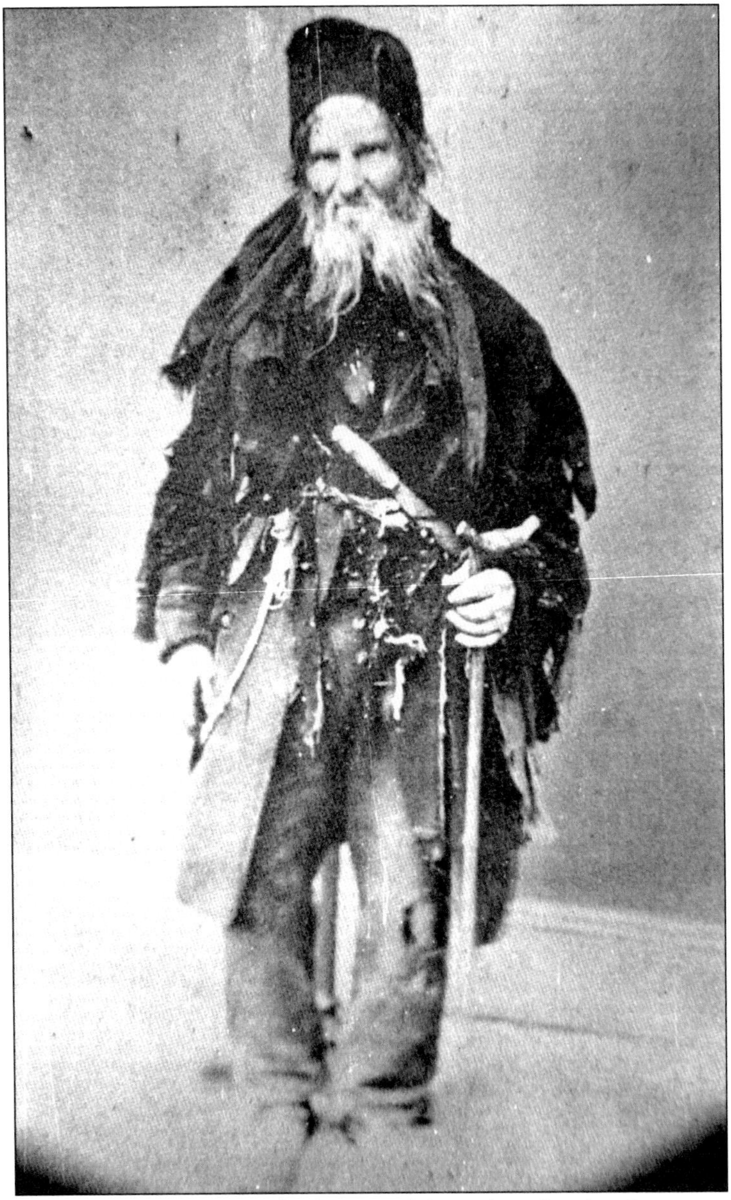

Legendary hermit Austin Sheldon made the peaceful woods and isolated cave on the outskirts of Dingmans Ferry his beloved home. Born into a family of Connecticut Yankees, in 1850, he married a woman he deeply loved. Tragedy destroyed their lives, however, when a violent summer thunderstorm struck. His wife sought escape in the basement, but the horror and fear caused permanent mental damage; she later died in an institution. Sheldon never recovered from losing her, and after spending years of wandering in Wayne and Pike, selling his knives and working as a blacksmith, he took his meager possessions and secured a hidden cave, where he communicated with God through reading the Bible and appreciating the beauty of nature. His wealthy sister persuaded him to come back to Connecticut, but he could not survive civilization and returned to the place he loved. A neighbor found Sheldon in a coma and took him to his (the neighbor's) home, where he died a peaceful death. Sheldon was laid to rest in the Dingman Township Cemetery. (Courtesy Pike County Historical Society.)

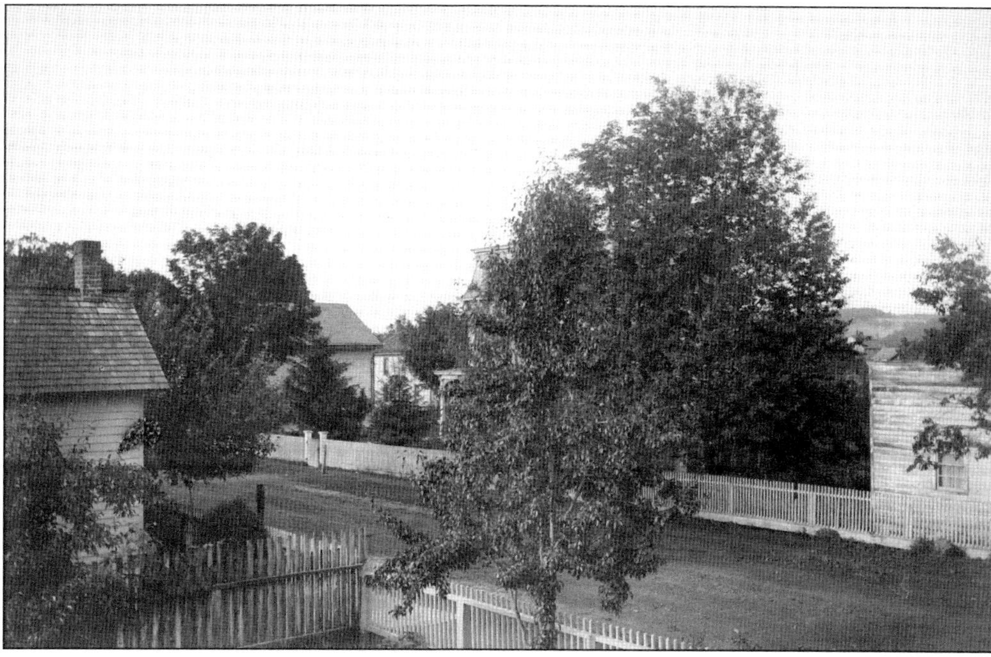

In 1889, Dingmans Ferry was a village of charming homes and white picket fences—the perfect image of a typical American town. (Courtesy Pike County Historical Society.)

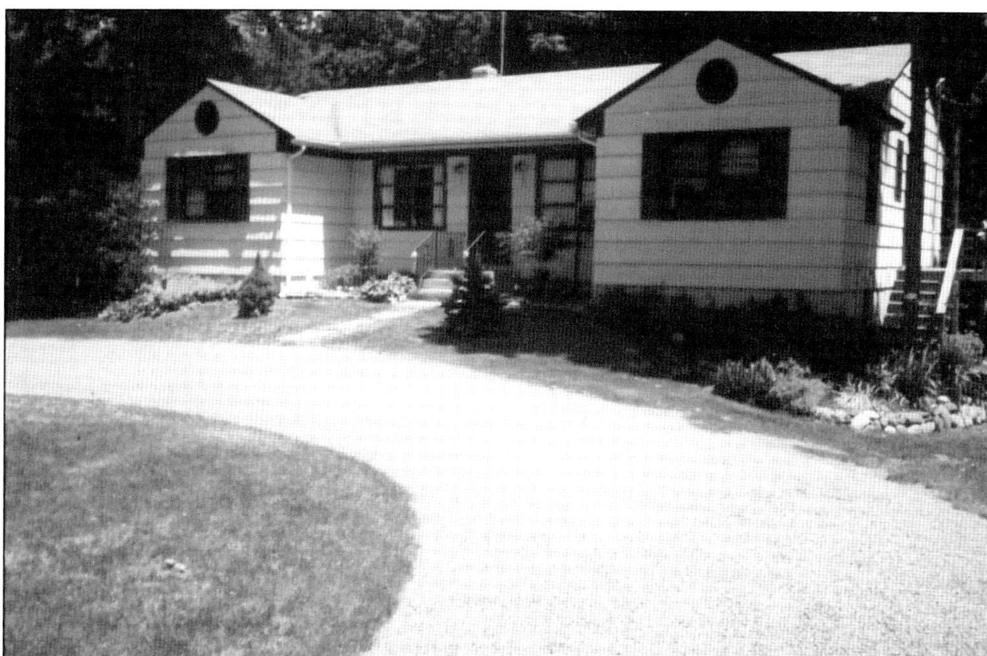

This Main Street home is one of the last residences still standing in the old Dingmans Ferry. The Malmquists, longtime locals, have lived here for many years. (Courtesy Helen Malmquist.)

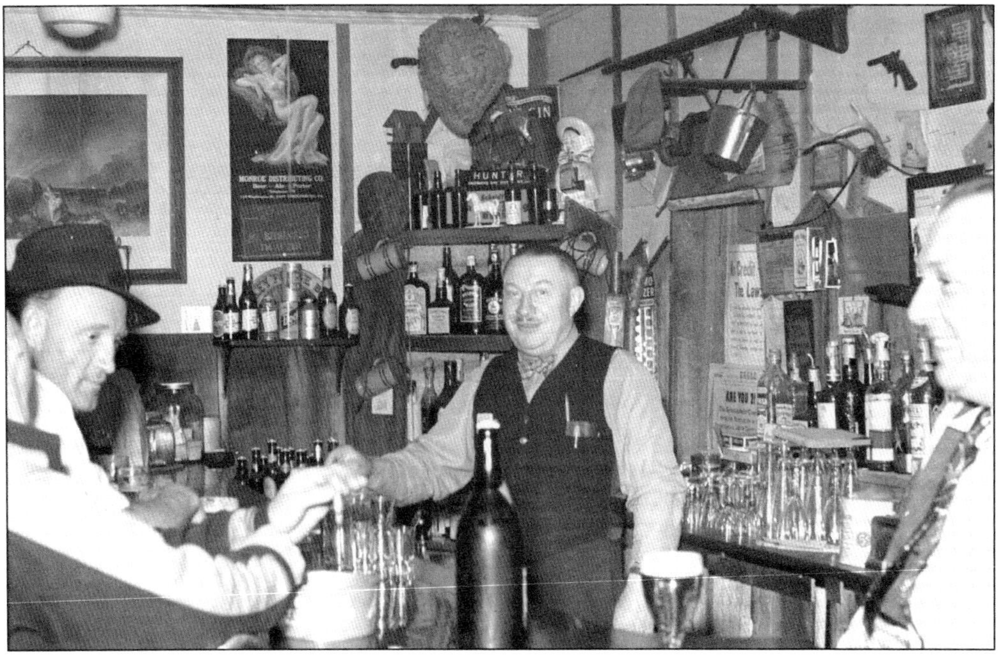

What better place to bid old Dingmans Ferry a fond farewell than at the Delaware House? Owner Karl Froese (center) serves up a few cocktails to friends and neighbors Ed Thurich (left), Rafferty Whittaker, and Carl Schnell (right). (Courtesy Marie Hoffman.)

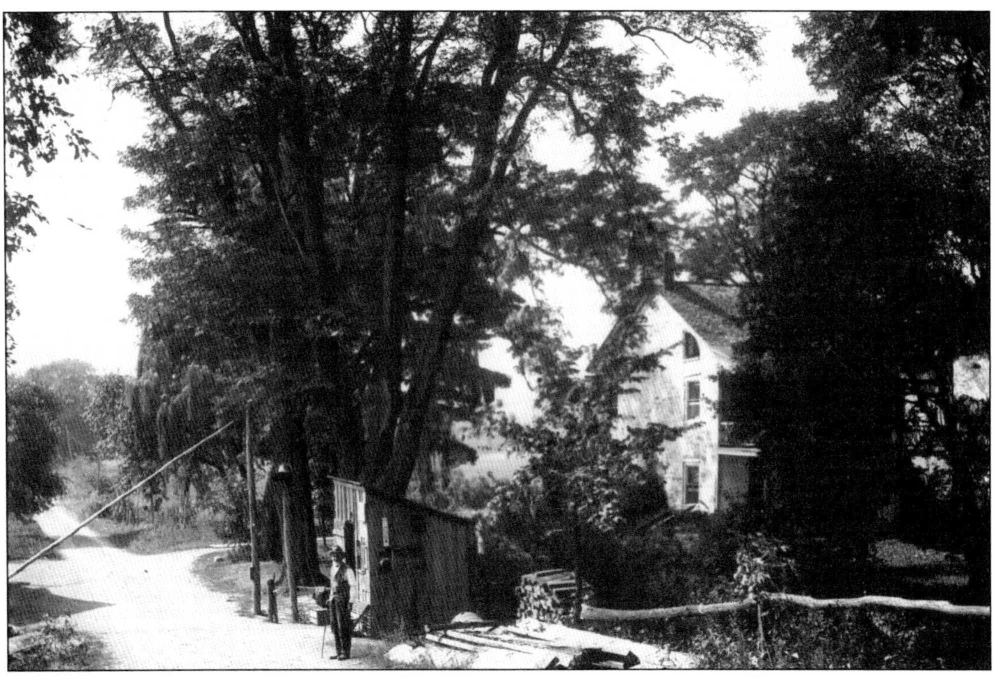

Though the village and all of its grand buildings are gone, its stories and memories continue in the people that called it home. Their love is felt when they tell of growing up in the small rural village of Dingmans Ferry. We say goodbye, with Johnny Kilsby standing guard at the Dingmans Bridge around 1900. (Courtesy Pike County Historical Society.)